OIL IN THE SEVENTIES

OIL IN THE SEVENTIES
ESSAYS ON ENERGY POLICY

Contributors include
WALTER MEAD, JAMES McKIE, DAVID QUIRIN;
CAMPBELL WATKINS and MICHAEL WALKER (Editors)

THE FRASER INSTITUTE
1977

Canadian Cataloguing in Publication Data
Main entry under title:
Oil in the seventies

Includes bibliographical references and index.
ISBN 0-88975-018-1 bd.
ISBN 0-88975-011-4 pa.
1. Petroleum industry and trade—Addresses,
essays, lectures. 2. Petroleum products—
Prices—Addresses, essays, lectures.
3. Energy policy—Canada—Addresses, essays,
lectures. 4. Energy policy—United States—
Addresses, essays, lectures. I. Watkins,
Campbell, 1939-   II. Walker, Michael, 1945-
III. Mead, Walter J., 1921-   IV. McKie,
James W., 1922-   V. Quirin, G. David, 1931-
VI. Fraser Institute, Vancouver, B.C.
HD9560.6.049   338.2'7'282   C77-002170-0

Contents

CANADIAN ENERGY DEMAND AND ECONOMIC GROWTH

Ernst R. Berndt, *Associate Professor of Economics, University of British Columbia*

7230
Canada

CANADIAN OIL AND GAS PRICING

7230
6130 Canada

G. Campbell Watkins, *President, DataMetrics Limited, Calgary,*
and Visiting Associate Professor of Economics, University of Calgary

86 /124

PART TWO — GOVERNMENT IN THE MARKETPLACE

PRIVATE ENTERPRISE, REGULATION AND GOVERNMENT ENTERPRISE IN THE ENERGY SECTOR

Walter J. Mead, *Professor of Economics, University of California, Santa Barbara*

NATIONS, COMPANIES AND MARKETS: INTERNATIONAL OIL AND MULTINATIONAL CORPORATIONS

Edward W. Erickson, *Professor of Economics and Business, North Carolina State University*

and

Herbert S. Winokur, Jr., *Associate Lecturer, John Fitzgerald Kennedy School of Government, Harvard University*

PART THREE — OIL IN THE SEVENTIES: POLICIES AND PROSPECTS

THE FINANCIAL POSITION OF THE PETROLEUM INDUSTRY

7230
6323
Canada

G. David Quirin, *Professor of Economics and Finance,*
University of Toronto
and
Basil A. Kalymon, *Professor, Faculty of Management Studies,*
University of Toronto

UNITED STATES AND CANADIAN ENERGY POLICY

James W. McKie, *Dean, College of Social and Behavioral*
Sciences, and Professor of Economics, University of Texas at Austin

7230
US
Canada

CHARTS

TABLES

xiii

UNITED STATES AND CANADIAN ENERGY POLICY —
JAMES W. MᶜKIE

THE AUTHOR

Michael A. Walker is the Research and Editorial Director of the Fraser Institute. Born in Newfoundland in 1945, he received his B.A. (Summa) at St. Francis Xavier University and his Ph.D. in Economics at the University of Western Ontario, 1969. From 1969 to 1973, he worked in various research capacities at the Bank of Canada, Ottawa and when he left in 1973, was Research Officer in charge of the Special Studies and Monetary Policy Group in the Department of Banking. Dr. Walker has also taught Economics and Statistics at the University of Western Ontario and Carleton University. Immediately prior to joining the Fraser Institute, Dr. Walker was Econometric Model Consultant to the Federal Department of Finance, Ottawa.

Dr. Walker was editor of, and a contributor to, five of the Fraser Institute's previous books: *Rent Control - A Popular Paradox* (1975), *The Illusion of Wage and Price Control* (1976), *How Much Tax Do You Really Pay?* (1976), *Which Way Ahead? Canada After Wage and Price Control* (1977) and *Public Property? The Habitat Debate Continued* (1977).

Preface

Michael Walker
Research and Editorial Director
The Fraser Institute

Preface

One of the most noticeable features of North American society is the extent to which most people are unaware of the mechanisms that provide them with their material standard of living. People need neither be aware nor concern themselves with the operations of the mechanism — the price or market system as it is called — because by and large the system is self-regulating and self-regenerative. A family does not have to concern itself with how cucumbers get from California to Winnipeg or how B.C. apples arrive in Ottawa. All that the family need concern itself with is the procurement of enough income to pay for the things that it wants. In the same way, a household in Montreal ordering its winter supply of fuel oil probably did not, until recently, give much thought to how it was that the local fuel oil dealer managed to have just the right amount of fuel oil to satisfy his customers each winter. Nor did the family give much thought to the fact that in terms of other goods and services, the price of fuel oil had been falling steadily. (In fact, by 1973 a gallon of fuel oil cost only 3.6 minutes of an average worker's labour.)

The events following the Middle East War of October 1973, (namely the Arab oil embargo and the subsequent quadrupling in international oil prices) were to change dramatically the attitude of the average Canadian toward the process by which fuel oil, gasoline and other petroleum requirements were met. The change in attitude was prompted by the realization that the prices of these products were rising sharply and likely to continue to rise in the future. This implied that in a well-established expenditure pattern room had now to be found for much larger outlays on petroleum based products.

For many, the oil squeeze meant financial discomfort, for some it meant real hardship, and for all it meant that "the government should do something" about what was quickly being labelled the energy "crisis".

This book of essays was commissioned for two reasons: first, to provide a view of petroleum and energy markets as seen through the economist's eyes. Secondly, to analyze a number of vital questions relating to the oil policies that governments have adopted or might enact in the future — particularly in response to radical changes in world conditions.

A crisis shortage

One of the most prominent features of public discussion about energy in recent times is the feeling that we - Canada, the U.S., the world - are running out of oil. Often, the implication is that as of a certain date in the not-too-distant future we shall pump out the last barrel of oil that we have and that will be that. Not surprisingly, this doomsday syndrome stuff of which headlines are made is not a very accurate depiction of the real situation. Since the issue is critical and an understanding of the oil supply process crucial, the first essay in the book is devoted to an examination of the nature of oil supply.

Of prime concern in this first essay by Professor R. Uhler, is the exact meaning of the commonplace assertion that we are running out of oil. Professor Uhler enumerates the various sources of supply and the conditions under which they will be tapped. In so doing, he demonstrates that it is meaningless to talk about the supply of oil unless the price of oil is known. In his words, "the question 'how many reserves?' prompts the question 'at what price?' " In other words, although there is a limited supply of oil that can be extracted for $8 per barrel, a limited supply at $9 and so on, the supply of oil at $100 per barrel would, in terms of current rates of usage, be practically unlimited.

This distinction between the geological stock of oil reserves and the supply that is economically feasible to exploit at any given time is a critical one. Lack of understanding of this difference has led to the presumption that a crisis is in the offing and has led to the adoption of crisis measures. Unfortunately, some of the policies that have been enacted by government have reduced the feasibility of augmenting the supply while at the same time encouraging more extensive use of oil. In other words, the net effect of the "crisis intervention" by government might well make the situation worse. The policy response is the subject of examination in several of the essays.

The quartermaster effect

Ignoring the fact that the supply of oil is dependent on the price (net of all taxes) that it will fetch on the market leads to a pessimistic supply outlook. By the same token, the view that we will use up all the oil that we do have is often based on the presumption that the intensity of oil consumption will continue to grow until the point of exhaustion is reached. This view ignores the fact that the demand for oil, like the supply, depends on, among other things, the price of oil.

In the second essay, Professor E. Berndt provides the first compilation ever of the attempts that have been made to estimate the extent to which Canadian consumption of energy in various forms will adapt as the prices of energy sources change and incomes grow. The unambiguous conclusion of Berndt's survey is that the demand for energy does depend on its price and that the rising price of energy sources performs the very valuable function of rationing the supply of energy sources.

In the context of the "spaceship earth" view that we are rapidly using up our rations, rising prices automatically perform the function of a firm-handed, impartial quartermaster to conserve remaining supplies. On the other hand, policies of government that successfully keep the price of energy down encourage the use of energy and, at the same time, discourage the production of alternative sources.

Professor Berndt also pursues the notion that energy supply constraints necessarily imply slower growth for industrialized nations. In the first section of his essay, it is demonstrated that the price of energy is a significant determinant of the extent to which various energy sources are utilized. On the basis of this fact Berndt concludes that as long as prices are allowed to perform their rationing role, economic growth can and will proceed in a less energy-intensive way. The key to meeting the two objectives of conservation and growth is efficient utilization of resources fostered by pricing resources according to their market value. It is Berndt's opinion that one of the main impediments to the attainment of growth-conservation bliss is current government policy and regulation.

The last essay of Part I ties together Parts I and II. This essay, by Campbell Watkins, describes the evolution of the pricing of petroleum and natural gas in the Canadian market and in the course of doing so provides inferences about the competitive structure of the industry. In considering the current situation in Canada he draws upon the analysis of supply and demand contained in the first two essays to spell out the implications of current government pricing policies and related matters. The most significant of these is the fact that the two-price system for energy resources involves a 'deadweight loss' or waste of resources. Watkins provides preliminary estimates of these losses.

Government steps in

To some extent the intervention by government into the energy marketplace was a purely political response to the fact of rapidly rising energy prices. As has often been observed, once a crisis atmosphere exists, government "can't do nothing". It is also clear that many Canadians would regard the oil industry as "fair game" for whatever measures government chose to impose upon them. Their image, whether deserved or not, as the "fat cats" of the industrial farm together with a suspicion in some quarters that they were ultimately responsible for the rising price of oil made it almost inevitable that in the wake of the crisis would come proposals for more direct involvement by government in the energy sector.

The establishment of Petro-Canada is a concrete expression of this sort of feeling as are the current proposals for splitting up the oil companies in the U.S. and recent demands that the Canadian industry be nationalized. Since it is not clear that proceeding in this way will rectify any of the perceived "problems" associated with the operation of energy markets we thought that it would be useful to devote a section of this book to an analysis of the role of the private sector in energy markets.

What is at issue in examining the structure of an industry is the extent to which the industry is competitive. Competition is not an end in itself, but is desirable because it yields the lowest possible price for consumers. To the extent that an industry is not competitive, prices to consumers will be higher and the profits of the firms in the industry will be higher than is required to maintain the desired supply of the product. It is relatively easy to speak in general terms about the conditions that would prevail in a particular market if there were free competition. It is quite another matter to infer from the operation of a market the extent to which the market is competitive. The best that one can do is to compare the price and profit performance of the particular market with the performance of other markets.

How much competition?

During the course of his essay, Campbell Watkins examines the price and profit performance of the Canadian petroleum industry. His conclusion is that throughout the period 1947-1961, before the involvement of government in the pricing process, the movement of prices to producers at the wellhead was consistent with the pattern expected under competition. This evidence, like his conclusion that the rate of profitability in the industry is consistent with the competitive case, does not necessarily prove the existence of competition. However, the broad impression is that the industry is not characterized by obvious inefficiency and those who advocate more intervention would do well to consider the evidence that Watkins presents.

Should the government step in?

Part II is a *tour de force* of the whole question of industrial structure, regulation and government ownership in the energy sector. In his lengthy essay, Professor Walter Mead discusses, in a clear and concise way, the conditions under which government intervention in the marketplace is called for. From a general statement of the objectives, Professor Mead moves to consideration of competition in the energy industry.

In large part the evidence examined by Professor Mead deals with the U.S. industry. This is because research in the area is much more advanced in the U.S. than it is elsewhere. (The partial Canadian evidence, examined by Campbell Watkins in his essay, yields conclusions broadly similar to those based on the U.S. evidence.) Surprisingly, Professor Mead concludes, "The most conclusive evidence of monopoly power in the oil industry that any objective research has been able to establish is due to market restrictions imposed by the Federal Government."

Government ownership and regulation

The net effect of current Canadian governmental involvement in the petroleum industry is to transfer oil revenues from the private sector to the government sector. This is done with the full realization that some of the revenues must be re-employed in the energy sector if Canada's energy needs are to be met - Petro-Canada is a reflection of this realization. To the extent that this happens, the effect of the taxation of petroleum revenues is not to cause a redistribution of resources away from the energy sector, but rather to augment the government's involvement in the energy industry at the expense of private sector involvement.

"If government policy is to be rational then prior to additional government regulation or ownership and management of the energy sector, evidence should be presented showing that there would be a net social gain accruing from such government activity." On the basis of this statement of objectives, Professor Mead surveys the evidence on the performance of government as a regulator and as an operator of enterprise. After a consideration of the social costs and social benefits of government ownership and government regulation, Professor Mead concludes that, "the record as well as the future of government regulation does not appear to be rewarding in terms of serving the public interest in the long run." This conclusion is tempered somewhat for certain cases. "In spite of its poor record of performance, where external costs are extremely large as in the case of nuclear electric power generation, regulation appears to be a necessity."

Professor Mead's analysis of the U.S. government as regulator is particularly relevant during the present time because of the insight that it provides into the recent gas shortages in the U.S. In his essay, written months before the current shortages arose, Mead points out that, "Today the demand for natural gas is far in excess of its supply at prevailing prices and *there is clearly a shortage.*" The cause of the shortage in his view is the fact that the price of natural gas has been artificially maintained by government controls at a level far below that dictated by demand and supply. Furthermore, "The dominant interest group calling the tune in natural gas price regulation has been the natural gas utilities as buyers and distributors, and consumers in non-producing states."

It is ironic to note that it is precisely consumers in non-producing states that are suffering most as a result of the current shortage.

From an examination of the role of government as owner and regulator, Professor Mead turns to a discussion of the performance of the private sector. In the course of his discussion he addresses a variety of vital questions, among them, "Have profits been excessive in the energy industry?" and "Have prices for energy products been excessively high?"

The overall conclusion reached by Mead in comparing the performance of private enterprise with government enterprise performance is, in Mead's words, "Churchillian". "Allocation of scarce energy resources by private decision-making is probably the worst economic system, except that the next best alternative, government enterprise, is an intolerable second best."

The OPEC puzzle

Taken together, the first section of Campbell Watkins' paper and the paper by Walter Mead provide insight into the economics of the structure of the domestic petroleum markets in Canada and the U.S. Current and recent happenings have, however, tended to focus an increasing amount of attention on the world oil market and its workings. The structure and function of the international market and the likely future course of oil prices are of more than passing interest to Canada which is both an importer and an exporter of oil. The second essay in Part II explores several alternative explanations of the workings of the world oil market and develops a "price leadership model" of the interactions between the OPEC countries in their attempts to set the world price of oil. This model explains, among other things, why it is that Saudi Arabia seems to be more conservative in its pricing policy than the other members of OPEC. The price leadership hypothesis seems to do a better job of explaining the behaviour of the OPEC countries than the prevailing cartel hypothesis.

After the Erickson-Winokur essay was written, the OPEC countries, in a real world test of the price-leadership model, began to behave exactly as the model predicts. Saudi Arabia, in an effort to make good its resistance to large increases in the price of oil, increased its production to offset the surge in oil demand caused by the record cold winter in the U.S. and the nascent world-wide economic recovery. In other words, the Saudis are performing the price-leadership role that the Erickson-Winokur hypothesis suggests.

In the process of examining alternative hypotheses, Professors Erickson and Winokur provide informative commentary on the conspiracy theory of world oil pricing, the splitting up of large multinational oil companies and a variety of other issues. Like the other papers that preceded it, the Erickson-Winokur essay lays some of the blame for current difficulties at the door of government. In particular, they are concerned about current preoccupation in the U.S. with splitting up the multinational oil companies. Not only is this activity of dubious social benefit, but to the extent that it distracts attention away from the central issue of improving supply potential it may impose a substantial long term cost.

Canadian oil prospects

Government policy and regulation are evolving as the dominant features of the economic landscape in the 1970's. This is particularly true of energy markets where governments have assumed a dominant profile. Part III of the book looks at aspects of government policy regulation with a view to providing some insight into the potential course of developments in the domestic petroleum industry.

The first paper in this Part, by Professors Quirin and Kalymon, addresses a variety of issues that are crucial for the formulation of a forward-looking Canadian energy policy. At the outset they examine the effectiveness of exploration expenditures in recent years as well as the cash flows currently available to the industry. A consideration of current taxation regimes and probable discovery costs lead Quirin and Kalymon to conclude that rates of return presently available are unlikely to induce the major step-up in exploration that would seem to be desirable. In fact, it is their view that current taxation is excessive and is unduly depressing returns on new discoveries.

It is easy to say that current returns are insufficient and quite another matter to say what return would be sufficient. In the words of the authors, "the only way to determine whether a given prospective rate of return in petroleum exploration is adequate to attract capital is to undertake a careful examination of the relative riskiness of petroleum exploration in comparison with other investment opportunities currently available. With a notion of relative risks in hand, a determination must then be made as to what rate of return premium, if any, over prospective rates of return available on these alternatives, is required to make investment in petroleum exploration as attractive as the alternatives."

The authors used information on the variability of companies share prices and returns per share to construct measures of the risk that petroleum companies face. By comparing the riskiness of investing in the petroleum industry with the riskiness of investing in regulated utilities, such as Bell Canada for example, they were able to construct an estimate of the rate of return that petroleum companies should earn (and offer to shareholders) if they are to compete successfully for investment funds in the capital market.

In comparing actual-prospective returns with required returns the authors conclude that there does not exist "an adequate incentive to invest" in petroleum development in Canada. This conclusion, combined with the fact that it is highly unlikely that the industry can be self-financing over the next five years yields a dreary prospect for the future of Canadian oil development. In the authors' view: "the industry will have to rely on the capital market to reach even moderate market growth and . . . unless rates of return, after tax, without reinvestment gimmicks, allow it to do so, Canada will become increasingly dependent on foreign sources of supply."

Canada-U.S. policy

The second paper in Part III is a partially retrospective - partially prospective - review of Canadian-U.S. oil policy. This essay by Dean James McKie provides a good summary of the evolution of Canada-U.S. energy policy and the view of an "outsider" as to the probable course of future developments. McKie's view of the potential for Canadian-American energy cooperation is not optimistic. However, he does identify some areas where mutually beneficial cooperation is possible, such as: reciprocity in transportation; petroleum exchanges; emergency measures in the event of oil embargoes; and United States capital investment in enterprises where mutual advantages can be negotiated.

Although there has been a tendency in recent years to downplay the benefits to Canada from energy cooperation, recent developments suggest that the areas for mutually beneficial cooperation outlined by McKie will become a reality. The recent role of Canada as an emergency supplier of natural gas to the U.S. has visibly altered the bargaining position of Canada in Canada-U.S. relations. The consequences of this could well be a more concerted effort toward collective emergency preparedness particularly in the stockpiling of petroleum. Other developments, such as the Kitimat pipeline in Western Canada, provide further evidence that the complexion of Canada-U.S. energy relations is changing in a way that McKie suggests would be mutually beneficial.

The preparation of this volume was made possible by the cooperation of Professor Campbell Watkins, whose essential contribution I gratefully acknowledge. As part of his editorial contribution, Professor Watkins has provided an introduction to each of the essays.

The Fraser Institute has been pleased to support the work reported in this volume in the interest of promoting informed public debate about this vital issue. However, owing to the independence of the authors, the views expressed by them may or may not conform severally or collectively with those of the members of the Institute.

Summer, 1977   Michael Walker

PART I
ENERGY IN THE MARKETPLACE

Editor's Introduction

One of the most important effects of changes in the price of energy is the effect they have on the quantity of energy supplied. This price sensitivity of energy supply is the main topic discussed by Professor Uhler. In his essay, he points out the necessity of treating petroleum supply in terms of different quantities available at different prices, rather than as a finite quantity irrespective of the cost conditions under which petroleum might be recoverable. Undoubtedly, higher prices bring forth more supply. Additional petroleum can be recovered from existing reservoirs. Previously non-commercial discoveries become economic. New exploration 'plays' become more attractive. But estimation of the magnitude of the price response is not easy to evaluate, especially in terms of new discoveries.

Professor Uhler discusses several methods used by industry, associations and government agencies to estimate future or new reserves. He finds all such methods lacking and cautions against their use without proper recognition of their limitations. An example of the way in which sanguine acceptance of such methods can provide misleading information is the estimation of future Canadian production potential provided by the Canadian government to the United States Oil Import Task Force in 1970 (see discussion by McKie in this volume). In the latter part of his essay, Uhler turns to the question of whether the rate and mode of exploration is optimal, measured by society's, rather than private, interests. He examines in particular three arguments which have been advanced as justification for government intervention. The first is whether the risks in petroleum exploration deter private investment, while spreading risk by public participation would produce a more bold approach. The second is whether government participation would make information more accessible. The third is whether a one 'firm' operation would avoid duplication of effort. Uhler concludes that the case for government intervention on these grounds is not proven.

Economic Concepts of Petroleum Energy Supply

RUSSELL S. UHLER

Associate Professor of Economics
University of British Columbia

THE AUTHOR

Russell S. Uhler is Associate Professor of Economics at the University of British Columbia. Born in 1937, Dr. Uhler was educated in California and graduated Ph.D. from Claremont Graduate School, 1967. He served as a consultant, 1973-74, to the Department of Energy, Mines and Resources, Ottawa, and as Visiting Professor at the U.S. Naval Postgraduate School.

Dr. Uhler's published works include "A Stochastic Model for Determining the Economic Prospects of Petroleum Exploration Over Large Regions," *The Journal of the American Statistical Association*, Vol. 65, June 1970, (with Paul Bradley); and "Costs and Supply in Petroleum Exploration: The Case of Alberta," *The Canadian Journal of Economics*, IX, No. 1, February 1976. His paper for the 1975 conference of the Economics of Oil and Gas Self-Sufficiency in Canada, at the University of Calgary, entitled "Forecasting Petroleum Supply: Methods and Aggregation Bias," is included in the published proceedings of the conference.

Economic Concepts of Petroleum Energy Supply

RUSSELL S. UHLER

Associate Professor of Economics
University of British Columbia

I. INTRODUCTION

Within the last five years, and in the midst of apparent plentiful world supply, crude oil prices have quadrupled, in some areas shortages of certain refined products such as gasoline have developed, natural gas prices have skyrocketed, and a sharp realignment of the relative prices of many kinds of goods and services has been set off. By almost any standard such changes reflect an economic upheaval of major proportions.

The basic reason for this upheaval is relatively simple. In 1971 the Organization of Petroleum Exporting Countries (OPEC) concluded the now famous Teheran-Tripoli Agreements in order to halt the secular decline in world crude oil prices which had begun in 1956. This action had immediate success and quickly led to a series of price increases so that today prices are approximately four times their 1971 level. It was not scarcity or high cost supply which caused this increase but simply the monopolistic power of the OPEC Cartel.

Although the world economy has managed to sustain the initial shock of the sharp increase in crude oil and natural gas prices and is apparently adjusting with a smoothness that many find surprising, a whole series of important energy policy questions have arisen as a result of these changes. Among them is the question of petroleum supply potential outside the OPEC group of countries. This is of particular interest to those countries with existing supply potential, such as Canada and the United States which would like to determine their capability for petroleum energy independence. But determining this capability is not an easy matter. In Canada's case it involves forecasting the remaining supply potential in already developed regions such as Alberta and British Columbia, and in the frontier regions of the Arctic and the continental shelf where only meagre amounts of information from actual drilling experience has been obtained. The United States has similar forecasting problems in its developed regions, on its own continental shelf, and in Alaska.

In both Canada and the United States the "energy crisis" has led to public concern that we are running out of petroleum resources. But what is generally not so well understood is that even though we are fast depleting our sources of low cost petroleum, there still exist substantial amounts of higher cost sources. Thus the appropriate supply question is not "how much petroleum is left?" but "how much petroleum is left at different prices?" Put another way, the appropriate question is "how much additional supply can we expect to be forthcoming at higher and higher levels of petroleum prices?" This is not an easy question to answer and today nobody can predict, for example, how much Canada's crude oil supply will increase (decrease) if prices rise (fall) by x dollars per barrel. The reasons for these forecasting difficulties will be discussed more fully later when I consider conditions associated with different sources of supply, but the most obvious one relates to the difficulty of forecasting the discovery rate of new reserves and determining how the discovery rate depends upon economic conditions.

It should be made clear at the outset that the answer to the "how many reserves at different prices" question does not just depend on our ability to forecast the supply potential of frontier regions. Although these regions are obviously of great potential significance the remaining potential of existing developed regions should not be overlooked. Moreover, our understanding of the petroleum supply process itself, and hence our ability to make accurate assessments of frontier regions, depends crucially on our understanding the development of existing producing regions and how this development has responded to changes in economic conditions.

Historically, most crude petroleum products have been located, developed, and processed by private firms. But renewed interest in future supply has brought into question the effectiveness of these institutional arrangements. It is claimed, for example, that private firms attempting to avoid risk may spend too little on exploration. This in turn may lead firms to discover new petroleum reserves at a rate which is slower than what is 'best' for society.

The exact opposite position has also been argued in that it has been suggested that competition among private firms to discover and control the limited petroleum resource stock has led to too much spending on exploration activity or to spending well in advance of what is 'best' for society.

It is for these reasons that some people think that government should seek a more active role in the petroleum industry, especially in exploration. But the formal basis or rationale for the arguments supporting government intervention are often couched in technical economic language and are, I believe, often misunderstood by the petroleum industry and the public. In the last section of this paper I will discuss the most common of these arguments.

7

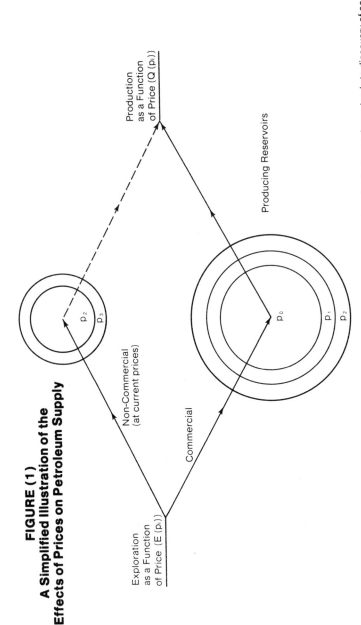

FIGURE (1)
A Simplified Illustration of the
Effects of Prices on Petroleum Supply

Exploration, which depends on the price to the producer, leads to discovery of commercial and non-commercial reserves. Commercial reserves can be brought into production at current prices while non-commercial reserves can only be produced at higher than current prices. At a price of p_1 none of the reserves in the non-commercial pools are producible, at p_2 some are, and p_3 all pools that were non-commercial at p_1 would be producible.

II. PETROLEUM SUPPLY

The concept of petroleum supply

Figure (1) is an attempt to present a much simplified overview of the petroleum supply process with particular emphasis on the effect of different price levels (as indicated by the p_i's in the diagram). This is not to say, of course, that other factors which we will consider in more detail later are not important in affecting this process.

Beginning at the far left of the diagram we see that exploration activity results in the discovery of new reservoirs (pools) of oil and natural gas. Exploration activity is affected by petroleum prices since, other things equal, (including royalties and other taxes) the higher the price the greater the economic reward of discovering new reservoirs and hence the greater the incentive to explore. At any given level of prices, say p_0, some discoveries will be commercial reservoirs, i.e., they will be economical or profitable to produce at current prices and costs. Such reservoirs become part of the pool of commercial reservoirs illustrated in the lower part of the diagram by a set of concentric circles. On the other hand, at current prices and costs some reservoirs will be uneconomical to produce and thus will become part of the pool of non-commercial reservoirs illustrated in the upper part of the diagram. As price increases from p_0 to p_1, in this illustration the stock of recoverable reserves in commercial reservoirs expands as indicated by the second and larger circle associated with the price p_1. If prices were to continue to rise to p_2 then still more reserves would be economically recoverable and, moreover, some previously non-commercial reservoirs would become economical to produce. This latter phenomenon is illustrated by the inner circle in the upper part of the diagram labelled p_2. If price increases still further then even more previously non-commercial reservoirs become economical to produce. The reason that increasing prices have this impact on supply (in both sectors of the diagram) is because of the simple fact that increasing portions of the reserves of petroleum reservoirs can, at least after some point, only be produced at higher cost. Thus, rising prices will make it worthwhile to recover a higher pro-

9

portion of initial reserves in place. In view of this it is reasonable to deduce that the amount of extra reserves which results from higher prices depends upon cost conditions in producing reservoirs and upon the costs of finding new ones. This is indeed true and it will be discussed in more detail later.

Referring again to the diagram in Figure (1) we note that the production of petroleum from reserves occurs simultaneously with the addition of newly discovered reserves and any additions due to changes in prices. We can also note that the production rate, $Q(p_i)$, from these reservoirs also depends upon prices. Thus it is clear that for any given price level the level of recoverable reserves, as indicated by our circles, is either expanding or contracting depending upon whether the production flow differs from the discovery rate of new reserves.

Since there is a finite amount of petroleum reserves which are economically recoverable at a given price level one would expect that eventually the inflow into the pool of reserves would dry up and that this would then set up forces leading to a rise in prices. As a result, as we have already noted, not only would it become worthwhile to recover higher proportions of producing reservoirs and begin production of some previously non-commercial ones, but exploration activity should also expand leading to a greater inflow of new reservoirs. Thus the rise in price acts as a mechanism for stimulating supply from several sources.

It is possible to derive two types of supply relationships from the overview presented in Figure (1). One type is associated with the right side of the diagram and is the usual variety where the quantity involved is the amount brought to the earth's surface (produced) per unit of time. The second type is associated with the left and middle portion of the diagram and involves relationships between price and petroleum reserves in the ground.

In the first type, such as illustrated in Figure (2a), each price will have associated with it a different quantity which producers will want to supply to the market. For example, at price, p_o, producers will want to supply quantity, $Q(p_o)$, and at a higher price, p_1, they will want to supply quantity, $Q(p_1)$,

FIGURE (2a)
The Effect of Price on Petroleum Production

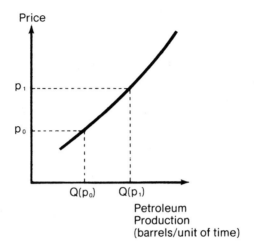

This diagram summarizes the relationship between the price of petroleum and the rate at which petroleum will be pumped from the ground. At price p_0 the quantity $Q(p_0)$ barrels per month, say, will be produced. At the higher price p_1 the larger quantity $Q(p_1)$ barrels per month, say, will be produced.

etc. Although it is easy to show that, other things equal, higher prices will induce greater production rates from existing reservoirs it is particularly hard to hold other things equal in this situation. In the first place, we know that the very act of production affects natural geophysical factors and tends to lower production rates over time. Alone, this would suggest that at any given price, production rates cannot be expected to remain steady but should instead decline. This is simply the natural decline phenomenon of producing petroleum reservoirs. But at the same time new reservoirs are being discovered which tends to offset this effect. Thus we see that the supply relationship in Figure (2a) is much more complicated than it appears and that it is shifting through time in response to the dynamics of natural decline and the discovery of new reservoirs. It is imperative that these factors be taken into consideration when estimating this type of supply or deliverability relationship.

The second type of supply relationship noted earlier is a relationship between the price and reserves in the ground rather than the rate at which they are produced. There are three kinds of supply relationships of this type. In two of them the quantity variable is a flow and in the third it is a stock.

We have noted previously that as price rises additional reserves would be forthcoming from several sources. Thus one kind of supply relationship relates price to the rate at which new reserves are added and is illustrated in Figure (2b). But since reserves also decline as a result of production

FIGURE (2b)
The Effect of Price on Gross Additions
to Petroleum Reserves

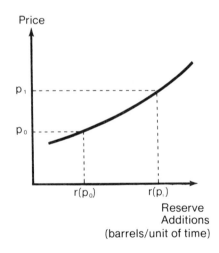

This diagram summarizes the relationship between the price of petroleum and the rate at which new petroleum reserves are added to the available stock. At price p_0 the stock of oil reserves will be added to at a rate of $r(p_0)$ barrels per month, say. At the higher price p_1 the stock will be expanding at the faster rate, $r(p_1)$ per month.

there is also a net supply relationship for reserves in the ground which is simply the difference between the curves in Figure (2b) and Figure (2a). The net supply curve is illustrated in Figure (2c). At p_0 the production rate exceeds the rate of additions to reserves so that the change in net supply of reserves in the ground is negative. In this example, if price were to rise to p_1 then the net supply rate would be positive as indicated in the diagram. This curve will also shift through time for the same reasons those in Figures (2a) and (2b) shift.

FIGURE (2c)
The Effect of Price on Net Additions
to Petroleum Reserves

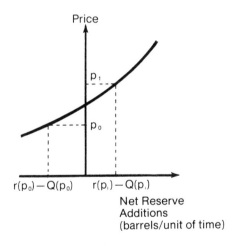

This diagram combines the information in Figures 2a and 2b. It shows the net effect of changes in the price of petroleum on reserves. At p_0 reserve additions $r(p_0)$ are smaller than petroleum production $Q(p_0)$ and as a consequence total reserves are shrinking — net change is negative. At the higher price p_1, reserve additions $r(p_1)$ exceed production $Q(p_1)$ and as a consequence total reserves are expanding — net change is positive.

FIGURE (2d)
The Effect of Price on Remaining
Recoverable Reserves

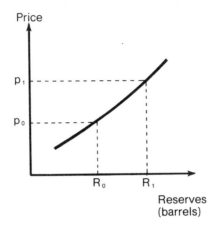

This diagram summarizes the relationship between the price of petroleum and the total stock of petroleum reserves in the ground. Other things remaining the same, an increase in the price of petroleum from p_0 to p_1 will increase the stock of recoverable reserves from R_0 barrels to R_1 barrels. (But see the discussion in the text.)

The third kind of supply relationship involving reserves in the ground is illustrated in Figure (2d). It is a relationship between price and remaining recoverable reserves. It is related to the net flow supply curve of Figure (2c) in the following way. At p_0 we saw that the production rate exceeded the rate of additions to reserves which must mean that recoverable reserves were declining through time. Thus, even though remaining recoverable reserves at p_0 are indicated as R_0 in Figure (2d) they must be declining since the additions are negative. On the other hand, at price p_1 additions exceed subtractions so recoverable reserves must be growing. On this basis we would then expect the supply curve in Figure (2d) to become more elastic (flatter) through time. But the situation is actually even more complicated than this. Since the net flow supply curve is itself shifting through time for reasons already noted it is an additional factor causing the supply curve in Figure (2d) to also be shifting through time.

We have already noted that additional recoverable reserves may come from several different sources but our discussion so far has been of the aggregate supply relationship in both flow and stock terms. In view of the rather complicated nature of the aggregate supply framework and the different supply concepts which are available, it is useful to consider in more detail the concepts which are most relevant to each of the major sources of potential petroleum supply which were noted earlier. These sources include: (1) additional reserves from producing reservoirs, (2) additional reserves from previously non-commercial reservoirs, and (3) reserves in new reservoirs discovered through exploration activity. A possible fourth source is reserves in previously abandoned reservoirs but this source can logically be included with the second source.

There are, of course, other possible sources of petroleum energy. The potential supply from such exotic sources as the gasification of coal and oil shale will depend upon the relative price to which petroleum energy eventually rises or on the availability of new cost reducing technology for exploiting these sources. The Athabasca oil sands is an example of a source which has become more attractive through a combination of price increases and advancement in technology. Further technological advances here, which might be all the more likely with the beginning of large scale production, could make this a vast source indeed. Although I mention them in passing, these potential sources will not be discussed further in this chapter.

Producing reservoirs as a source of additional supply

The recoverable fraction of initial petroleum reserves is not a known constant but an economic variable which can change with economic conditions. If petroleum prices rise, for example, it often becomes worthwhile to recover a higher fraction of the reserves in a reservoir. But typically, an attempt to recover a higher fraction of reserves can only be accomplished at a higher incremental or marginal cost. In other words, each extra fraction of reserves recovered is at a higher cost, at least after a particular recovery fraction has been reached. Figure (3) illustrates the cost conditions of an imaginary oil reservoir which has initial reserves-in-place of 100 million barrels. The upward sloping curve is the marginal cost of recovering additional barrels of oil and the horizontal line at p_2 is the current price per barrel. The correct economic decision is to expand recovery until the marginal cost of recovering an additional barrel is just equal to its price, in other words, where the two curves intersect. If price rises from p_2 to p_3 it then becomes worthwhile to recover an additional increment $R_3 - R_2$.

It is clear that the magnitude of the additional increment which becomes worthwhile to recover due to the rise in price depends crucially on the position and shape of the marginal cost curve. If it is very steep near the current point of intersection then the effect of a price increase on additional supply will be small; if the curve was relatively flat in this region, as it is between p_1 and p_2, then the effect of a price increase on additional supply will be larger. It should be noted that this marginal cost curve is nothing more than the supply curve illustrated in Figure (2d) for an individual reservoir since it tells us the level of remaining recoverable reserves at each price level. It should also be recalled that production from an individual reservoir causes the supply curve to shift leftward through time and that the supply curve for several such producing reservoirs is just the horizontal summation of the supply curves of each reservoir.

FIGURE (3)
The Effect of Price Increases
on Recoverable Reserves

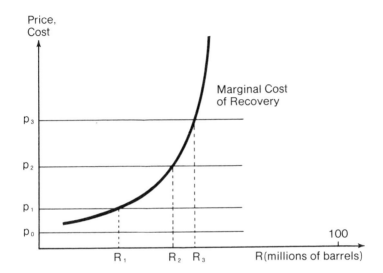

The amount of oil that will be extracted from a reservoir of given size (100 million barrels) depends on the cost of producing each additional barrel and the price that the additional barrel will fetch for the producer. At price p_0 none of the oil in the reservoir will be recoverable. At price p_1, a total of R_1 barrels will be recoverable. At the higher price p_2, a larger total R_2 will be recoverable.

Even though Canada has thousands of producing reservoirs whose additional potential would have to be individually evaluated in order to build up an aggregate supply relationship from this source, the job is certainly not insurmountable. For example, in 1973 the Alberta Energy Resources Conservation Board (ERCB) reported on its estimates of the effects of higher natural gas prices on recovery from 120 non-associated gas reservoirs which have over 50 per cent of the proven initial gas in place in the province. Their estimates indicated that increases in prices from mid-1960's to 1973 levels resulted in an increase of 2.7 trillion cubic feet (tcf) of recoverable reserves from these reservoirs. A less detailed part of the study indicated that these price effects on additional recoverable associated and other non-associated reserves was in the order of 0.4 tcf.[1]

Even though the ERCB stresses the tentative nature of some of its conclusions in this study the results do indicate the potential importance of producing reservoirs as a source of additional recoverable reserves. The study also indicates the feasibility of constructing a supply relationship from this source. It would simply be necessary to estimate additional recoverable reserves for still higher prices to determine more points on the supply relationship.

Non-commercial reservoirs as a source of supply

In the process of petroleum exploration it is common to discover reservoirs which are non-commercial. This means that current economic conditions are such that it simply is not profitable to make the necessary investment to begin production. Such reservoir discoveries might be viewed as going into an inventory, to be taken out if and when economic conditions warrant it. Many natural gas reservoirs in Alberta have been of this type. Discoveries were made, evaluated, and wells capped because of unfavorable market conditions. With subsequent expansion in demand and the rise in price many of these previously non-commercial reservoirs have been "taken out of inventory" and brought into production.

An excellent recent example is the Southeastern Alberta Field. The Medicine Hat Number 1 reservoir was discovered in 1904, the Milk River reservoir was discovered in 1911, and other smaller reservoirs were subsequently discovered in this field. Even though these reservoirs contained large reserves, economic conditions were such that they were non-commercial until 1973 when prices and demand were sufficient to begin production. The potential importance of such sources is indicated by the following data. Of the 6.5 trillion cubic feet (tcf) increase in recoverable natural gas reserves in 1973 as estimated by the ERCB, 2.2 tcf was due to this one field and of the 5.2 tcf increase in 1974, 3.0 tcf was from this field, a full 34 per cent and 58 per cent respectively. Still other previously non-commercial reservoirs offer potential for the future.

Let us use Figure (3) again to illustrate the kind of situation which makes a reservoir non-commercial initially but allows it to become commercial under a new set of economic conditions. Initially the marginal cost of production is everywhere above the current price, p_o, so that the indicated recoverable amount is zero. But if the price rises, say to p_1, then it becomes worthwhile to recover an amount R_1 of reserves from this reservoir. As indicated earlier, further price increases can be expected to lead to still larger recoverable amounts.

It was noted earlier that abandoned reservoirs are also a potential source of additional reserves and that the analysis of their potential is formally similar to this case. This is true since an abandoned reservoir is nothing more than one which has reached a non-commercial stage in its life. Price increases can, in some cases, cause these reservoirs to again become commercial ventures.

It should also be noted that cost-reducing recovery technology can lead to abandoned reservoirs again becoming commercial and to increases in recoverable reserves in producing reservoirs or to non-commercial reservoirs becoming commercial. In terms of our diagrams the effect of cost-reducing technological change is to shift the marginal cost curve downward so that for any given price it becomes worthwhile to recover a higher proportion of the reserves in a reservoir.

New reservoirs as a source of supply

So far we have discussed producing reservoirs, non-commercial reservoirs, and abandoned reservoirs as possible sources of additional petroleum supply. The remaining source of supply which we will consider is from the discovery of new reservoirs. This source might be expected to account for the greatest amounts of additional reserves, but at the same time it is the least certain and most difficult source to analyze. A number of different methods of analysis have been proposed, each with a certain objective in mind and each with its own strengths and weaknesses.

1. Volumetric analysis of supply

This method uses the fact that petroleum reservoirs are only found in sedimentary rock formations. Given that one can determine the reserves per unit volume of the sediments in one region, for a particular set of economic conditions it should be possible to apply the same recovery fraction to the volume of sediments in another partially developed or undeveloped region and thus determine the remaining recoverable reserves in that region.

An extension of this approach recognizes that recovery fractions depend upon prices and costs as we have noted earlier. This extension therefore presumes that it is possible to establish a relationship between real price (price deflated by an appropriate cost index) and the recovery fraction per unit volume of sediments and use this price-recovery fraction relationship in other regions.

The major weakness of the usual volumetric approach and its extension is the assumption that even for very large sedimentary regions the law of large numbers will result in similar recovery fractions per unit volume of sediments. I know of no empirical support for this hypothesis. It is also often argued that even if a suitable analogue region could be found, the data on recovery fraction would be unreliable since the recovery fraction in the analogue region is obviously a function of economic conditions. But as noted earlier, if recovery fractions as a function of economic conditions could be forecasted in the analogue region then these fractions might be usefully applied to the region of interest. I think, however, that it is now widely accepted that the volumetric approach or extensions of it should only be used in obtaining a very rough approximation to recoverable reserves. Whenever possible it should be supplemented with other methods.

2. Geological analysis of supply

Although volumetric analysis is a rudimentary kind of geological survey method, newer methods which require more detailed geological knowledge of a region are slowly beginning to take its place. Instead of simply using information on the volume of sediments, seismic and other geophysical data are used to evaluate the potential of sedimentary formations. Estimates of the amount of recoverable reserves at various price levels are made in order to establish the supply relationship. The uncertainty of supply at each price level can be introduced by placing subjective confidence limits on the quantities involved. This then produces a supply band of probable recoverable reserves at each price level.[2]

A refinement of this method is currently under development by the Geological Survey of Canada.[3] It focuses on the potential of individual petroleum plays in a region. Within each play are prospects having characteristics such as surface area, porosity of sediments, trap fill, etc., all of which are subject to uncertainty. A prospect potential equation of the following form is postulated:

Prospect Potential = Volume of Pores in Trap × Hydrocarbon Fraction × Recovery × Engineering Factors

The quantities on the right side of the equation are characteristics of the prospect which affect its ultimate size but, as noted above, they are subject to uncertainty. The level of uncertainty is, of course, dependent upon the amount of information which is available to geologists and is measured by their subjective estimates of the probabilities of various outcomes. An example may help to clarify this point. Consider the variable 'area of the trap' which is part of the first factor in the prospect potential equation given above. Based on their best information, geologists may feel that the following probabilities regarding area of the trap should be assigned to prospects in the play being evaluated. Let these probabilities be indicated by the diagram in Figure (4). The diagram shows that the probability of a prospect with an area greater than or equal to one square mile is .8, the probability of a prospect greater than or equal to ten square miles is .76, etc., and the probability of a trap being greater than fifty square miles is zero. A similar set of subjective probabilities could be constructed for each of the variables in the prospect potential equation.

FIGURE (4)
An Illustration of the Probability
of Occurrence of Prospects of Given Area

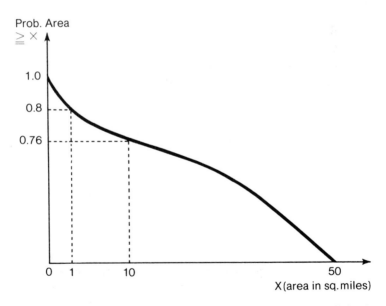

This diagram represents the likelihood of finding a petroleum "trap" or basin of a given size. Exploration is very likely to lead to the discovery of a trap that is at least one square mile in area — eight out of ten times a trap will be greater than or equal to one square mile in area. Although less likely, traps with an area of 10 square miles in area occur seventy-six per cent of the time. Traps greater than 50 square miles in area occur so infrequently that the chances of finding one are negligible (zero probability).

Each variable is also viewed as having a minimum value, or cutoff point, below which the prospect would have zero potential. In other words, if any of the variables in the prospect potential equation took on a value less than the specified cutoff value, the value of the equation is zero.

The next step is to combine all of this information, using the Monte Carlo method and the prospect potential equation given above, to obtain probabilities that a prospect will be greater than or equal to a particular size.[4,5]

The final step is to evaluate the size of the petroleum play from the distribution of prospect potential and information on the number of prospects in the play. The number of prospects in a play is, of course, also uncertain but the best information available is used to evaluate the probabilities of various possible numbers of prospects. Again the Monte Carlo method is employed to arrive at an estimate of the reserves in prospect to finally determine a range of values for the size of the play which would occur at various levels of probability.

If one were interested in extending this to estimate the potential of a region, or basin, similar methods could be used in adding up the potential of various plays.

There is no question that this method has considerable appeal. It uses the best information which is currently available to obtain its estimates and its flexibility is excellent. It has the capability of being modified as new information concerning the variables in the prospect equation comes in and minimum cutoff values for the variables can be changed as warranted by economic conditions. However, as it now stands, the method has one potentially significant technical problem. In the language of the statistician the problem is that the variables in the prospects potential equation are assumed to be independent when they undoubtedly are not. In everyday language this means that when the value of one variable is high the value of another also tends to be high (or low), i.e., they are correlated. Unless this correlation structure can be built into the Monte Carlo sampling framework the answers which come out will be subject to error. But identifying and building in such a structure is certainly possible and is an avenue for future development of this approach which should prove fruitful.

3. Analysis of petroleum supply based on drilling results

Several attempts have been made to build a "model" of the petroleum supply process and then use the data derived from actual drilling experience to estimate its parameters. Once estimated, the quality of the model can then be determined by observing how well it fits the data.

M.K. Hubbert (1962) was an early advocate of this approach stating that "the only possible way we have of determining how much oil the United States will produce is by pure empiricism, based on our actual experience in exploration and production of petroleum. The United States experience can then be used to estimate what may be expected from other comparable regions". This claim was made in a categorical rejection of the volumetric method as a useful way of estimating supply potential. Presumably Hubbert would feel similarly about other geological methods whose estimates are not strictly based on drilling results. Such a criticism is too strong, however, since we will always be able to make better forecasts if more data are available. Moreover, if one argues that it is appropriate to use the results from one region to estimate the potential of another then one can hardly criticize the geological methods on these grounds since this is exactly what they do. How can the subjective probability distributions of the prospect characteristics discussed earlier possibly be formed unless from past experience? Thus it is clear that all methods use past data to one degree or another and we should not be surprised if those models which use the most data relevant to a particular region or play do best. But even though the data-intensive models have the capability of improved forecasts certain weaknesses are still apparent. Thus it will prove instructive to consider several of these models in further detail. Let us begin with the method of M.K. Hubbert.

Hubbert's method was introduced as an alternative to volumetric analysis and makes use of the empirical observation that cumulative discoveries of reserves and cumulative production in a play follow a logistic pattern of behavior as a function of time. As is illustrated in Figure (5a), cumulative discoveries grow initially at an increasing rate because the

FIGURE (5a)
Logistic Pattern of Cumulative Discoveries

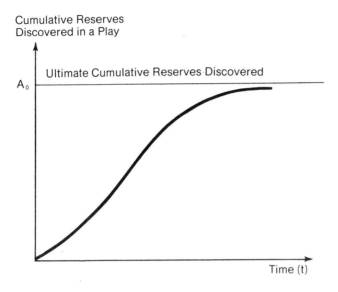

Cumulative Reserves
Discovered in a Play

A_o — Ultimate Cumulative Reserves Discovered

Time (t)

This diagram represents the hypothesis that the total amount of reserves discovered in a given area depends on the length of time that has elapsed. Initially, the cumulative total of discovered reserves increases at an increasing rate. As the total volume of petroleum left to be discovered (petroleum as yet unfound) gets smaller and smaller, the total of discovered reserves increases at a decreasing rate. The flat, upper portion of the curve represents a situation where no new discoveries are being made.

discovery rate is growing, but eventually, due to a reduced number of undiscovered reserves in the play, the discovery rate begins to decline. This causes the cumulative level of discoveries to rise at a slower rate toward a limit such as indicated by the horizontal line A_o in the Figure. The associated "rate of reserves discoveries curve" is shown in Figure (5b).

It is apparent from Figure (5a) that if one could estimate ultimate cumulative reserves discovered A_o from the data on a particular play, then A_o could be considered as the

25

level of ultimate recoverable supply from the play. However, there are several difficulties. In the first place it seems too simple to let time serve as a variable explaining discoveries. A more suitable alternative would be a variable which reflected the impact of cumulative exploration effort such as cumulative exploration wells drilled or cumulative exploratory footage drilled. This substitution is easily accomplished, however, without substantially altering the basic nature of the approach.

The second difficulty has to do with the use of the data in estimating such a relationship. First of all it is clear that the play must be relatively mature before enough data are available to estimate its remaining supply potential since it is necessary to have data points in the range of declining discovery rate, i.e., beyond the point at which the cumulative curve in Figure (5a) begins to bend toward the horizontal line A_0. Thus the method is only useful for plays which are relatively mature and not at all useful if little or no drilling information were available. Secondly, even if we were interested in the supply potential of a mature play (which we often are), the method fails to recognize that the data which it uses are also affected by changing economic conditions. For example, if we were to imagine wellhead price and exploration costs remaining constant over the period of the exploration of a play a set of data would be generated which would allow us to obtain an estimate of the supply potential parameter, A_0. Now suppose a different set of economic conditions in which price were doubled and costs were the same as before. This set of data would result in exploration activity which showed a different pattern and a different value of A_0 would be estimated since higher prices would affect both the rate of exploration and the level of ultimate supply of recoverable reserves. Thus, as in this case, if a model does not have the capability of accounting for the effects of changes in economic conditions and the data are generated in and affected by the presence of such changes the parameter estimates will probably be in error.

Although Hubbert did not use this model to estimate the potential of individual plays, he assumed that the supply potential of the United States, which includes many such

FIGURE (5b)
Discovery Rate Associated with Logistic
Pattern of Cumulative Discoveries

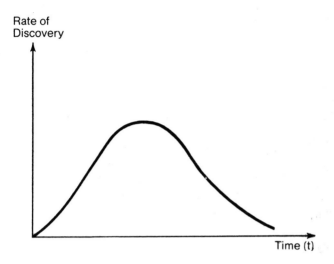

This diagram plots the rate at which new reserves will be discovered in a given play. It is derived from Figure 5a. The hump in this figure corresponds to the middle portion of the "s" shaped curve in Figure 5a. The discovery rate rises to the middle point in the "s" shaped curve and falls thereafter.

plays, could be determined using this model. But even though the aggregated cumulative discoveries data may follow the logistic pattern fairly well there is no a priori reason to expect that this is anything but an accident or that cumulative data tends to smooth out fluctuation. After all, the aggregated data are the summation of discoveries in many plays which are all in different stages of development and there is no reason to suppose that the aggregated data will look anything like that for an individual play. Indeed, a plot of the aggregated discovery rate data shows this to be the case. It is accented by large surges which occur at the beginning of major new plays and does not fit the bell-shaped discovery rate curve illustrated in Figure (5b) well at all.

27

In my view these weaknesses make the application of Hubbert's method to aggregate data useful only to obtain very rough estimates of remaining supply potential. Moreover, it is subject to the same weaknesses as noted earlier when the method is applied to individual plays. In particular, it takes no account of the effects of changing economic conditions.

J.T. Ryan (1974) has criticized Hubbert's method because:

> "there is no fundamental law of physics insuring that cumulative discoveries or cumulative production will follow a logistic pattern in the future . . . This curve was chosen instead on the purely empirical ground that it provided a good fit to past data. The fact that a particular analytical function may appear to the eye to provide a good fit to past data provides no assurance that it will continue to do so in the future."

Ryan postulates instead that "the rate at which oil is discovered is proportional to the amount of undiscovered oil and the knowledge of where it resides" and, after including a logistic function explaining the growth of knowledge, goes on to determine the relationship between reserves discoveries and cumulative wells drilled. As in Hubbert's model for the United States, he finds that the actual discovery rate data in Alberta do not at all fit well the estimated discovery rate relationship which is derived from this hypothesis. The relationship, as one would expect, is a smooth function of cumulative wildcats drilled whereas the actual data are characterized by many spikes and troughs. Noting that the spikes in the data tend to be associated with the beginning of new plays, Ryan then postulates that "the rate of discovery of oil in a play is proportional to the undiscovered oil in a play and the knowledge of the existence of a play", introduces a step function to account for the knowledge of a play, and then develops and estimates the new implied relationship between reserves discoveries and wells drilled. As might be expected, the reserves discovery rate relationship which results from this reformulation does a much better job of explaining the observed data. Of course, the model now requires that the well at which a new play begins be identified thus making its prediction capability depend partly on the ability to predict new plays, a possibility which Ryan sees as remote.

It is also noteworthy that Ryan does not indicate in his hypothesis that economic factors may play a role in determining the discovery rate in a play. But surely one would expect that if relative prices or costs were to change during the exploration of a play, these factors would be important in explaining the rate of exploration effort and hence the rate of discovery of petroleum reserves in the play. It therefore seems worthwhile to consider another model of the petroleum supply process which makes use of the contributions of Hubbert, Ryan, and others but focuses on the effects of changing economic conditions.

I have recently proposed a model with just such an objective in mind.[6] Moreover, I explicitly recognize that the petroleum reserves discovery process is subject to uncertainty. In other words, for a given rate of exploratory effort the amount of reserves discovered is not a specific quantity but instead follows a probability distribution. In this respect it resembles the geological method described earlier in which the potential of a play was described as a probability distribution generated by Monte Carlo methods. But in this model the reserves discovery process is represented by what economists call a production function; that is a relationship between the quantities per unit of time of physical factors of production such as labor and capital equipment, and the amount of product or service produced per unit of time. In the case of petroleum exploration the production process involves the use of exploratory inputs (labor and capital equipment involved in drilling and predrilling operations), and the output is the rate of discovery of reserves in new reservoirs. As we will see later this kind of formulation allows the determination of the implied supply relationship, that is, the relationship between price and the rate of new reserves discovery.

In order to simplify the problem let us represent the multiplicity of productive inputs in the exploration process by a single aggregate we call exploratory effort. It can be approximated by a physical measure such as exploratory feet drilled or wildcat wells drilled per unit of time. Such a production function is illustrated in Figure (6a). As the rate of exploratory effort rises the rate of discovery of new reserves also rises but is subject to diminishing returns as indicated by the shape of the curve. But this diagram is much too simple and needs further elaboration to make it more realistic. Firstly, we have already noted that unlike the manufacture of steel, for example, where a given rate of effort (as measured by the rate of use of labour, capital equipment, and raw materials inputs) produces a known output rate of steel, in this production process the output rate cannot be known with certainty. Thus the curve in the diagram may at most only represent an expected rather than a certain amount.

Another difficulty with the diagram is that a single curve does not represent the relationship between that rate of effort and the discovery rate at all times. As we have already seen, it is believed that for any given level of current exploratory effort the reserves discovery rate at first grows, reaches a peak, and ultimately declines. This is, of course, the essence of the bell-shaped curve shown in Figure (5b). In terms of the diagram in Figure (6a) this phenomenon has the effect of first shifting the whole curve upward until some point is reached after which it shifts downward again. It should be noted, however, that as before this is an approximate representation of the production process in a particular play. Any aggregation will distort the picture since the beginning of several plays would be out of phase with respect to time or to cumulative exploratory effort.[7]

The nice feature of this model is that it leads to just what we are looking for: a short-run and a long-run relationship between the price of petroleum reserves and the rate at which they are expected to be discovered. These supply relationships are constructed from the marginal cost curves which can be calculated from the production function. To see how this is done assume that the cost per unit of exploratory effort is constant and consider the diagram in Figure (6a). Remember also that the output rate is an expected rather than a certain amount. The total cost of finding various expected amounts per unit of time is easily determined by simply multiplying the constant unit cost of effort by the rate of effort and plotting this against the ex-

FIGURE (6a)
Petroleum Production Function

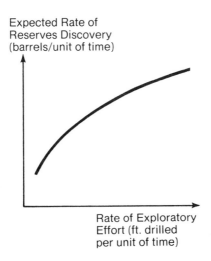

Expected Rate of
Reserves Discovery
(barrels/unit of time)

Rate of Exploratory
Effort (ft. drilled
per unit of time)

This figure represents the relationship between the extent of exploratory effort and the expected rate of reserve discovery. Other things being the same, the greater the effort expended in exploration, the higher will be the discovery rate. Exploratory effort yields diminishing returns and this is reflected in the flattening of the curve.

pected discovery rate as shown in Figure (6b). The short-run marginal cost curve, which is defined as the incremental cost due to an incremental change in the discovery rate, can then be determined from the total cost relationship. Because total costs are increasing at an increasing rate in this example, the marginal cost curve is increasing as the discovery rate increases as shown in Figure (6c). Under reasonable assumptions we can identify the marginal cost curve as the short-run supply curve using reasoning similar to that used earlier; that is, that the discovery rate will expand until its marginal cost equals the price of reserves. Note, however, that this price must be the price of reserves in the ground, i.e. roughly the wellhead price less development costs.

FIGURE (6b)
Petroleum Total Cost Function

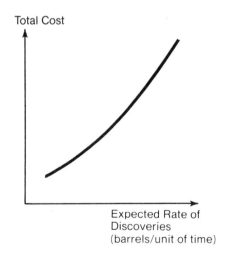

This figure is the dollar cost equivalent of Figure 6a. Given that the cost of drilling stays constant, the greater the exploratory efforts, the greater the cost. From Figure 6a we find that a given effort produces a given expected rate of reserves discovery. Figure 6b represents the fact that the higher the expected rate of discovery, the higher the total cost.

But just as the production function illustrated in Figure (6a) is shifting due to the acquisition of geological knowledge and the reduction of undiscovered reservoirs in a play so will the cost curves also be shifting. Thus it is unreasonable to suppose that a rise in price will result in a substantial movement up the short-run supply curve since more current effort causes the supply curve to shift. In particular, we know that eventually the short-run supply curve will begin to shift upward as reservoirs in a play become more difficult to locate. Thus the long-run supply curve is determined by the speed and the magnitude of the shifts in the short-run curve. In mature plays such shifts are such that it is unreasonable to suppose that even substantial price in-

FIGURE (6c)
Short-run and Long-run Supply Curves
for New Discoveries

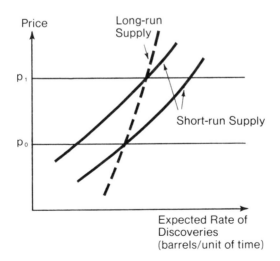

In the long run, the increase in supply from a given change in price will be less than that experienced in the short run. This decline in the responsiveness of supply is caused by the exhaustion of easy-to-locate and, hence, lower-cost reservoirs.

33

creases will yield significant increases in the discovery rate of new reserves. On the other hand, in new plays the supply curve may even be shifting downward so that price increases lead to very significant increases in discoveries. This then suggests further the importance of analyzing petroleum supply on a play by play basis.

Probably the best known attempt in the economics literature to estimate the effect of increased oil or natural gas prices on the supply of these resources is the so-called econometric model.[8] Since I have recently presented a detailed statement of my views on the strengths and weaknesses of this approach I will only outline the argument here.[9]

The econometric model can be viewed as a direct method of analyzing the impact of prices on the discovery of petroleum reserves. In order to do this observations on prices and other relevant variables are gathered to form a time series of data. These data are then analyzed, using a statistical method called regression analysis, to determine the independent effect of price changes on reserves discoveries; that is, holding the affects of all other factors constant the method isolates the effect of price changes. This is exactly what we want. If we could rely on the accuracy of the results the approach would be powerful indeed and we would not have to go beyond these results. Unfortunately, however, in my opinion the basic model to which the regression analysis is applied has serious weaknesses. Let us consider what I believe to be some of the major difficulties.

Recall that I have emphasized the importance of using the petroleum play as the most natural unit of aggregation. The reason is that we know a good deal about how the rate of reservoir discovery in a petroleum play behaves with respect to the current and cumulative levels of exploratory effort. We also know that the largest reservoirs in a play tend to be found early and that their average size declines over the course of the play. This information allows us to say something about the cost of future reserves discoveries and hence their supply price. The econometric studies, however, have constructed models of the supply process which are designed to use data which is aggregated over many plays. Thus the discovery rate of reserves in the aggregate data consists of the summation of the discovery rates in all the plays which are currently active. Such an aggregation will tend to bias the effect of cumulative effort on the discovery rate downward and hence the effect of price changes will be biased upward. To see the common sense of this argument consider a large area in which several plays are simultaneously unfolding. But just as it becomes more difficult to find new reservoirs in a play thus leading to a decline in the discovery rate within the play, it also eventually becomes more difficult to find new plays. They run out as well. But the estimates based on historical aggregate data will forecast plays to unfold more or less as they have in the past. Thus the basis for suspecting bias is that for some reason the discovery sequence of past plays does not reflect the future. I think this is quite likely to be the case. Suppose, for example, that one estimated an econometric model for all of Alberta using a series of data beginning in the late 40's and ending in 1969. Several plays were discovered in the 50's and 60's with the last major play in full swing in Northern Alberta in the mid-60's. The estimates from these data would forecast discovery rates not just based upon what was happening in the developing plays which had already been discovered but they would depend upon plays continuing to unfold more or less as they had in the past. This is a strong assumption to be sure and, in fact, a major new play has not been discovered in Alberta since.

Thus we see that though these aggregate models seem to be one way to incorporate the effect of new play discoveries on the reserves discovery rate, in my view it is quite likely that they will lead to erroneous forecasts. I am convinced, for example, that the strong positive effect of increased prices on discoveries of natural gas and oil which has been forecast for onshore areas in the United States (excluding Alaska) based on these models have an upward bias.

4. Government involvement in the search for petroleum products

In the previous section in this essay I have indicated how one might go about determining how the discovery of new petroleum reserves responds to changes in market prices. The presumption has been that the exploration activity necessary for such discoveries comes from the private sector of the economy. As in the usual market analysis, price changes act as signals to private producers to expand or contract exploration activity. However, recent interest in energy shortages has focused attention on the levels of exploration investment actually chosen by the private sector in response to price changes. The riskiness of such ventures and the hypothesis that risk leads to under-investment relative to the social optimum has led to the suggestion of more extensive government involvement in petroleum exploration.

When confronted with this suggestion, petroleum industry officials are often scornful, and hostile at the implication that they have failed to adequately do their job. But it has been my experience that even though many of these officials are familiar with such phrases as, risk-averse behavior and expected value decision-making, many are much less sure of the logic of the argument which they see as being used against them. Thus, my first objective in this section of the essay is to present the logic of this argument. I will then finish up by discussing other arguments for government involvement.

At any one time firms in the petroleum industry have before them a number of possible exploration programs which could be undertaken, each with different levels of expected costs and revenues. It is common to envisage different levels of revenues or returns to the investment program as occurring with subjective probability with the probability of reserves discoveries being greater than or equal to a low value fairly high, and the probability of a truly mammoth discovery quite low. Some subjective notion of the discovery rate and subsequent production must also be formed so that the expected present value of the revenue flow can be compared with expected costs. Such a comparison is necessary in order to make the decision.

FIGURE (7)
Relationship Between Utility and Gross Return

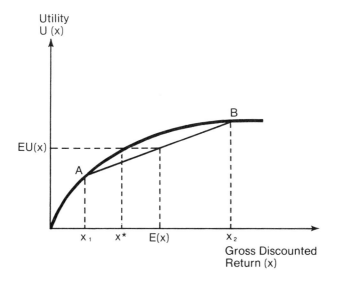

This figure represents the relationship between "utility" or satisfaction and gross returns from an undertaking. The higher the gross return expected, the higher the utility attaching to the undertaking. However, as gross returns increase, utility rises less than in proportion.

Let us pick just one such possible program and simplify further by assuming that the gross return to the exploration program can take on only two possible values, an amount x_1 and a higher amount x_2. These two outcomes can be said to occur with probability $P(x_1)$ and $P(x_2) = 1 - P(x_1)$ respectively. Now let us suppose that what economists call a utility function or utility ordering is defined over all possible gross returns and that this utility function is something like the curve depicted in Figure (7). Utility is simply a reflection of the importance or value (in non-money terms) of the outcomes. Note that the utility function is always increasing with the level of returns but the increments to its level decline with equal increments to net return. This assumption is important since "declining marginal utility" says that a unit reduction in return reduces utility more than a unit in-

37

crease adds to it. It is this shape of the utility function that characterizes risk-averse behavior.

The risk averter will not be willing to make an investment equal to the expected (average) value of the risk even though in the long run the return from such a risk will average out to the expected value. To see this consider the diagram in Figure (7). The straight line between points A and B indicates the expected utility of the risk for different levels of the probability of the outcomes x_1 and x_2. Suppose that for the sake of illustration $P(x_1) = 1/2$ so that the expected value of the risk is midway between x_1 and x_2. The expected utility of the risk is $EU(x)$. Now note that this utility is the same as the utility of a lesser, but certain amount x^*. Thus the rational decision-maker in this situation would not invest an amount greater than x^* since he would be giving up more utility than he could expect to get back from taking the risk.[10] This means that an exploration program which had a present value of expected return of $E(x)$ but costs (discounted) an amount greater than x^* but less than $E(x)$ would not be undertaken by the risk-averse decision-maker. On the other hand, a risk-neutral decision-maker, such as the government is sometimes argued to be, would be willing to adopt the exploration program as long as investment costs were less than or equal to $E(x)$. Thus, it is in this sense that under-investment in risky ventures is likely to occur. Certain programs are simply not undertaken by the private sector when on an expected value basis they should be.

Another way of looking at the same thing is to say that the risk averter puts too high a discount rate on the probable returns from a risky venture. This results in some programs being rejected when in the interest of society they should be undertaken.

We have seen that rational decision-making of a risk averter leads to under-investment in exploration. But even though we believe that risk aversity predominates in our society as evidenced by the tendency for even the very largest of firms to buy insurance against insurable losses, we do not know that petroleum exploration firms exhibit risk aversity in their petroleum exploration decisions.[11]

Although they do not have the risk-spreading capability of a major government, large firms have many stockholders and hence engage in substantial risk-spreading.[12] Many also have substantial investment diversification which allows them to reduce the impact of unsuccessful ventures on general revenues. Moreover, it is not clear that government petroleum exploration companies would actually exhibit less risk aversion than private companies even though their risk-spreading capability is immense. After all, these companies like their private counterparts, are typically run by professional managers whose performance is subject to the scrutiny of the public. There is plenty of evidence of the replacement of high level management in government crown corporations on the basis of poor performance. All of this suggests then that the government involvement may not improve the situation. Decision-makers in these enterprises would probably have utility functions similar to their private counterparts in that unit reductions in the return to an exploration program outweighs the benefits of unit increases in the returns. In fact, on average it may be that the personality type that leads people to government employment may be of a more risk-aversive nature than the private decision-maker.

Another argument for government involvement in petroleum exploration relates to the condition of "information spillover". The problem, it is argued, is that information from exploration operations is so easily transmitted that it is difficult for the firm discovering it to capture its entire social value. In other words, its private value to the firm is typically less than its social value. This leads firms to hold back on exploration, as they wait for other firms to produce costless but valuable information for them. If this characterizes the attitudes of the majority of firms then a level of exploration below the socially optimal level will result. The fact of the matter seems to be, however, that most of the value of information, especially that from pre-wildcat drilling operations, can be captured by exploration firms. Thus information spillover prior to lease bidding may be insignificant.

Some people take the view that over-investment rather than under-investment in exploration activity is a more important problem. They argue that the way in which firms gather geophysical and geological information results in unnecessary duplication of effort. Wouldn't it be better to have a single government monopoly or a private firm chartered by the government produce the necessary geophysical information which would then become public knowledge? Lease bids could then be made on the basis of this information and the duplication of effort would be eliminated. Although this proposal seems reasonable, we must first ask if there are any benefits associated with the duplication of effort to obtain information, or more accurately, do the incremental benefits exceed their extra costs? Although this is difficult to answer, one thing that is clear from the data is that excellent petroleum prospects have been overlooked on an initial pass. I have heard geologists argue that it is essential that several exploration crews (which participation by different firms would provide) be allowed to investigate the same area lest we fall into the "conventional wisdom trap" and thereby forever possibly pass up golden opportunities.

It has been argued that the existing system of competition among private firms for a finite amount of petroleum resources may also lead to over-investment in exploration. The argument is the usual one of the over-exploitation of a common property resource. Private firms competing for such resources will not take their future value, if left unexploited to a future time, into proper account. The firms feel individually that if they do not secure control now they will lose the opportunity to their competitors forever. Therefore, such a situation leads firms to search for petroleum resources in advance of what they would in situations of sole-proprietorship. A public or private monopoly firm would not encounter prospective loss of control of resources and hence would have no incentive to accumulate inventories of petroleum prospects in advance of what was necessary.

In this section I have presented several economic arguments suggesting the non-optimality of current institutional arrangements of searching for petroleum resources. All of these arguments have merit. While some of them suggest over-investment others suggest under-investment and we simply do not know the relative importance of each. Government intervention may help, but is the magnitude of the payoff worth it? In order to answer this question we need additional empirical research to test and determine the economic importance of these hypotheses.

Notes

[1]See AERCB, Report 74-18.

[2]This is essentially the method used by the Geological Survey of Canada to obtain the supply relationships for Arctic regions reported in *An Energy Policy for Canada, Phase I*, (1973).

[3]See for example, Roy (1975) and Roy, Proctor, and McCrossan (1975).

[4]The Monte Carlo method involves using a computer to select values for the variables in the prospect potential equation in accordance with a specified set of subjective probabilities for each. The equation is evaluated for each set and after many such selections and evaluations the distribution of prospect potential is determined.

[5]Actually the Geological Survey of Canada uses a slightly different framework than I have described here. They prefer to define a conditional probability structure for each variable in the prospects potential equation. These probabilities are conditional on each of the variables taking on a value equal to or greater than a certain minimum value. The Monte Carlo method is then used to obtain a conditional prospect size distribution which is then "risked" using the product of the probabilities that each variable is greater than or equal to its prescribed minimum value. It is easily shown, however, that this framework is equivalent to that described above.

[6]See Uhler (1976).

[7]The dangers of aggregation will be examined in more detail later in connection with econometric models.

[8]See Fisher (1964), Erickson and Spann (1971), and MacAvoy and Pindyck (1973) for example.

[9]A more detailed statement can be found in Uhler (1975).

[10]The amounts x_1 and x_2 are the discounted flow or gross returns where the discount rate is the socially optimal one.

[11]Of course, there is also clear evidence of risk lovers in our society. Taking part in unfair gambles on the part of individuals is a common observation as long as there is only small loss involved. The fact that people simultaneously buy insurance and gamble may seem irrational but see Friedman and Savage (1952) on this question.

[12]Firms also engage in joint ventures as a way of spreading risk.

41

References

Canada, Dept. of Energy, Mines and Resources, *An Energy Policy for Canada* (Ottawa: Information Canada, 1973).

Energy Resources Conservation Board, *Reserves of Crude Oil, Gas, Natural Gas Liquids and Sulphur, Province of Alberta*, Dec. 31, 1973, Report 74-18 (Calgary, 1974).

Erickson, E.and R. Spann. "Supply Response in a Regulated Industry: The Case of Natural Gas", *The Bell Journal of Economics and Management Science* (Spring 1971) pp. 94-121.

Fisher, F. *Supply and Costs in the U.S. Petroleum Industry: Two Economic Studies* (Baltimore, Johns Hopkins Press, 1964).

Friedman, M. and L. Savage. "Utility Analysis of Choice Involving Risk", in *American Economic Association Readings in Price Theory*, (Richard Irwin, 1952).

MacAvoy, P.W. and R.S. Pindyck. "Alternating Regulatory Policies for Dealing with the Natural Gas Shortage", *The Bell Journal of Economics and Management Science* (Autumn 1973) pp. 454-98.

Roy, K.J. "Hydrocarbon Assessment Using Subjective Probability and Monte Carlo Methods", Geological Survey of Canada, Unpublished (1975).

Roy, K.J., R.M. Proctor, and R.G. McCrossan. "Hydrocarbon Assessment Using Subjective Probability" Unpublished (1975).

Ryan, J.T. "An Analysis of Crude Oil Discovery in Alberta", *Bulletin of Petroleum Geology*, Vol. 21, No. 2, 1973, pp. 219-233.

Uhler, Russell S. "Costs and Supply in Petroleum Exploration: The Case of Alberta," *The Canadian Journal of Economics* (Feb. 1976), pp. 72-90.

Uhler, Russell S. "Forecasting Petroleum Supply: Methods and Aggregation Bias", *Proceedings of the Conference on the Economics of Oil and Gas Self-Sufficiency in Canada*, Calgary, Alberta, pp. 49-54 (Oct. 1975).

Editor's Introduction

The issue of the extent to which the amount of energy consumed is affected by the price of energy is critical in the formulation of public policy. Professor E.R. Berndt's essay looks at Canadian energy demand studies which attempt to estimate the degree of response of demand to variations in price (price elasticity of demand). He then discusses the implications of these studies both for projecting energy demand and in terms of current controversies over conservation, economic growth and resource constraints. The evidence he cites suggests that the price of energy is an important determinant of the amount of energy consumed in Canada, but that the response is more muted in the short run than in the long run. The conclusion is that the price of energy can be an effective instrument in rationing energy demand. Policies which emasculate the role of price are potentially inefficient and distortive. Failure to use the price mechanism requires imposition of alternative, less preferable, controls.

Since energy prices appear to have significant effects, Professor Berndt suggests energy projections must make price assumptions explicit and incorporate estimated price effects. It also follows that energy conservation and economic growth are not necessarily incompatible. Energy consumption is not simply a function of income and habit. As long as prices are allowed to perform their rationing role, economic growth can proceed in a less energy-intensive way and thus satisfy conservation objectives. Berndt points out that one of the main impediments to energy conservation is current government policy and regulation; price subsidies on oil and gas; utility rate structures that reward higher energy consumption with lower prices and tax policies that discriminate against energy-conserving equipment.

Canadian Energy Demand and Economic Growth

ERNST R. BERNDT

Associate Professor of Economics
University of British Columbia

THE AUTHOR

Ernst R. Berndt was born in 1946 in Argentina. He graduated (B.A. Honors) from Valparaiso University, Valparaiso, Indiana, in 1968 and from the University of Wisconsin, M.S., (Economics), 1971, and Ph.D., (Economics), 1972.

Professor Berndt was appointed Associate Professor of Economics at the University of British Columbia in 1974. In 1971 and 1972 he was a research economist with the U.S. government in Washington, D.C. He was recently named to the National Academy of Science - National Research Council Committee on Nuclear and Alternative Energy Sources.

Among Professor Berndt's publications are: "Forecasting North American Energy Demand: Issues and Problems," in Peter Pearse, ed., *The Mackenzie Pipeline: Arctic Gas and Canadian Energy Policy*, Toronto, McClelland and Stewart, 1974; and, with David O. Wood, "An Economic Interpretation of the Energy-GNP Ratio," in M.S. Macrakis, ed., *Energy: Demand, Conservation, and Institutional Problems*, Cambridge, M.I.T. Press, 1974.

46

Canadian Energy Demand and Economic Growth*

ERNST R. BERNDT

Associate Professor of Economics
University of British Columbia

I. INTRODUCTION

The purpose of this essay is to survey the existing economic literature on factors affecting Canadian demand for energy. Section II introduces an analytical framework drawn from basic economic theory. It is hoped that the concepts presented will be comprehensible to those readers not familiar with economic jargon. Section III moves from theory to evidence based on historical Canadian data. The results of a number of statistical studies are presented, compared, and assessed.[1] Section IV derives implications for methods of projecting future Canadian demand for energy. This section also comments on the reliability of a number of much publicized forecasts of Canadian energy demand. Section V attempts to synthesize the previous sections by discussing relations among energy demand, economic growth, and the rationing role of the price system. The central issue considered is whether economic growth, full employment, and energy conservation are compatible goals.

*The helpful comments of David Brooks, J.A. Coombs, John Helliwell, Robert McRae, G. Campbell Watkins and Leonard Waverman are gratefully acknowledged. Responsibility for opinions expressed in this essay and for any remaining errors rests with the author.

II. FACTORS AFFECTING THE DEMAND FOR ENERGY

It is convenient to discuss domestic demand for energy by distinguishing two end users. Demand for energy from an intermediate sector is typically a derived demand of a business firm; the firm's demand for energy is derived from demand for its output (product). More generally, firms demand inputs of labour, capital, materials and energy because these inputs are needed to produce the firm's output. Demand for energy from the final demand sector includes household energy demanded for heating, lighting, use of appliances, and transportation services. This form of demand is final in the sense that energy is not being used as an input to produce goods and services sold in the marketplace.[2] In addition to these two types of domestic demand, energy is demanded for export to other countries. For example, in 1973, total Canadian crude oil consumption was 1.67 million barrels per day; it exported 1.13 million barrels per day to the United States, and imported .86 million barrels per day.[3]

Table I below provides an indication of the relative importance of the domestic intermediate and final demand sectors for energy. In 1973, intermediate demand for energy (including commercial, industrial, and transportation) accounted for approximately 78 per cent of total Canadian domestic demand for energy, while final demand (residential) constituted the remaining 22 per cent.[4]

To better understand factors affecting total demand for energy in Canada, it will be useful to examine the various components in some detail. I begin with the intermediate demand sector.

A. Demand for energy in the intermediate sector

Earlier it was noted that a firm's demand for energy as an input is derived from demand for the firm's output. Obviously energy is not the only input entering the firm's production

TABLE I
Canadian Domestic Demand for Energy, 1958 and 1973

	Trillions of BTU's		Share of Total BTU Demand (%)		Average Annual Growth Rate (%)
	1958	1973	1958	1973	
Intermediate Demand:					
Commercial	186	744	8.4	15.0	9.24
Industrial	662	1666	29.9	33.5	6.15
Transportation	735	1461	33.1	29.4	4.58
Road	496	1120	22.4	22.6	5.43
Rail	127	96	5.7	1.9	-1.87
Air	40	120	1.8	2.4	7.32
Marine	72	125	3.2	2.5	3.68
Total Intermediate Demand:	1583	3871	71.4	78.0	5.96
Final Demand:					
Residential	634	1095	28.6	22.0	3.64
Total	2217	4966	100.0	100.0	5.38

Source: Detailed Energy Supply and Demand in Canada (Statistics Canada: 57-207)

process; inputs such as capital equipment and structures, labour and materials are also required. Technological relations constrain the way in which inputs can enter the firm's production process. For example, the production of paper is characterized by technological relations among lumber, equipment, chemicals, other materials, energy, and labour. Thus, it is technologically possible to produce a given quantity of paper with different combinations of inputs.

In general, the number of alternative input combinations used to produce a given level of output will vary with the particular product. The comprehensive set of relations among technologically efficient combinations of inputs and output is called the *production function.* Essentially the production function is a menu of alternative methods for producing output using technologically efficient methods of production. It does not indicate, however, what particular input combination a firm will choose to produce its output.

Economic theory suggests that competitive firms will choose the combination of inputs that produces the desired output at minimum cost. This implies that cost-minimizing firms will devote considerable attention to input prices. For example, if a firm observes that wages are high and energy prices are low, then, other things being equal, it will tend to choose a production process that is more energy-intensive and less labour-intensive than if energy prices were high and wages were low. In short, the derived demands for inputs depend on the level of output, the substitution possibilities among inputs allowed by the production technology, and the relative prices of all inputs.[5] Economic theory suggests, therefore, that the derived demand for energy will be affected by changes in the prices of inputs, the level of output, and the extent to which the technology (production function) permits substitution among energy and non-energy inputs.

The degree to which energy demand responds to a change in its price is of course very important. Price responsiveness is typically measured by own price elasticity, defined as

$$\epsilon_{ii} = \frac{\text{Own Price Elasticity}}{\text{of Demand for Energy}} = \frac{\text{\% Change in Quantity of Energy Demanded}}{\text{\% Change in Price of Energy}},$$

where output quantity and all other input prices are held constant. Economic theory predicts that the own price elasticity of demand for energy will be negative, i.e., as the price of energy increases, output and other prices held constant, the quantity of energy demanded will fall. In Section III of this paper estimates of this price elasticity will be presented.

One other definition will prove to be useful here. It is often of interest to examine the effect on the derived demand of one input when the price of another input changes.

This cross-price effect is typically measured by the *cross-price elasticity*, defined as

$$\epsilon_{ij} = \begin{array}{l}\text{Cross-Price Elasticity}\\ \text{of Demand}\end{array} = \frac{\text{\% Change in Quantity of Input i Demanded}}{\text{\% Change in Price of Input j}}$$

where output quantity and all other input prices are assumed to be constant. If two inputs were substitutable in the production process, then the cross-price elasticity would be positive; on the other hand, if two inputs were complementary, then the cross-price elasticity would be negative. To illustrate, let the price of labour increase; if the quantity of fuel demanded increases while labour demand decreases, given the level of output, then fuel and labour are substitutes. On the other hand, if the price of labour increases and the quantity demanded of both labour and fuel decreases, then fuel and labour are complements. Substitutable inputs are rival or competing factors, while complementary inputs are cooperating commodities. Energy and labour are likely substitutes, while energy and certain specific types of equipment may be complements.

The above discussion has dealt with energy as an aggregate or composite input. There are, of course, different types of energy inputs: electricity, coal, natural gas, gasoline, fuel oil, and many other refined petroleum products. In most cases one would expect the own price elasticity of a particular fuel to be larger (in absolute value) than the own price elasticity of aggregate energy. The reason for this is that fuels can frequently be substituted for one another in the production process without significantly affecting the quantity of aggregate energy consumed. For example, if only the price of natural gas increased, a firm could generate heat by substituting en masse toward a different energy type such as oil or coal. Aggregate energy demand would not be affected as greatly.

One would not expect firms to adjust input demand instantaneously to changes in prices. A number of circumstances mitigate short-run price responsiveness. First, the firm may view an input price change as only temporary and may therefore decide to live with it in the short run rather than bear the costs of adjusting factor proportions. In some cases costs of adjustment are substantial, e.g., laying off or hiring of new labour, drawing up of plans for new plant and equipment, and searching for appropriate materials. Second, even if the firm viewed the input price changes as permanent, it may be inhibited in the short run from adjusting fully to the desired input levels. Reasons for this partial adjustment include the firm's contractual commitment to the purchases of materials and certain salaried labour, and the presence of fixed plant and equipment which cannot easily be varied in the short run. Over the longer term, however, the firm will be more able to adjust demands to desired levels.

The implication of the above for energy demand is that short-run own price elasticities of demand for energy will be smaller (in absolute value) than long-run own price elasticities. This is likely to be particularly true for specific fuel types, e.g., if a firm does not have dual burning capacity in its heat generation plant, it may substitute from natural gas to oil or coal only after a considerable lag in time. The firm may find it economical not to change equipment until its present stock becomes obsolete or worn out. Nevertheless, short-run price responses are likely to be present. If the price of a certain fuel rises, the firm will often be able to conserve on that fuel even in the short run by making temporary changes in utilization rates. Furthermore, since there are literally thousands of firms in Canada, at any time a substantial number are considering investment in new fixed plant and equipment. For these firms energy prices will play an important role in the choice of new production techniques. Thus even in the short run one can expect the aggregate quantity of energy demanded to respond to changes in its price.

In the very long run one might expect technological innovations to take place which conserve on inputs whose costs are increasing greatly. Some recent evidence bearing on this issue of induced innovation will be discussed in Section III below.

B. Demand for energy in the final demand sector

As discussed earlier, household energy demanded for heating, lighting, use of appliances, transportation, etc. is in the final demand sector in the sense that energy is not being demanded as an input to produce goods and services sold in the marketplace. In a strict sense, however, even in the household,energy is a derived demand. Households demand natural gas, not for its own sake, but because natural gas is an "input" in the "production" of household heating. Similarly, electricity is demanded because households wish to consume the services of electricity-using appliances such as refrigerators and televisions. The implication is that household demand for energy must be viewed in the context of household demand for the services of appliances and other consumer durables.

In general, household demand for energy will depend on income, consumer preferences, and prices of energy and other commodities. Since a substantial portion of household energy demand is related to heating and air conditioning, household energy demand will also be affected by temperature and weather variations.[6]

Economists typically assume that households purchase bundles of goods so as to obtain maximum satisfaction, given their preferences and budget constraints. When the income of a household increases while preferences and prices remain fixed, the budget constraint is relaxed and the household is able to purchase more goods. The response of quantity demanded to a change in income is measured by the *income elasticity*, defined as

$$\text{Income Elasticity of Demand for a Good} = \frac{\%\text{ Change in Quantity of Good Demanded}}{\%\text{ Change in Income}}$$

where preferences and prices are held constant. We would expect the income elasticity of demand for aggregate energy to be positive. It is worth mentioning that if the income elasticity of demand for a good were greater than unity, the *share* of the household budget spent on that good will increase with income.[7] On the other hand, if the income

53

elasticity of demand for a good were greater than zero but less than unity, household expenditures on that good would increase with income, but the *share* of the household budget spent on that good would decrease with income. *A priori*, one might expect the income elasticity of household demand for aggregate energy to be within the zero-one interval, i.e., the share of household income devoted to energy expenditures is likely to decrease with income, unless use of energy intensive appliances is extremely responsive to changes in income. The income elasticity of demand for a particular fuel (e.g., electricity) may be greater than unity, or possibly even less than zero (e.g., coal). Empirical evidence on this issue will be discussed in Section III below.

Household demand for energy is also likely to be price responsive. When the price of one commodity increases, the household's bundle of goods will be more costly than before, and normally consumers will attempt to allocate the resulting fall in real income (money income adjusted for inflation) by demanding less of a number of goods. Further, consumers are likely to attempt to substitute away from the more costly commodity. Thus own price elasticities of household demand for energy are negative.

Short-run own price elasticities of household demand for energy are smaller (in absolute value) than long-run price elasticities. The reason is that in the short run a substantial portion of household demand for energy is tied to existing stocks of appliances and durables such as refrigerators, heaters, and stoves. In the longer term as these appliances age and wear, consumers adjust their stocks of durables to the new energy prices. Even in the short run, however, energy demand is likely to be price responsive, for households can adjust thermostats downward, install insulation, turn lights off more quickly, etc.

Earlier it was noted that household demand for energy is typically used to produce services in the household. Such services can often be produced in a number of ways. To provide additional insight into factors affecting household demand for energy, one can envisage a household production function, analogous to that of the firm. For example, households can produce refrigeration services in a number of ways. Frost-free refrigerators require less cleaning time than do ordinary refrigerators, but use considerably more energy. The substantial increase in the share of households using frost-free refrigerators implies that, given the recent trends of increasing wage rates and lower energy prices, consumers have decided to substitute energy for household labour. Indeed, it appears that many household labour-saving devices and appliances are energy-using.

The above discussion suggests that aggregate household demand for energy in Canada is affected by consumer preferences, prices of energy and other goods, existing stocks of durables and appliances, weather variations, income and wage rates, technological changes in the production of household services, the number and size of composition of Canadian households, and the housing stock (apartments versus single family dwellings).

C. Export-import demand for energy

Over the last decade Canada has exported a substantial quantity of oil and natural gas to the United States. At the same time, eastern Canada has imported oil from Venezuela and the Middle East and coal from the U.S. These sources have helped satisfy intermediate and final demands for energy in both the U.S. and Canada. Factors affecting U.S. demand for energy are of course largely the same as those affecting Canadian demand.

If barriers to international trade and issues of national security were not present, Canadians and Americans would tend to purchase energy at the lowest available price, regardless of whether it was produced in the U.S., Venezuela, or Canada. Free trade would likely result in predominantly north-south gas flows between the U.S. and Canada rather than the present west to east flow within Canada. Eastern Canada would import more from the United States and less from Western Canada, while Western Canada would export more to the United States.[8]

For a number of reasons, complete free trade in energy does not exist between Canada and the United States. Ottawa has imposed export taxes on crude oil products and has restricted the quantity of both natural gas and crude oil exported to the United States.[9] Washington has also intervened in the energy marketplace. A full discussion of reasons for these actions is outside the scope of this paper. However, an implication of these export restrictions is that the quantity of Canadian energy exported to the U.S. is not likely to be determined by the free market, but rather by policies worked out among governments — federal, provincial, and state.

D. Interaction of demand for energy in the intermediate, final, and export-import sectors

I now summarize and complete our discussion on factors affecting Canadian demand for energy. In column 1 of Table II I list those factors affecting domestic intermediate demand, in column 2 those affecting domestic final demand, and in column 3 those affecting export demand.

TABLE II
Principal Factors Affecting Aggregate Demand For Energy in Canada

Domestic Intermediate Demand Sector	Domestic Final Demand Sector	Export Demand Sector
Total volume and composition of production (output of Canadian firms)	Household income	Same factors affecting domestic intermediate and final demand
Structure of technology and possibilities for substitution among energy and non-energy inputs	Consumer preferences, attitudes and sentiments	Quantity exported largely affected by actions of federal and provincial governments, e.g., tariffs and quotas
Prices of energy and non-energy inputs	Temperature variations (heating and air conditioning)	
	Possibilities for substitution among energy and non-energy inputs in the production of household services	
	Prices of energy and non-energy goods and services	
	Number, size, and composition of Canadian households	

Table II is incomplete, however, because it fails to portray fully the interactions among the final, intermediate, and export demand sectors. These interactions can be illustrated by distinguishing initial or direct effects from transmitted or induced (indirect) effects.

Suppose, for example, that the price of energy in Canada increased substantially. The first effect of the higher priced energy is a direct one. Households and firms would attempt to substitute away from the higher priced energy. This direct effect would bring about a reduction in the quantity of energy demanded — both from intermediate and from final demand sectors. The direct effect, however, is only one part of the economy's total response.

The second set of responses results because of changes in the composition of goods produced. Faced with higher energy prices, cost minimizing firms will attempt to substitute away from energy to other inputs. The extent of this adjustment will of course be constrained by the production technology. Firms will find costs of production increasing, and will attempt to pass these higher costs on to consumers in the form of price increases. Industries whose production technology is highly energy-intensive (e.g., aluminum products) will be hardest hit; in order to remain profitable these industries will be forced to raise product prices substantially. In turn, the customers of these energy-intensive firms (households and other firms) will attempt to circumvent the higher prices by substituting toward goods whose prices have not increased as substantially, i.e., toward goods produced by less energy-intensive methods. The final result of this process will be a change in the composition of goods demanded by domestic and foreign firms and households toward goods whose production uses less energy. This indirect effect is likely to be important — it may even be larger than the direct response.

The magnitude of the direct and indirect effects will depend of course on the size of the own and cross-price elasticities of demand. In order to measure these effects, empirical evidence on price elasticities is necessary. Empirical studies based on Canadian data are discussed in the next section.

III. HISTORICAL EVIDENCE ON FACTORS AFFECTING CANADIAN DEMAND FOR ENERGY: AN ECONOMIST LOOKS AT THE DATA

Because values of price elasticities are important, it is essential that they be measured and estimated with great care. The task of estimation is frequently assigned to an econometrician. The econometrician gathers numbers, observes the data carefully, then specifies equations in such a way that they incorporate the distinctive features of economic theory, and finally subjects the data and theoretical model to statistical testing.

A number of econometric studies have focused on demand for energy in Canada. In this section I survey the results of these studies. First, however, I sketch the salient trends found in recent Canadian data.

Over the 1958-1973 time period aggregate demand for energy in Canada increased at an average annual rate of 5.1 per cent (see Table I, page 49). This annual growth rate in energy demand was larger than the 5.0 per cent average annual increase in real gross national product and was also greater than the 1.7 per cent average annual growth rate of population. In summary, during the 1958-1973 time period the Canadian economy became increasingly energy-intensive.

Such an increase in energy intensity is not at all surprising, given the historical relationship of energy prices relative to other prices. For example, from 1961 to 1971 in the manufacturing sector the price index for fuels and electricity fell by 30 per cent relative to average wage rates. Similarly, in the residential sector the price index of fuels and utilities relative to the consumer price index fell from 1.035 in 1958 to 0.886 in 1971.[10] Thus, in both the industrial and residential sectors, the price of energy fell in real terms. The finding that Canadian households and firms became more energy-intensive during this period of time is not surprising; rather it is exactly what would be predicted on the basis of economic theory.

A critical observer would not likely be convinced that this increase in energy demand was due solely to low-priced energy, for it is likely that many other factors could have been involved. The above time series data merely show a quantity series increasing over time and a price series decreasing over the same time period; the inverse correlation between the two series could be due to other unspecified factors. Skepticism would tend to persist even if data for different regions of Canada at a single point in time (cross-sectional data) provided similar inverse correlations. It would be comforting if supporting cross-sectional and time series evidence were obtained based on more sophisticated statistical procedures that included additional explanatory variables and thereby isolated the effects of price from other factors.

One important additional variable that must be included in an aggregate energy demand equation is the level of aggregate economic activity (GNP). The relation between aggregate demand for energy and GNP in Canada was first examined by John Davis.[11] Davis hypothesized the following relationship:

"Energy consumption . . . tends to move along more or less in line with GNP. In a few cases, it has been known to exceed the rate of growth of GNP for a period of years. But in the great majority of cases, as economic development proceeds, it is known to lag progressively behind the total output of goods and services."[12]

It was Davis' contention, then, that as a country developed, the ratio of energy consumption to production — the energy-GNP ratio — would tend to fall, other things being equal. At the time Davis wrote his book (1957), evidence available for Canada was consistent with his notion. For example, Davis reported that over the 1929-1953 time period, the energy-GNP ratio in Canada fell slightly.[13,14] In his projections for 1955-1980, Davis anticipated that the ratio of energy to GNP would continue to fall slightly or would possibly remain constant. He did not, however, anticipate the remarkable change that took place in the energy-GNP ratio, namely, that it would actually increase even as the Canadian economy matured and developed. I have already argued above that one reason for the increasing energy intensity in this later period was the lower price of fuels. The Davis conjecture may have been realized had the relative price of energy remained constant; however, in fact, this relative price fell.

In the next few pages I will briefly survey the findings of econometric studies using Canadian time series and cross-sectional data. The results, though in some cases fragmentary, are reasonable and surprisingly consistent. I begin with a survey of studies on demand for energy in the intermediate demand sector.

A. Principal findings of econometric studies on demand for energy in the intermediate demand sector

To the best of my knowledge, the first detailed econometric study of Canadian industrial demand for energy was done by James A. Coombs.[15] Coombs examined 1964 regional data on electricity, coal, oil (including gasoline), and natural gas for seventeen manufacturing industries. Data on energy consumption were related to energy prices and output (value-added) using the statistical method of multiple regression analysis. Coombs confined his attention to the four energy types and did not examine possibilities for substitution among energy and non-energy inputs. His estimates of the 1964 average own price elasticities of demand in the seventeen manufacturing industries were -.71 (electricity), -4.17 (coal), -1.44 (oil and gasoline), and -2.13 (natural gas). Coombs also found that gas and oil were quite substitutable but that electricity and the fossil fuels were largely non-substitutable and independent. In addition, Coombs obtained results consistent with the notion that output and energy consumption tended to grow at the same rate, assuming real energy prices remained constant.

These cross-sectional findings of Coombs are notable in that they suggest that Canadian industrial demand for energy in 1964 was strongly price responsive. Further, Coombs' model was able to explain a substantial amount of variation in energy consumption across Canada on the basis of regional variations in output levels and energy prices.

Related empirical results were reported in 1973 by J. Daniel Khazzoom, based on industrial gas consumption by province, 1960-1968.[16] Khazzoom found that gas demand declined as gas price increased, but that the decline proceeded at a slower and slower pace as gas prices continued to rise. He found this result reasonable, " . . .since the shift to other substitutes becomes more and more costly as the less and less vital layers of gas consumption are shaved off."[17] Unfortunately, Khazzoom did not report estimates of own and cross-price elasticities of demand.

The Coombs and Khazzoom studies focused attention on intermediate demand for certain specific fuels — oil, coal, gas and electricity. It is also of interest to examine intermediate demand for total energy, where total energy is measured in BTU's. Aggregate industrial-commercial demand for energy in Alberta, 1951-1972, was analyzed in a study by DataMetrics Limited.[18] The principal authors of that study, E.R. Berndt and G.C. Watkins, found that energy demand was moderately responsive to a change in its price; the estimated own price elasticity was -.30. Berndt-Watkins also found that energy and labour were substitutable or rival inputs and that this substitutability increased over time as the relative price of energy fell. The relative downward trend in the energy price tended to make energy and capital less substitutable, and eventually, about 1969, the two inputs became complementary.

In another study based on data for all provinces, 1961-71, F.W. Gorbet obtained an estimated own price elasticity for total energy demand of -.59.[19] Energy-labour substitutability and energy-capital complementarity were also reported by Gorbet. In particular, Gorbet found that when output was held constant, the quantity of energy consumption and the level of capital stock were positively related, while energy and employment were negatively related.

Other more recent empirical studies have buttressed the above findings. M. Denny and C. Pinto estimated the own price elasticity for aggregate energy in the industrial sector to be -.59,[20] while M. Fuss, R. Hyndman, and L. Waverman obtained an estimate of -.36.[21] Both studies concluded that energy and labour were substitutable inputs.

The demand for specific fuels was integrated with the demand for aggregate energy in a recent study by M. Fuss.[22] Fuss' results on demand for aggregate energy in Canadian manufacturing are virtually identical with those cited above: the own price elasticity of demand for energy is -.49, energy and labour are substitutes, while energy and capital are complements. In addition, Fuss obtains estimates of the own price elasticities for specific fuels: -1.48 (coal), -2.39 (LPG), -1.30 (fuel oil), -1.30 (natural gas), -.74 (electricity), and -1.59 (motor gasoline). A particular feature of Fuss' results is that they illustrate that price elasticities for specific energy types are larger (in absolute value) than price elasticities for total energy, since some substitutability is possible among individual fuels.

Another recent study incorporating demand for specific fuels with demand for aggregate energy is that of Robert McRae.[23] McRae separately specifies energy used for production of other energy (for example, oil and gas used for thermal generation in electric power plants) from other energy demand, but aggregates all end uses. Furthermore, supply constraints of gas availability are taken into account. The estimated average non-thermal own and cross-price demand elasticities for specific energy types vary by region and year. For the non-Atlantic provinces in 1973, the estimated own price elasticity for total energy is -.41. The own price elasticities for crude oil, natural gas, and electricity all fall within the -.3 to -1.0 range, while the cross-price elasticities among the three energy types all fall within the .15 to 1.0 interval.

I now summarize the above findings. A number of studies have been cited which vary with respect to data base — cross-section, time series, or a combination of both — and in terms of statistical methodology. The principal findings, however, are remarkably similar.[24] Demand for energy in the intermediate demand sector in Canada is price-responsive. Own price elasticity estimates vary from -.3 to -.6, energy and labour tend to be substitutable inputs in the production process, while energy and capital appear to have become complementary, especially in recent years. Finally, demand for specific fuels is even more price responsive because of possibilities for inter-fuel competition.

Agreement of findings among studies using different data bases is comforting, but it does not ensure that the common results are correct. This is particularly true when the studies share certain shortcomings. Further research is needed on the sensitivity of the above results to alternative model specifications. For example, none of the cited studies specifies alternative paths of adjustment of demand to change in price. The interrelated aspects of lagged adjustment between energy and fixed plant and equipment remain to be carefully specified and measured.

A second common drawback of the cited studies is that they have not considered the effects on factor demands of technological change. When technological progress occurs, it becomes possible to produce a given level of output with less of one or more inputs . Technological progress may of course be non-neutral in the sense that some inputs are augmented or conserved more than others. A recent study by E.R. Berndt and David O. Wood finds that technological change in post-war U.S. manufacturing has been labour-saving and energy-using.[25] An intriguing aspect of this result is that the pattern of technological change has been to conserve on the input whose price has risen the greatest (labour), and to utilize most extensively the input whose price has risen least (energy). This suggests that even the bias of technological innovations may be price-responsive.

I now turn to a brief survey of econometric studies on final demand for energy.

B. Principal findings of econometric studies of demand for energy in the final demand sector

In the short run the typical household is limited in its attempt to adjust energy demands to changes in price because normally energy demand is tied to the services of long-lived appliances. Over the longer period of time, however, appliances wear and purchases of new appliances are likely to be affected by changes in energy prices. Empirical studies of demand for energy in the residential sector should take these "stock effects" into account.

Although issues of data reliability and accuracy arise in all areas of empirical energy research, data considerations are particularly troublesome in the analysis of household or residential demand for energy. Unfortunately "household" demand does not correspond neatly with the typical data breakdown of residential, commercial, and industrial customers. Small apartment blocks and duplexes are frequently classified as residential, but virtually all large apartment blocks are categorized as commercial. This means that a substantial portion of commercial energy demand is in fact household demand from large apartment blocks. Researchers have also encountered substantial difficulties in obtaining reliable statistics on the decomposition of gasoline sales to households and commercial customers, for retail gasoline stations typically do not record such statistics. Because of these data problems, empirical studies of demand for energy have usually combined the residential and commercial sectors. I now turn to a discussion of empirical results on residential-commercial demand for specific fuels. I begin with natural gas.

The principal use of natural gas is of course space-heating. An implication of this is that aggregate demand for natural gas will depend on the number and size of households, average income, variations in weather, price, and the stock of existing appliances.

The first econometric study of Canadian residential and commercial demand for natural gas was done in 1973 by G. C. Watkins.[26] The model specification incorporated "stock" effects and separately identified "free" and "captive" demand for natural gas.[27] Based on annual data for B.C., Quebec, and Ontario, 1959-71, Watkins obtained short run own price elasticity estimates of -.28 (Quebec), -.30 (Ontario), and -.29 (B.C.). The Watkins framework was generalized by E.R. Berndt and G.C. Watkins to isolate the effects of weather variations and to allow for non-linearities.[28] Using 1959-74 data for B.C. and Ontario, Berndt-Watkins obtained short-run (one year) price elasticity estimates of about -.15, and long-run price elasticity estimates of -.59. The estimated income elasticity was .03 in the short run and .16 in the long run. This indicates that demand for natural gas has tended to respond negligibly to increases in income, i.e., natural gas tends to be more a "necessity" than a "luxury". Berndt-Watkins also found that natural gas demand varied, as expected, with temperature; if the temperature fell by 1 per cent (as measured in degree days), demand for natural gas increased by about .75 of 1 per cent. This result is reasonable, since a similar proportion of gas demand is used for space-heating purposes.

Residential demand for electricity and fossil fuels has been analyzed by M. Fuss, R. Hyndman, and L. Waverman.[29] These authors have attempted to construct separate data for the residential and commercial sectors. In the residential sector they estimated the own price elasticity of demand to be -.14. Further, electricity did not appear to be substitutable with any of the fossil fuels. The estimated income elasticity for electricity is 1.25, which suggests that electricity demand has been very responsive to changes in average per capita income. Such a result, however, may be due to the effect of income on purchases of energy-using appliances.

In the commercial sector, Fuss-Hyndman-Waverman obtained an electricity own price elasticity estimate of -.31. The authors also estimated a fossil fuel (natural gas plus petroleum) demand equation and found that the own price elasticity in the residential sector was -.73. It should be noted that all their elasticity estimates did not distinguish between short and long run.

In contrast to the above studies on residential-commercial demand for specific fuels, F.W. Gorbet has investigated factors affecting demand for aggregate energy (measured in BTU's) in the residential sector.[30] Based on 1958-71 annual data by province, Gorbet estimated the own price elasticity estimate to be -.31, while the estimated income elasticity was .98.

In summary, evidence on Canadian final demand for energy is somewhat fragmentary but reasonable. In the short run, prices have only a small effect but in the longer run the own price elasticities appear to be in the -.3 to -.6 range. Income elasticity estimates vary considerably by fuel; for natural gas (used primarily for heating purposes), the elasticity estimate is about .16, but for electricity (used with many appliances) the elasticity is about 1.25.

While the results of these studies seem reasonable, a number of issues remain to be investigated. Estimates of the long-run energy demand elasticities must be related explicitly to factors affecting demand for appliances and other durable goods. At this time I am not aware of any Canadian study relating choice of appliances to relative fuel costs.[31] Secondly, household demand for energy has been affected strongly by the preferences of consumers for labour and time-saving appliances, which in most cases have been energy-using. Empirical studies have not yet incorporated the value of time as a variable affecting household demand for appliances and for energy.

C. Integration of results on demand for energy in the intermediate and final demand sectors

The results of studies cited above strongly support the notion that demand for energy is affected by, among other things, prices, income, and technology. In the context of the intermediate demand sector, it has been found that when output is held constant, a fall in the price of energy is likely to induce substitution away from labour and toward energy and perhaps capital. In the context of the final demand sector, it has also been found that demand was price responsive. The results are tabulated in Table III (opposite).

Each of the cited studies, however, is partial in the sense that a large number of factors were being held constant. A more general analysis would not only measure direct effects, but would also incorporate the indirect effects — the changes in output composition and income — that would likely accompany the energy price change. This more general analysis requires detailed information on interactions and trade among intermediate and final demanders in Canada. To my knowledge, no study of this kind has been done in Canada, primarily because of data constraints.[32] Such a study is desirable but difficult, because it requires a detailed and consistent specification of interactions among domestic and foreign sectors in the nation's economy.

TABLE III
Summary of Findings on Factors Affecting Demand for Energy in Canada

Author	Data Base	Principal Findings
Intermediate Demand Sector:		
Coombs	1964, 17 manufacturing industries, by region	Price elasticities of $-.7$ (electricity), -4.2 (coal), -1.4 (oil and gasoline), -2.2 (natural gas)
Khazzoom	Total industry, by province, 1960-68	Demand responsive to price; elasticity estimates not reported
Berndt-Watkins	Alberta, industrial and commercial, 1951-72	Own price elasticity for total energy of $-.3$; energy-labour substitutability; energy-capital become complementary as price of energy continues to fall
Gorbet	Total industry by province, 1961-71	Own price elasticity for total energy of $-.6$; energy-labour substitutability and energy-capital complementarity
Denny-Pinto	Total manufacturing, 1949-70	$-.6$ estimate for own price elasticity of total energy demand; energy-labour substitutable, energy-capital complementary
Fuss-Hyndman-Waverman	Total manufacturing by province, 1958-71	$-.4$ estimate for own price elasticity of total energy demand; energy-labour substitutable, energy-capital slightly substitutable
Fuss	Total manufacturing by province, 1961-71	Own price elasticity for total energy of $-.5$; energy-labour substitutability and energy-capital complementarity, own price elasticities of -1.5 (coal), -2.4 (LPG), -1.3 (fuel oil), -1.3 (natural gas), $-.7$ (electricity), and -1.6 (motor gasoline)

continued

TABLE III (continued)

Final Demand Sector:		
Watkins	Residential and commercial, B.C., Quebec, Ontario, 1959-71	Short-run own price elasticity for natural gas of about −.3
Berndt-Watkins	Residential and commercial, B.C., Ontario, 1959-73	Own price elasticity for natural gas of −.6 in long run, −.15 in first year; income elasticity estimates of .15 (long run) and .03 (short run); degree-day elasticity of .75
Fuss-Hyndman-Waverman	Residential by province, 1958-71	Own price elasticity for electricity of −.14, in-come elasticity of 1.25, own price elasticity for fossil fuels of −.7
″ ″	Commercial by province, 1961-71	Own price elasticity for electricity of −.31
Gorbet	Residential by province, 1958-71	Own price elasticity for total energy demand of −.31, income elasticity estimate of .98
Total Demand (Not distinguished by end-use sector):		
McRae	By province, 1961-73; non-thermal separated from energy used to generate secondary electricity	Non-thermal uses: own price electricity for total energy demand of −.41; own price elasticities for crude oil, natural gas, and electricity in −.3 to −1.0 range; cross price elasticities among fossil fuels in the .15 to 1.0 interval; above interfuel elasticities vary by province and year.

IV. IMPLICATIONS FOR PROJECTION OF CANADIAN ENERGY DEMAND

A salient feature of energy supplying industries is that the length of time required to develop production facilities is usually considerable. In order to meet projected demands in the 1980's, in many cases decisions must be made now. For example, British Columbia Hydro and B.C. provincial officials are presently deciding whether to proceed with construction of the massive Revelstoke dam which would begin providing electricity in the mid-1980's. The duration of time from beginning of construction to full capacity throughput for portions of the Syncrude project is about ten years. At the present time, hearings on the Mackenzie Valley pipeline are still underway. If construction were approved, gas would not begin flowing through the pipelines until 1981-83, and full capacity would not be reached until five years later. These examples illustrate that energy supply decisions require long planning horizons.

A critical issue facing industrial and governmental planners is the likely magnitude of future energy demand. If demand in the coming decade will continue to grow at recent rates, then to meet future demands, substantial construction activity must be implemented forthwith. On the other hand, if lower energy demand growth rates will prevail, the extensive construction now of such high-cost production facilities would be potentially wasteful. In the latter case, revenues would be less than costs, and pressures would mount on governments to provide large subsidies to producers and consumers.[33] It is extremely important, therefore, that projections of energy demand be made with great care.

It is well known that forecasting is a hazardous occupation. Dramatic events, new social goals and lifestyles, novel products and processes, and major political movements are typically difficult if not impossible to predict. Our ability to foresee the future in more than highly aggregate terms is still limited. At the same time, failure to scrutinize the uncertain future and to model it carefully could lead to costly excesses

69

or shortfalls in capital accumulation, to unnecessary environmental degradation, or to the rapid depletion of energy supplies without a viable successor. The costs of myopia are so large that forecasts have high value, even if they embody considerable uncertainty.

Future demand for energy will not be entirely capricious. To be sure, projections are embedded in uncertainty, but they can be made more reliable by incorporating recent advances in our knowledge of factors affecting demand for energy. Additional information and reliability can be obtained by checking the sensitivity of projections to alternative assumptions. This latter procedure can be used to obtain reasonably reliable upper and lower bound estimates of future demand, which often are of considerable value to government and industry planners.

Recently a number of forecasts of Canadian energy demand have been published. How reliable are these forecasts? How can the projections be improved? Space limitations rule out a full discussion of these issues. However, in the few remaining paragraphs I will outline some of the more obvious problems and procedures.[34]

First, it is important that the phrase "future energy requirements" be discarded. How much energy is to be demanded in years to come is still largely a matter of *choice*, not necessity.[35] Economic growth need not be as energy-intensive as in recent years, because future energy demand will depend on tastes, technology, output, and relative prices.

The most common procedure for projecting industrial energy demand has been the simple energy-GNP ratio. This method has been used in the much-publicized 1969 National Energy Board Forecast of energy demand in Canada to 1990.[36] Under the assumption of a constant energy-GNP ratio, a projection is computed by simply multiplying the forecasted value of GNP in some future year by the energy-GNP ratio. Such a procedure completely ignores the rationing role of higher energy prices.[37] The energy-GNP method would be valid only if demand were completely unresponsive to changes in relative price or if relative prices remain unchanged. However, as discussed in Section III above, all the empirical evidence in Canada suggests otherwise.

Another projection of Canadian energy demand, that prepared by the Department of Energy, Mines, and Resources,[38] frequently mentioned the likely moderation of future energy demand due to rising prices, but never stated precisely how price was incorporated into the projections. Although several variations of the standard forecast were considered, the EMR study did not discuss how future energy demand would be affected if relative energy prices increased slowly, moderately, or very rapidly.

Both the NEB and EMR forecasts have recently been updated.[39] The new NEB forecast still relies heavily on trend extrapolations, energy-GNP ratios, and "expert judgment", and does not appear to take into account explicitly the effects of changes in relative energy prices.[40] On the other hand, the new EMR projections explicitly link future demand for total energy to assumptions about future demographic and economic activity, including future energy prices. Once total energy demands are estimated for each end user sector of the economy, demands for specific fuels are calculated by EMR on a "market share" basis. This procedure is preferable because it incorporates substitution among energy types and ensures that the sum of the demands for specific fuels equals total energy demands. The principal problem with an alternative procedure — building up energy demand projections from specific commodity forecasts — is that interfuel substitution is ignored, and thus the sum of the individual projections may yield total energy demands that are inconsistent with the underlying demographic and economic trends. Not surprisingly, the new EMR projections incorporating price effects are considerably smaller than the new NEB forecasts for oil and gas.[41]

The survey of Canadian energy demand projections, though admittedly brief, is sufficient to demonstrate that the approach of the new EMR forecast has the desirable property of explicitly accounting for effects on energy demand of increases in energy prices. Other things being equal, failure to incorporate effects of higher priced energy would lead to overestimation of future energy demands.

Inclusion of price effects into demand projections is necessary, but not without its own problems. First, future energy prices must be projected. Some disagreement still exists over the likely pattern of future oil prices, and the possibility of the OPEC cartel disintegrating.[42] An obvious method of handling this problem is to prepare and then compare projections based on alternative future prices.[43] Second, even if agreement is reached on future energy prices, price elasticity estimates must be utilized. Although the empirical estimates based on historical Canadian data are reasonably consistent, problems remain in specifying paths of adjustment to higher energy prices. In this regard, econometricians are eager to examine carefully data from 1974 and 1975, years in which energy prices increased dramatically. Until more years' data becomes available, however, it will be difficult to separate the effects of a dramatic price increase from those of an unusually sharp recession. Unfortunately, at the time of this writing (October 1976), 1974-1975 data is not yet available in sufficient detail. The more rapid publication of energy price and quantity data could contribute substantially to the improvement of energy demand analysis and projections.

V. ENERGY CONSERVATION, ECONOMIC GROWTH AND THE PRICE SYSTEM

In the preceding pages I have presented historical evidence on factors affecting demand for energy in Canada and have discussed how this evidence should be embodied in projections of future energy demand. I now turn to a discussion of present policies for energy conservation, the relationship between economic growth and the demand for energy, and the rationing role of the price system. The central issue is whether economic growth, full employment, and energy conservation can be compatible goals.

It is a well-known fact that the world's most industrialized and affluent countries are also the most energy-intensive. Some analysts contend that this correlation is necessary. The availability of low-cost energy supplies has been vital to rapid economic growth, they argue, and in turn consumers in the affluent industrialized nations have chosen to purchase large quantities of energy-intensive goods. To these observers a mechanical link exists between relative affluence and high levels of energy consumption. Using this argument, some industry spokesmen contend that provincial and federal governments should provide large subsidies to the energy-producing industries to induce further development of new energy sources, thereby ensuring continued economic growth.

On the other hand, a substantial number of writers currently argue that contemporary attitudes of North Americans towards economic growth are irresponsible and suicidal. Recent trends in economic growth cannot possibly continue, they write, because finite non-renewable resources will soon be exhausted. Based on this argument, some critics have suggested that citizens of the world's affluent nations must lower their expectations, recognize the finiteness of the earth's resources, and adapt to a "no growth" mentality.[44]

Although the political positions of these two groups differ, a common view seems to be that if we wish to conserve on energy in years to come, we must do so at the cost of reducing the rate of growth of GNP. Thus it is not surprising that debates surrounding energy conservation easily expand into vehement arguments concerning the desirability of prolonged economic growth.

Economists have an important contribution to make in this debate. To be sure, whether sustained economic growth is *desirable* is outside the domain of scientific economic analysis; as social scientists, economists cannot take a position on that issue, for any position involves numerous value judgments.[45] On the other hand, economists can use their analytical tools to examine carefully the relations among energy demand, economic growth, and the rationing role of the price system.

A critical issue in the controversy surrounding energy conservation and economic growth is the *energy-intensity* of future growth. In Section III of this paper evidence was presented which indicated that since the mid-1950's economic growth has been increasingly energy-intensive. This recent pattern differed from that of earlier stages in Canadian economic development, when growth in energy demand lagged behind growth in GNP. If the more recent trend were to continue, that is to say, if future energy-GNP ratios continue to increase or at best level off, growth in GNP will ultimately be constrained by the availability of energy supplies. Proponents of such a position contend that with present GNP growth rates, this "ultimate reckoning" may well occur within the next thirty to fifty years. In this context, debate over energy conservation and economic growth simply degenerates to controversy over the dating of the apocalyptic "doomsday".

A more reasonable and enlightened point of view is that energy-GNP ratios vary with changes in relative energy prices. Future economic growth will be less energy-intensive than that of the 1950's and 1960's, because the world relative price of energy has increased dramatically, and will likely continue to increase in years to come. In the longer term, relative energy prices might possibly flatten out. Thus a substantial amount of energy conservation will occur in coming years, simply because energy has become increasingly expensive and adjustments are now beginning to take place. For this reason economists contend that the higher energy prices provide a socially useful rationing function: because relative energy prices are increasing, industry and consumer demand for energy will be mitigated and the apocalyptic day of "ultimate reckoning" will be postponed.[46] Aggregate demand for energy will likely continue to rise with increases in GNP, but energy intensity will fall. Thus because of the rationing function provided by a smoothly operating price and market system, the goals of energy conservation and economic growth can be consistent with one another.

The view that energy conservation and economic growth need not be incompatible is now beginning to take hold. For example, at the Second Conference on Industrial Energy Conservation in March 1976, Canadian industry spokesmen presented briefs outlining ways in which they planned to reduce energy consumption per unit of output in 1980 by 15 to 20 per cent.[47] A similar positive attitude was reflected by the *Canadian Consumer*.[48] Comparisons with industrial energy use in other countries with historically higher relative energy prices indicate that such energy conservation targets are feasible. For example, energy intensity in industrialized West Germany in 1972 was about 70 per cent of that in Canada.[49]

In the above paragraphs I have argued that higher energy prices provide the socially valuable function of conserving future demand for energy. Public response to the higher energy prices seems to be somewhat uncertain, however, for a number of issues still remain. Among the disturbing questions are three common queries: (1) will not poor Canadian families suffer more from energy price increases, while large multinational corporations prosper? (2) will not the higher energy prices bring about greater unemployment? (3) are energy price increases sufficient, or must further government intervention be encouraged and must "conservation lifestyles" be imposed on Canadians? These three questions are worthy of further discussion. I begin with the issue of income redistribution.

I have argued above that higher energy prices are socially useful in that they ration scarce resources. In doing so, I have emphasized the allocating or efficiency function of the price system. I have not discussed equity on distributional issues concerning who will benefit and who will lose because of the higher energy prices. The evidence suggests to me that higher energy prices will impose a greater relative burden on poorer families. It is useful to review briefly the relevant evidence. I begin with the supply side, and then discuss the demand side.

Individuals holding shares in oil company stocks for several years may have benefited from higher profits accruing to the energy industries in recent years.[50] A portion (approximately 25 per cent) of these shareholders are Canadian, and of these most are likely to be in the upper income brackets. Thus, to the extent that these shareholders benefited, the likely impact of higher energy prices on the income side was to accentuate income differentials among Canadians. This argument is admittedly naïve, however. For example, the governments — federal and provincial —

have benefited enormously from the higher oil prices through leases, royalties, and export taxes. If these substantial additional governmental revenues are used in such a way as to benefit poor more than rich, the regressive impact of higher energy prices would be mitigated. It should be noted that Ottawa has returned some of the additional revenues to eastern provinces in the form of equalization payments. Clearly more research is needed on the income distribution effects of higher energy supply prices. For purposes of the present discussion, I will assume that supply side effects of higher energy prices on income distribution are approximately neutral.

Viewed from the demand side, the available evidence suggests that the income redistribution effects of higher energy prices are regressive. The issue here is whether the share of a family's budget spent on energy decreases, remains the same, or increases with greater income. Waverman has produced calculations based on 1969 data for energy expenditures by income class.[51] For Canada as a whole, direct energy consumption accounted for 6.22 per cent of the expenditures for an average family, 8.86 per cent of the expenditures for the poorest family (income less than $3,000 in 1969 dollars), and 4.34 per cent for the richest family (income class $12,000 and above in 1969 dollars). Hence expenditure on energy as a proportion of total expenditures falls as incomes rise. The implication is that poorer families will bear a disproportionately larger burden of the higher energy price.

These averages across a country as large and diverse as Canada can, however, be misleading. Waverman reports that the relationship between energy expenditures and income occasionally varies with income and by province. He concludes that higher energy prices would produce the largest relative burden on the poorest groups in the Prairies and Atlantic Provinces and on the middle class in Ontario, Quebec and British Columbia. Other evidence suggests that natural gas price increases would be the most regressive, while electricity price may be less regressive, due to the fact that the demand for electricity-using appliances is more income elastic.

If one combines both approximately neutral supply and regressive demand side income redistribution effects, the net result is that higher energy prices impose a greater relative burden on poorer families. This unfortunate aspect does not imply, however, that considerations of compassion require that energy prices be kept low. Such a policy would only contribute to excessive energy consumption by all Canadians, regardless of income levels, and might well impose a greater burden on future generations. Rather, to the extent that income redistribution effects of higher energy prices are regressive, neutralizing changes in the income tax structure should be implemented immediately. One possibility is to provide an additional tax credit or subsidy to low income families.[52] The conclusion must be then, that income redistribution considerations do not constitute a valid excuse for keeping energy prices low.[53]

A second concern of many citizens is whether higher energy prices will bring about greater unemployment. In the short run, it is likely that some firms will respond to the dramatic energy price increases by reducing scale of operations and laying off some workers. Other firms, however, will attempt to make their production process less energy-intensive and more labour-intensive. This latter result is explained by the empirical evidence cited in Section III above which consistently showed that energy and labour are substitutable inputs. Hence, as the relative price of energy increases, the economy will become less energy-intensive and more labour-intensive. The goals of energy conservation and full employment may conflict in the short run, but as the economy adjusts to a more labour-intensive production process, the goals may become compatible. In this context it is interesting to note that a major U.S. study recently examined the direct and indirect effects of a moderate BTU tax on energy. The result of such a tax was to make the U.S. considerably less dependent on imported energy, and to increase the demand for labour.[54] Thus energy conservation policies are not inconsistent with policies designed to reduce unemployment.

A third concern of many Canadians is whether the price increases are "sufficient", or whether additional government intervention is desirable.

At the outset, it is worth remarking that in some cases present governmental policies actually militate against energy conservation. Take, for example, the rate structures of crown-owned utilities that sell electricity and natural gas. The present rate structure of these utilities is such that price per kilowatt hour of electricity or thousand cubic feet of natural gas falls as the quantity demanded increases. That is to say, large energy users pay a lower price per unit than do small energy users. The effect of such a policy is of course to encourage higher levels of energy consumption. A more reasonable policy would be to charge users on the basis of the additional long-run social cost incurred by providing an additional unit of energy.[55]

Another example of policies militating against energy conservation is the federal government's two-price policy for oil, in which the price to domestic users is lower than the "world price" in the export market. Since eastern Canada imports oil from Venezuela and the Middle East at the world price, the cost of oil to Canada is the world price, not the lower domestic price.[56] The effect of the two-price system is to make the composition of output from Canadian industry overly energy-intensive. Indeed, the two-price system should simply be recognized as a subsidy to domestic energy-intensive consumers and industries.[57]

A final set of examples of governmental policies contributing to excessive energy consumption is the federal corporate tax structure. The allowable rate of depreciation for tax purposes on investments for on-site electricity generation and for most heat recovery equipment has been 6 per cent; the allowable rate of depreciation for almost all other comparable investments in the manufacturing sector has been 50 per cent. Such a tax policy obviously discriminates against the adoption of more efficient energy-conserving equipment. It should be noted that this particular feature of the corporate tax structure was recently changed in the May 25, 1976 budget of Finance Minister MacDonald. However, other energy-using biases still remain. For example, as noted above, the federal government grants accelerated write-off provisions and other investment incentives to industry. In the past the capital-energy complementarity meant that these investment incentives actually increased the demand for both equipment and energy. The final effect of such policies was to make the economy more capital and energy-intensive and less labour-intensive. To the extent that these investment incentives induce substitution toward capital (regardless of whether it is "energy-saving"), the investment incentives conflict with the goal of energy conservation. Future investment incentives must be implemented with care so that energy demand is not exacerbated.

Strangely enough, the payroll tax system also contributes to greater energy consumption. In recent years employers have been required to pay an increasing proportion of wages and salaries to the Social Insurance Plan. The effect of these larger payroll tax rates is to increase the price of labour to firms. Since the empirical evidence cited in Section III suggests that energy and labour are substitutable, increases in payroll taxes reduce labour-intensiveness and increase energy demand.

The above examples illustrate that some of the present policies of provincial and federal governments conflict with the goal of energy conservation. This should not be surprising, however, since energy conservation is but one of many goals. For example, if energy conservation were the sole target of governmental policy, wartime measures such as direct energy rationing could be implemented. Such an "overkill" policy would bring about numerous bottlenecks, inefficiencies, and administrative nightmares; as a result, production, employment and standards of living for Canadians would suffer needlessly. Alternatively, some have suggested that the federal government should impose "conservation lifestyles" on Canadians. Proponents of this position implicitly state that Canadians will continue to waste energy, even when energy prices reflect social costs because consumers lack "correct information". Such arguments need to be analyzed carefully to determine whether the principal argument states precisely what type and amount of information is "sufficient".

There is of course an important and critical positive role for governmental action: to help ensure that the market prices and user fees paid by informed consumers and industries accurately reflect the cost of resources used in producing and consuming energy. To the extent that present prices differ from costs, utility rate structures and tax policies should be amended accordingly. When such policies are followed, the goals of energy conservation, economic growth, and full employment can be compatible.

Notes

[1]Although I have attempted to provide an exhaustive survey, I may have omitted some studies inadvertently.

[2]However, as will be discussed later, household demand for energy is also derived in that demand for energy typically results from household demand for services of appliances, etc.

[3]Source: Statistics Canada 57-207.

[4]These figures undoubtedly understate final demand, for household demands are partly included in the commercial and transportation sectors. Further discussion of data is found in Section III of this paper.

[5]Recently a B.C. Hydro official pointed out to me that the British Columbia forest industry is considerably more energy-intensive and less labour-intensive than its European counterparts. One reason for this, he suggested, was that in Europe electricity was more expensive and labour less costly than in British Columbia.

[6]The portion of intermediate energy demand used for heating will of course also be sensitive to weather conditions; but space heating demand is a less important share of total energy used in the business than in the final demand sector.

[7]Obviously the income elasticity for a good cannot remain greater than unity indefinitely, for eventually as income rises the budget share expended on that good would approach unity.

[8]See Leonard Waverman, "National Policy and Natural Gas: The Costs of a Border", *Canadian Journal of Economics* (August 1972), pp. 331-348.

[9]Further discussion of these issues is found in "U.S. and Canadian Energy Policy," by James W. McKie, in this book.

[10]These statistics are drawn from F.W. Gorbet, "Energy Demand Projections for Canada: An Integrated Approach", paper presented at the 1975 American Institute of Mining Engineers meetings, New York, February 16-20.

[11]John Davis, *Canadian Energy Prospects*, Royal Commission on Canada's Economic Prospects, Ottawa, March 1957.

[12]*Ibid.*, p. 24.

[13]*Ibid.*, p. 31.

[14]International comparisons of energy consumption are found in Davis, *op. cit.*, and in Joel Darmstadter, *et al., Energy in the World Economy* (Baltimore: Johns Hopkins Press (Resources for the Future), 1971).

[15]James Allen Coombs, "A Cross-Sectional Study of Energy Demand in Canadian Manufacturing Industries, 1964", Master of Arts Thesis, Department of Economics, Queen's University, September 1969.

[16]J. Daniel Khazzoom, "An Econometric Model of the Demand for Energy in Canada, Part I: The Industrial Demand for Gas", *Canadian Journal of Statistics*, Vol. 1, No. 1, 1973, pp. 69-107.

[17]*Ibid.*, p. 106.

[18]DataMetrics Limited, "Projections of Alberta Aggregate Energy Demand, 1974-1985", Joint Submission of Pan Alberta Gas Limited and the Alberta Gas Trunk Line, Limited, to Proceeding 6147, Alberta Energy Resource Conservation Board, May 1974.

[19]F.W. Gorbet, *op. cit.*, Appendix A-3.

[20]M.G.S. Denny and C. Pinto, "The Demand for Energy in Canadian Manufacturing, 1949-1970", mimeographed, University of Toronto, 1975.

[21]M. Fuss, R. Hyndman, and L. Waverman, "Residential, Commercial, and Industrial Demand for Energy in Canada; Projections to 1985 With Three Alternative Models", in William Nordhaus, ed., *Papers and Proceedings of the Conference on Energy Demand* (Laxenburg, Austria: International Institute for Applied Systems Analysis, 1975). These results were also presented at the 1975 meetings of the Canadian Economics Association in Edmonton.

[22]M. Fuss, "The Demand for Energy in Canadian Manufacturing: An Example of the Estimation of Production Structures with Many Inputs", Institute for Policy Analysis Working Paper 7505, University of Toronto, December 1975; forthcoming, *Journal of Econometrics.*

[23]Robert McRae, "A Quantitative Analysis of Some Policy Alternatives Affecting Canadian Natural Gas and Crude Oil Supply and Demand", draft manuscript, Department of Economics, University of British Columbia, July 1976.

[24]Results from American and Canadian studies are also quite consistent with one another. For a comparison of findings from Canadian and American studies, see L. Waverman, "Estimating the Demand for Energy: Heat without Light", in Conference Proceedings, *The Economics of Oil and Gas Self-Sufficiency in Canada*, University of Calgary, October 1975.

[25]E.R. Berndt and David O. Wood, "Tax Policy, Technological Change, and the Derived Demand for Energy", mimeograph, University of British Columbia, Department of Economics, August 1975.

[26]G.C. Watkins, "Canadian Residential and Commercial Demand for Natural Gas", University of Calgary Discussion Paper Series No. 30, May 1974. An earlier version of this work appeared in a submission to the National Energy Board hearings, AO-1-GH-3-71, June 1973.

[27]For an earlier study using similar methodology but American data, see Pietro Balestra, *The Demand for Natural Gas in the United States: A Dynamic Approach for the Residential and Commercial Market* (Amsterdam: North Holland Co., 1967).

[28]E.R. Berndt and G.C. Watkins, "Demand for Natural Gas: Residential and Commercial Markets in Ontario and British Columbia", forthcoming, *Canadian Journal of Economics* (Spring 1977). An earlier version of this paper appeared under the title "A Residential and Commercial Natural Gas Demand Model for Ontario and British Columbia", in Proceedings of the Conference on *The Economics of Oil and Gas Self-Sufficiency in Canada*, University of Calgary, October 1975, pp. 57-63.

[29]M. Fuss, R. Hyndman, and L. Waverman, *op. cit.*

[30]F.W. Gorbet, *op. cit*, Appendix A-1.

[31]For an American study, see Martin Baughman and Paul Joskow, "The Effects of Fuel Prices on Residential Appliance Choice in the United States", *Land Economics* (February 1975), pp. 41-49.

[32]An American study of this nature is now being completed by E.R. Berndt, E.A. Hudson, and D.W. Jorgenson in a forthcoming book. A first version of one of the chapters has been published; see E.A. Hudson and D.W. Jorgenson, "U.S. Energy Policy and Economic Growth, 1975-2000", *The Bell Journal of Economics and Management Science*, Vol. 5, No. 2 (Autumn 1974), pp. 461-514.

[33]Ironically, the energy demand forecasts could possibly be self-fulfilling. For example, if utilities will be unable to sell the energy at a high price that covered costs, they could lower price and increase demand to the level originally projected. Such a lower price would of course be a subsidy to energy consumers.

[34]A more detailed discussion can be found in Ernst R. Berndt, "Forecasting North American Energy Demand: Issues and Problems", in Peter H. Pearse, ed., *The MacKenzie Pipeline: Arctic Gas and Canadian Energy Policy*, (Toronto:McClelland and Stewart), 1974, pp. 71-79.

[35]It is noteworthy that the National Energy Board publishes energy demand forecasts with the title "requirements"; see, for example, *Canadian Oil Supply and Requirements*, NEB, September 1975, and *Canadian National Gas Supply and Requirements*, NEB, April 1975.

[36]National Energy Board, *Energy Supply and Demand in Canada and Export Demand for Canadian Energy, 1966 to 1990* (Ottawa: Information Canada, 1969).

[37]For further discussion, see E.R. Berndt and D.O. Wood, "An Economic Interpretation of the Energy-GNP Ratio", Chapter 3 in Macrakis, ed., *Energy: Demand, Conservation, and Institutional Problems* (Cambridge: M.I.T., Press, 1974).

[38]Department of Energy, Mines, and Resources, *An Energy Policy for Canada, Phase I* (Ottawa: Information Canada, 1973).

[39]National Energy Board, *Canadian Natural Gas Supply and Requirements*, 1975; and NEB, *Canadian Oil Supply and Requirements*, September 1975; Department of Energy, Mines, and Resources, *An Energy Strategy for Canada: Policies for Self-Reliance*, Ottawa, 1976.

[40]Further comparison of the 1969-75 NEB forecasts can be found in John Helliwell, "Costs and Benefits of Self-Sufficiency in Oil and Gas", in *Proceedings of the Conference on the Economics of Oil and Gas Self-Sufficiency in Canada* (Calgary: University of Calgary), 1975, pp. 18-20.

[41]The new NEB forecast is considerably less than that projected by the Canadian Petroleum Association (see their submission to the NEB 1974-1975 natural gas supply and requirements hearings).

[42]Most observers feel that the recent higher oil prices will remain, if not increase. An articulate spokesman for the minority view is Morris A. Adelman. See, for example, M.A. Adelman, "U.S. Energy Policy", in *No Time to Confuse:* A Critique of the Final Report of the Energy Policy Project of the Ford Foundation, *A Time to Choose* (San Francisco: Institute for Contemporary Studies, 1975), pp. 27-42.

[43]Such a procedure has been adopted in the 1976 EMR forecasts.

[44]It is interesting to note that recently the well-known Club of Rome reversed its original position and called for selective economic growth to speed the development of the world's poorer countries. See "Club of Rome Revisited", *Time*, 26 April 1976, p. 45.

[45]A discussion of some of these issues is found in Gideon Rosenbluth, "Economists and the Growth Controversy", *Canadian Public Policy*, II (2), Spring 1976, pp. 225-239.

[46]Furthermore, as world supplies of specific finite resources fall, their relative prices will rise. These price increases will make economically feasible substitutable energy sources that were not feasible at lower energy prices. For a useful discussion of "backstop technologies" and the intertemporal pricing of exhaustible resources, see William D. Nordhaus, "The Allocation of Energy Resources", *Brookings Papers on Economic Activity*, 3:1973, pp. 529-570.

[47]See the "Condensed Reports of the Industry Task Forces", Second Conference on Industrial Energy Conservation, March 24, 1976 (Ottawa: Department of Industry, Trade and Commerce).

[48]See "Energy: Our Decision, His Legacy", *Canadian Consumer* (February 1976), Vol. 6, No. 1, pp. 30-33.

[49]See "Comparison of Energy Consumption Between West Germany and the United States", Conservation Paper No. 33, Washington, D.C., Federal Energy Administration, Office of Marketing and Education. Canadian-U.S. comparisons are found in Darmstadter, *op. cit.* Some of the Canadian-West Germany energy consumption differences may be due to climatic factors, distances between major population centres, and variations in output mix.

[50]It appears, however, that prices of shares in Canadian oil companies (e.g., Gulf Oil Canada, Imperial Oil, Shell Canada) have not risen as rapidly as those of the American oil companies (e.g., Atlantic Richfield, Exxon, Mobil, Standard Oil Indiana). Furthermore, share prices of the Canadian companies in late 1976 are still less than their peak prices of late 1972 - early 1973, prior to the embargo. The share prices of the U.S. oil companies peaked in late 1974 - early 1975, after the embargo. Source: *The Investment Index*, Burns Fry Limited.

[51]Leonard Waverman, "The Two Price System in Energy: Subsidies Forgotten", *Canadian Public Policy* (Winter 1975), pp. 76-88, Tables 2 and 3.

[52]An alternative possibility is to incorporate a direct energy payment into the Family Allowance programme. However, such a procedure would still implicitly constitute a subsidy to energy, and would therefore conflict with the goal of conservation.

[53]For further discussion on this point, see Chapter 3 in this book by G. Campbell Watkins, "Canadian Oil and Gas Pricing".

[54]See E.A. Hudson and D.W. Jorgenson, *op. cit.*, especially Section 6. The Hudson-Jorgenson analysis was confined primarily to demand, and did not examine potential problems in primary energy supply.

[55]It should also be noted that utilities frequently find it necessary to utilize extremely energy-intensive processes to supply energy during periods of peak demand. Utilities could bring about a substantial energy conservation by charging higher prices to all users during periods of peak demand. Such peak load pricing policies have been implemented by telephone companies.

[56]See Chapter 3 in this volume by G. Campbell Watkins, "Canadian Oil and Gas Pricing".

[57]Also see Leonard Waverman, *op. cit.*

Editor's Introduction

At the present time, Canadian domestic oil and gas prices are set by the federal government at levels below world oil equivalence; oil imports are subsidized, exports are taxed. Mr. Watkins' essay reviews the development of Canadian oil and gas pricing and discusses current policy issues, especially those typified by such price regulation. Evidence - albeit incomplete - which has been accumulated on the petroleum industry suggests it is sufficiently competitive to allow market prices to perform their function as an allocator of scarce resources, unless prevented by government intervention. Watkins finds that up until 1961, Canadian oil prices conformed to a pattern consistent with competitive price formation. Since then, the Canadian government has increasingly influenced prices, first indirectly, then directly. In the 1960's, producers (and consumers) were protected from 'low' cost oil. In the 1970's, consumers (and producers) are protected from 'high' cost oil.

On the question of current subsidization of crude oil (and natural gas) prices within Canada, Watkins argues that efficiency losses under such a policy should preclude its continuation. Non-market pricing systems such as the application of public utility pricing concepts to petroleum production and pricing systems, which distinguish between 'new' oil and 'old' oil, are found wanting. Application of formulae such as commodity value to set the price of gas can be justified as an interim measure, but not as a long-term solution. Continuing government involvement in regulating exports of oil and gas will be required, but pricing should revert from the government arena to the marketplace.

Canadian Oil and Gas Pricing

G. Campbell Watkins

President
DataMetrics Limited, Calgary

and

Visiting Associate Professor of Economics
University of Calgary

THE AUTHOR

Gordon Campbell Watkins, born in Cheshire, England in 1939, is President of the economic consulting firm of DataMetrics, Calgary, and is also Visiting Associate Professor of Economics at the University of Calgary. He graduated from Leeds University, Honours B.A. Economics and Statistics, 1960; took degree courses in accountancy at Manchester University, 1961; and received his M.Phil., 1972, from Leeds University.

After two years as statistician with an English engineering firm, Professor Watkins came to Canada, and from 1962 to 1972 he served as an economist with several government agencies and corporations. He joined DataMetrics in 1973. Professor Watkins' involvement in economic research spans a wide range of projects and positions: Chief Economist at the Oil and Gas Conservation Board (1965-1969); Associate Economist, Royal Bank of Canada (1970-1971); Economic Advisor and Co-ordinator of Economic Studies - Gas Arctic Group (1971-1972). As well as his involvement in petroleum research, Professor Watkins has also directed and participated in studies related to road transport, aviation, cost-benefit analyses and regional economic impact studies.

Professor Watkins has published papers in a wide range of professional and academic journals, including the *Canadian Journal of Economics, Journal of Industrial Economics, Journal of Environmental Economics and Management, The Journal of Canadian Petroleum Technology,* and such trade journals as *Oilweek* and *Canadian Petroleum.*

Canadian Oil and Gas Pricing*

G. Campbell Watkins

President
DataMetrics Limited, Calgary

and

Visiting Associate Professor of Economics
University of Calgary

I. INTRODUCTION

This essay reviews historical Canadian crude oil and natural gas pricing mechanisms and discusses some current policy issues. It is divided into four main sections. Section I deals with general aspects of oil and gas supply, demand and prices. Section II concerns the pricing of Canadian oil and gas in the context of the market developments since World War II. In Section III the focus is on some current policy issues: subsidies and export taxes; pricing according to timing of discovery ('vintage' pricing); public utility pricing concepts applied to oil and gas; and the pricing of natural gas by 'commodity value'. Some concluding remarks are made in Section IV. An Appendix develops a diagram relating to certain points raised in Section III.

*I am indebted to comments made by P.G. Bradley, F.J. Anderson, E.R. Berndt, A.J. MacFadyen and F.R. Anton, but do not implicate them in any opinions expressed below. I also wish to thank Ms. B. Hansen and Mrs. K. Sharp for statistical assistance.

II. PETROLEUM DEMAND AND PRICING[1]

It is common to refer to the amount of crude oil demanded by refiners at any point in time as depending, among other things, upon its price. Yet frequent assertions are made about formulating a policy to meet oil requirements without any allusion to the pricing structure in which such requirements are defined.

The economist's conventional demand schedule lists the quantities of oil refiners might wish to purchase at various assumed prices over a given period of time. No reference is made to whether demands at a particular price will be met. In other words, the demand schedule is considered to be independent of supply conditions. The demand schedule is simply an expression of the preference of users given various prices of petroleum.

For example, at a price of $1 per barrel, demand for crude oil would be very high.[2] The associated low gasoline prices would encourage the intensive use of large automobiles; industrial consumers of fuel oils would seek to substitute oil for other higher-priced alternative fuels; fuel oil would be preferred as a source of energy for space heating; and energy-saving behaviour would be discouraged. At a price of $12 per barrel - and given no change in other determinants of demand - consumption patterns would be rearranged to reduce the use of oil. Automobiles and trucks with more frugal fuel appetites would be preferred. Where feasible, industries would favour other fuels. Better insulation of residences and other buildings heated by fuel oil would be encouraged.

Thus, in general the relationship between the volume of crude oil demanded and its price is inverse: the higher the price, the less the quantity demanded, and vice versa. This sort of relationship is depicted by the downward sloping curve labelled DD in Figure 1.

The demand schedule shown isolates the effect of price on quantity demanded. Other factors affecting demand - incomes, households, consumer tastes, technology and prices of alternate fuels - will affect the levels of demand at which the price relationships are valid. For example, in general if real incomes were to rise or industrial output expand, the curve DD in Figure 1 would shift to the right. If the price of a fuel considered a substitute for fuel oils in certain end uses - such as natural gas - were to decline, the curve DD would shift to the left, since some consumers previously preferring fuel oil would now switch to natural gas, given its relatively more attractive price.

FIGURE 1
Petroleum Demand and Supply

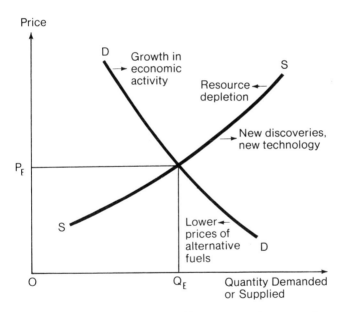

The price of petroleum depends on the demand for petroleum and the supply of petroleum. Shifts in supply caused by depletion of reserves (decreased supply) and new discoveries (increased supply) cause the price to rise and fall respectively. Shifts in demand caused by lower prices of alternative fuels (decreased demand) and growth in economic activity (increased demand) cause the price to fall and rise respectively.

The task of estimating the character and degree of response of the demand curve to changes in the variables which determine it, for instance changes in real incomes, prices of other fuels and in the composition of industrial output, is the subject of another essay in this volume.[3] The point of primary concern here is that the demand schedule expresses a hypothetical ranking of consumer needs, and the 'agent' for ranking these needs is the price. Price is essential information for consumers to evaluate the various purchase options open to them.

So much for demand. What of supply, and in particular its relationship to price? In a manner analogous to the demand schedule, the supply schedule labelled SS in Figure 1 signifies how much oil suppliers would be prepared to produce as its price varies, given production costs, technology, price expectations, tax regimes and the like. As price increases between periods, desired output rises. Higher prices will bring forth more output from existing sources of supply and render operation of higher cost deposits economic. For instance, higher prices may well make attractive further development drilling on the flanks of already developed oil reservoirs and also promote additional exploratory activity at deeper horizons or in more remote regions. Hence the supply schedule as depicted in Figure 1 rises from left to right.[4] It expresses how much crude oil suppliers would seek to produce, not how much they might sell at a given price. The latter is governed by the demand curve.

In the context of crude oil (and natural gas), the rate of production from a given reservoir tends to decline for physical reasons as production proceeds, and thus the curve SS may shift to the left as a function of cumulative output. Alternatively, new technological developments or new discoveries may shift the curve to the right. An especially important determinant of the shape of a petroleum supply curve is the type of taxation regime imposed.[5] If taxes depress incremental returns too much, the degree of supply response to higher prices will be minimal.[6]

Where markets operate with little interference, at any given period of time the market price will gravitate towards the equilibrium level of P_E in Figure 1. At this price, consumers' demands will be met by producers' supplies. At a price lower than P_E, consumers will seek to satisfy uses for which supply is insufficient. The shortfall in supply would be allocated among consumers by devices such as rationing and queuing. At a price above P_E, supply will exceed the amount consumers would wish to purchase. The excess supply could be eliminated by production quotas. Given a market for the product and sufficient interchange or availability of information by consumers and producers, prices will fall or rise to eliminate excess demand or supply, until an equilibrium price (P_E) is reached.

The function of the price mechanism, then, is to allow expression of the aggregation of the valuations of all consumers, to encourage shifts in resources as such valuations change or as supply conditions alter, and to act as a rationing device and in this way eschew arbitrary regulation which might otherwise be required to bring supply and demand into balance. In short, where markets are sufficiently developed and competitive, prices enable consumers to express their preferences and induce producers and consumers to alter their behaviour as conditions vary.

This, then, is the theory. To what extent can the pricing and marketing mechanism be expected to perform its social role as an allocator of a scarce resource in the context of the institutional and other characteristics of the oil and gas industry? This topic, among others, is covered in the next section.

III. CANADIAN OIL AND GAS PRICING AND MARKETS

This section discusses theoretical aspects of delivered pricing mechanisms and then reviews developments in Canadian oil and gas pricing in the light of the theory. Finally, the competitive structure of the oil and gas industry is briefly examined.

Delivered pricing[7]

In a competitive market, the 'net back' at a given source of supply (delivered market price less transportation costs to supply source) will be the same irrespective of eventual market destination. If the net back from shipping to any one market exceeds another, producers would find it attractive to sell there to take advantage of the wider margin of profit. But under competition such differences would be eroded, and prices at the supply source would tend to fall until all net backs were equalized.

Before large scale development of indigenous production, the Canadian prairies were supplied in the main by crude oil from the United States. The Prairie crude oil price was the field price of oil from the main source of incremental supply - the United States - plus the cost of transportation.[8] Consider Alberta as a new source of supply, but one which has the initial capability of supplying only a portion of the demand for oil in Alberta. Under the type of delivered pricing system outlined above, the price of Alberta oil would be the prevailing delivered price from the alternative source of supply - the United States. It would not be more, because no Alberta oil would be sold. It would not be less, because all Alberta output could be sold at the prevailing price.

Suppose new discoveries continued to increase Alberta's supply capacity. Output expansion would entail displacement of alternative supplies in areas increasingly beyond Alberta. Westward expansion could be accommodated by the existing price structure if prices to the west of Alberta were set on the same basis as Alberta prices. However, expansion in an eastward direction would require acceptance of lower net backs, since the delivered price of oil from the alternative source of supply - the United States - falls the closer the delivery point to such supply sources, as shown in Figure 2.

FIGURE 2
Delivered and Net Back Prices

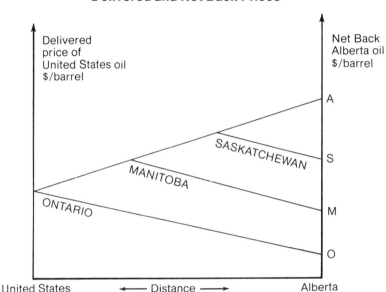

The price of oil in various local Canadian markets is determined by the price of U.S. oil delivered to that local market. The net price to Alberta producers (the net back) from sales in any local market (e.g. Manitoba) is determined by the price of U.S. oil delivered to that market (the line running from left to right indicating higher delivered prices for U.S. oil the farther the market is from Ontario) minus the costs of transportation (the slope of the lines running from right to left represents the effect of transportation costs by associating each U.S. delivered price with a lower net back on Alberta oil).

In Figure 2 the line sloping upward from left to right indicates the increasing delivered cost of United States oil the further the market satisfied is from United States supply sources. If Alberta oil were only sufficient to serve Alberta needs, the price of oil for Alberta producers would be A. If Alberta oil were to supply some or all of the Saskatchewan market, the net back in Alberta for such movements would be S, the net back from Manitoba would be M, and so on for points further east (e.g. Ontario).[9]

Reduced Alberta net backs for supplying such markets as Saskatchewan, Manitoba and Ontario would still be attractive if the increased output sold were profitable. Monopoly or collusion in the marketing of Alberta production would tend to result in the maintenance of different net backs according to markets served: the farther east the market, the lower the Alberta net back. Under competitive marketing, different net backs cannot be sustained. A uniform net back will prevail, based on the market at which the delivered price of Alberta oil equalizes with supplies from alternative sources. This is called the competitive 'interface'. If the resulting Alberta net back were still significantly above costs and output could be further expanded, the Alberta price would be further reduced to achieve additional eastward market penetration. Such an evolution of prices is consistent with the presence of competitive forces. The attraction of higher profits has expanded output and lowered prices: consumers have gained. In a perfectly competitive situation, output would be expanded until the incremental cost of Alberta oil supply (marginal cost) would equal the net back from the 'interface' market.

Developments in Alberta oil pricing

The extent to which the competitive model described above applies to the evolution of Canadian oil prices, and in particular to prices from the major source of supply, Alberta, is examined below.

Before 1947, the growth pattern of the Alberta petroleum industry was erratic; peak production had been reached in 1942, stimulated by wartime requirements. Secular growth of the industry commenced with the discovery of the Leduc field in 1947. Subsequently, substantial discoveries were made at Redwater (1948), Joarcam and Golden Spike (1949), Fenn Big Valley and Acheson (1950), and at other locations.

In 1947, Alberta oil supplied Alberta requirements and a portion of Saskatchewan's. By 1948, Alberta oil had begun to penetrate the Manitoba market and in 1951 deliveries to the Ontario market commenced, as did exports to the United States.

Alberta crude oil prices reflected these market developments, as shown in Table 1.

TABLE 1
Salient Alberta Crude Oil Prices, 1947-1962

	$/barrel*
1947	$3.20
1948 (Dec.)	$2.68
1951	$2.44
1953	$2.645
1955	$2.485
1957	$2.67
1958	$2.42
1962	$2.62

*With the exception of 1947, all prices are wellhead prices for the Redwater reservoir (API gravity 35°) in Alberta. Source of data: Alberta Energy Resources Conservation Board (AERCB). Numerous other adjustments took place up to 1962, reflecting changes in the Canadian dollar exchange rates.

In 1947, the price of Alberta oil was $3.20 per barrel. By December 1948, this price had been reduced to $2.68 to make Alberta oil competitive with the delivered price in Manitoba of United States supplies from Illinois, Oklahoma and Texas. Alberta oil prices fluctuated in 1949 and 1950, according to changes in the exchange rate of the Canadian dollar. The reduction in price in 1951 was intended to make Alberta crude competitive with Illinois crude at Sarnia. The price rise in 1953 reflected an increase in equivalent delivered prices of United States and world oil at Sarnia. The price fell in 1955 with a change in the price of Illinois crude oil and exchange rate adjustments, but rose in 1957 as world oil prices increased. Subsequently, the 1958 decline in world oil prices induced a fall in Alberta oil prices. In 1962, the devaluation of the Canadian dollar to a pegged rate resulted in an Alberta (Redwater) wellhead price of $2.62. This price held until 1970.

Up to 1960, the behaviour of Canadian oil prices is compatible with the competitive model outlined beforehand.[10] The build-up in supplies induced market expansion. Prices for *all* markets were reduced as the competitive interface for Alberta oil shifted eastwards to displace United States supplies. Also, up until 1960 changes in world crude oil prices were directly reflected in Alberta prices.

A different picture emerges in the 1960's. The Canadian Government's National Oil Policy reserved markets west of the Ottawa Valley for Canadian oil, whether such oil was competitive with the delivered price of imported oil or not. Exports to the United States grew significantly, but at a regulated rate under the aegis of the United States Oil Import Quota Policy. The competitive interface for Alberta oil shifted south to the Detroit-Toledo area in the United States in the early 1960's, but no changes in Alberta oil prices were induced. The important point is that the United States oil import policy insulated United States prices from the downward trend in world oil prices. The combination of the special status accorded to Canadian oil within the United States policy and the National Oil Policy protected Canadian oil prices from the fall in world oil prices experienced in the 1960's.[11] By 1970, Ontario refiners were paying some $0.27 more per barrel for Alberta oil compared with the delivered price of offshore imports.[12]

Developments since 1970 are briefly summarized as follows. Over the period 1970 to 1973 several adjustments were made to Alberta oil prices such that by the spring of 1973 equality had been established between Canadian and United States delivered prices at Chicago.[13] These adjustments reflected increases in United States oil prices and the changed terms by which Canadian oil gained access to United States markets: all restrictions were dropped by early 1973. Delivered price equality at Chicago was a response consistent with competition, within constraints set by the

Canadian National Oil Policy and the United States Oil Import Policy.

Such changes were realized within the context of abrupt changes in world oil markets. The Teheran-Tripoli Agreements of 1971 reversed the decade-long competitive decline in world oil prices, and laid the groundwork for more intensive, and later dramatic, action by the Organization of Petroleum Exporting Countries (OPEC) to raise world oil prices. Further increases in United States prices and strong demand in United States markets provided scope for further rises in Alberta wellhead prices to a level of some $4.00 per barrel by August 1973.

Beyond August 1973, competitive relationships in the Chicago market have been sustained by the imposition of export taxes on Canadian oil.[14] Corresponding Canadian prices at the source of supply (wellhead prices) have been held at levels below world oil equivalent prices. The export tax commenced at $0.40 per barrel in September 1973, rose to $1.90 per barrel in December 1973 (given the then increase in world oil prices), to $2.20 per barrel in January 1974 and then to $6.40 per barrel in February 1974, after the dramatic rise in world oil prices imposed by OPEC in the preceding month. In 1975, Alberta oil prices were raised to some $8.00 per barrel, and the export tax was correspondingly reduced; a similar adjustment was made in July 1976.

The current situation (August 1976) is that the export tax on light and medium crude oils shipped to the United States is $3.65 per barrel; Alberta wellhead prices are $9.175 per barrel;[15] and the landed price of overseas supplies at Montreal is $13.29 per barrel.[16] Importers of oil into Eastern Canada are subsidized to the equivalent of the difference between the import price and the implicit delivered price of domestic supplies.

In conclusion: throughout the period 1947 to 1960 wellhead price movements were consistent with the *pattern* expected under competition: equal net backs on all sales and changes in wellhead prices reflecting changes in the market interface.[17] In the 1960's, Canadian oil prices were indirectly insulated from world oil prices. In the 1970's prices have been increasingly subject to direct government regulation.

Developments in Alberta natural gas pricing

The period after Leduc was also characterized by a rapid build up in natural gas reserves in Alberta, and to a lesser extent in British Columbia. This reflected the discovery of gas both in conjunction with crude oil (associated gas) and on its own (non-associated gas). In Alberta, by the year end 1947 remaining gas reserves were some 5.1 trillion cubic feet, but the current rate of production was only some 33 billion cubic feet per year: a reserves-production ratio of 155 years.[18]

Given this substantial inventory, in 1949 the provincial government appointed a commission (the Dinning Commission) to recommend a policy for natural gas marketing. On the basis of the Commission's report, the Province passed an Act[19] providing for the possible export of 'surplus' gas from Alberta. In essence, the surplus was defined as the difference between known reserves and Alberta's cumulative forecast gas requirements over a thirty year period. Subsequently, this definition of surplus was relaxed as the continued development of the industry encouraged more reliance on anticipated reserves[20] to match future Alberta requirements.

Exports of gas from the Province grew rapidly with the award of permits predicated on the building of three major gas trunklines: the TransCanada pipeline system serving Canadian provinces east of Alberta (including Quebec) and certain U.S. markets in the northern tier states as far east as New York state; the Alberta and Southern system, serving Northern California; and the Westcoast system, serving the United States Pacific Northwest. Alberta gas marketed beyond the province and all Canadian gas exported to the United States was assigned under long-term export permits. This reflected in part the type of commitment required for financing such major developments. Normally, for gas committed to a permit, prices were constant but with some provision for minor escalation and for periodic redetermination. By 1970, only 17 per cent of Alberta gas production was consumed within the Province; 39 per cent was marketed in other Canadian provinces (especially Ontario) and the remaining 44 per cent was exported. Of total Canadian gas production in 1970, 56 per cent was consumed within Canada, 46 per cent outside.[21]

Natural gas prices up to the late 1960's were relatively stable. The average Alberta field price was 10.2¢/MCF in 1957, 12.7¢/MCF in 1962, and 15.7¢/MCF in 1967.[22] These low prices in terms of BTU equivalence compared with crude oil[23] reflect higher unit BTU transportation costs for natural gas vis-à-vis oil, the need for natural gas to achieve rapid penetration in relatively distant energy markets - especially Ontario - to ensure viable transportation costs over long distances, and restrictions on natural gas prices in the United States imposed by the Federal Power Commission (F.P.C.).

By the late 1960's, nascent shortages of United States natural gas encouraged more United States companies to look to Canada as a source of supply. These shortages in part reflected an absence of competitive pricing of natural gas in the United States resulting from the field price controls exerted by the Federal Power Commission. Consolidated Natural Gas - a subsidiary of Northern Natural Gas of Nebraska - began an aggressive gas purchase programme in Alberta. In 1969, prices for new supplies of natural gas were placed under increasing pressure. This effect would have become more widespread over time, as contractual arrangements disseminated higher prices among already marketed supplies. The nub of the matter, however, was whether increased United States competition for gas supplies would be translated into actual marketing arrangements. This depended on whether the Canadian National Energy Board (NEB) would issue new permits for export of gas. In 1970, additional export permits were awarded, but, significantly, the request by Consolidated Natural Gas was refused. Finally, in 1971 requests for further exports by Alberta and Southern (serving northern California) and by Consolidated Natural Gas were rejected: any surplus of gas was deemed insufficient, if non-existent.[24]

This closure of export markets and associated curtailment of competition for gas supplies in Canada had important consequences for Canadian gas pricing, especially at a time when the price of the main alternative fuel - crude oil -

began to increase. *A priori,* the absence of a surplus under the NEB's export formula arithmetic suggested increasing domestic competition for limited natural gas supplies would replace pressures exerted by the export market. However, closure of the export market left gas buying activities in Alberta in a situation tantamount to monopsony (monopoly buying), given TransCanada PipeLines 'role as a sole buying agent for most distributors east of Alberta, and in particular for the big Ontario distributors - Northern and Central, Consumers Gas and Union Gas Ltd. A similar situation existed in British Columbia, where the sole buyer was Westcoast.

In 1972, this situation induced the Alberta Government to request the Alberta Energy Resources Conservation Board to report on Alberta gas prices. The prime conclusion reached by the Board was:

> "The current average field price for gas in Alberta . . . is some 16 cents per Mcf. The Board considers this to be less than the field value of the gas by at least 10 cents per Mcf and thus finds that the current field price is not in the Alberta public interest . . . For gas to be placed under contract in the future, if there were effective competition in purchasing, the future price will reflect the field value and be in the Alberta public interest."[25]

The Alberta Government acted to ensure price became a specific factor to be considered in any decision to issue new export permits, and in effect imposed higher prices on existing supplies through price redetermination clauses in gas purchase contracts.[26] Requests by TransCanada for additional gas to be placed under permit were approved by the AERCB, but were shelved by the Alberta government.

In the summer of 1972, a new gas buyer, Pan Alberta Gas Ltd., entered the arena. It offered initial field prices of 38¢/MCF — some 15¢ more than those offered by TransCanada at that time. Moreover, pressures on gas prices were exacerbated by the continuing rises in oil prices, which affected decisions on gas prices under arbitration proceedings.[27] In particular, a major arbitration between Gulf Oil Canada and TransCanada PipeLines in the spring of 1975 precipitated action by the Federal government. The pricing impasse between TransCanada, the Alberta government and the Federal government was resolved by an agreement which set a Toronto City gate price for gas at $1.25/MCF for November 1975.[28] At the same time export prices at the Canadian border were set at $1.60/MCF. The difference between the export gas price and the price in the domestic market - after royalty deductions - was to be shared among gas producers. As these various influences permeated industry contracts, average wellhead gas prices in Alberta rose to 17.0¢/MCF in 1972, to 30.0¢/MCF in 1974, to 66.0¢/MCF in 1975 and to 99.0¢/MCF in mid 1976.[29]

The situation in British Columbia - which produces about 13 per cent of Canada's gas[30] - is different. Here, a publicly-owned company, the British Columbia Petroleum Corporation (BCPC), has replaced Westcoast as a monopsony buyer. However, in turn the BCPC sells gas to Westcoast at prices which reflect market prices of alternate fuels less the cost of transportation. In effect, the BCPC acts as an agency to collect the difference between the market price and purchase price of the gas.[31] Average wellhead prices of natural gas in British Columbia have increased from 10.9¢/MCF in 1970, to 11.9¢/MCF in 1972, to 18.3¢/MCF in 1974 and 39.0¢/MCF currently.[32]

In summary, the situation in gas is more complex than in oil. In effect, the Federal government levies an export tax, but all its proceeds are repatriated to the provinces. Domestic delivered prices for natural gas are set by mutual agreement between the Federal and Alberta governments, using a Toronto basing point. The price for the Alberta producer is the net back from Toronto plus a pro rata share of incremental revenue from exports. In British Columbia, the wellhead price is directly set by the B.C. government through the auspices of the BCPC.

Competition in the petroleum industry

The preceding material illustrates the extent to which, especially at present, government regulation both at the provincial and federal level acts to prevent, distort or even substitute for competitive responses to changing circumstances. The purpose of this section is to examine to what extent the structure of the industry itself militates against or mutes competitive action.[33]

In the producing sector of the Canadian petroleum industry several hundred distinct companies are active. This activity is not concentrated in few hands. In natural gas production, the largest producer in 1974 accounted for only 10 per cent of total Canadian production; the top ten accounted for 62 per cent and the top twenty for 75 per cent. The corresponding figures for oil in 1974 are 17 per cent, 67 per cent and 85 per cent.[34] The structure of the producing sector, then, is sufficiently competitive. However, government regulations impose important constraints on the degree to which the industry can respond to competitive pressures.

While the sellers of natural gas are many, the buyers - at present - are few. Within Alberta, several utilities purchase gas, but, in essence, this is undertaken under the umbrella of the protective policy of the Alberta government. Effective competition depends, therefore, on out-of-province purchasers. However, as mentioned beforehand, the United States buyers cannot expect to receive export permits at this time and the major Canadian buyers are represented by one buyer: TransCanada PipeLines. Hence, the buying structure remains close to monopsonistic - or at least oligopsonistic.

The situation for crude oil is different. Here many sellers are pre-empted by quota regulation of oil production (proration) in the main producing province of Alberta. Thus competitive supply pressures within Alberta are inhibited.[35] Buyers of crude oil - including export buyers - are many[36] and competition prevails here to the extent government policies permit.[37] However, the domestic refining industry tends towards an oligopolistic structure,[38] although exposure to imported product competition, even to some extent in Ontario, acts to offset tendencies towards oligopolistic pricing. Note also that certain petroleum product markets - particularly those for fuel oils - are subject not only to intra fuel competition, but also to inter fuel competition, for instance from natural gas.[39]

The rate of return on capital employed is an important indicator of the degree of competition prevalent in an industry. Restrictions on competition tend to produce above average returns. Data examined by Jenkins[40] indicate that over the period 1965-69, real private after tax returns on investment by the mineral fuel and refining industry averaged 5.34 per cent. The corresponding figure for manufacturing was 6.45 per cent; for all activities it was 5.82 per cent. However, normal returns are a necessary rather than sufficient condition for competition. Thus the prevalence of returns slightly below average levels as shown by Jenkins is consistent with, but does not necessarily demonstrate the existence of, competition. It does suggest that if there were market power, it was not being abused by the earning of excess profits.[41]

To summarize: the framework of the exploration and producing sector of the Canadian oil and gas industry is competitive, but government regulations governing oil production and natural gas marketing are impediments to a fully competitive situation. The buying sector for oil is competitive; for gas it is monopsonistic. Transportation systems are regulated, explicitly or implicitly, as are gas distributors.[42] Petroleum refining tends to oligopoly, but is also subject to inter fuel competition. Overall, on an integrated basis, industry rates of return are consistent with but do not necessarily prove the existence of competition. The past performance of the industry sketched beforehand shows it is able to respond in a competitive way to changing circumstances, to the extent government policies allow.

IV. SOME CURRENT CANADIAN OIL AND GAS PRICING ISSUES

The section examines three current questions concerning Canadian oil and gas pricing. The first is the question of subsidies on the domestic price of Canadian crude oil and associated export taxes. The second is whether different prices should obtain for crude oil discovered at different points in time ('vintage' pricing) and whether public utility pricing concepts are applicable to petroleum. The third reviews natural gas pricing and the concept of 'commodity value'.

Subsidies and export taxes

As outlined earlier, at the time of writing (August 1976) Canada imposes an export tax of $3.65 per barrel on oil exports.[43] Domestic importers of oil are correspondingly subsidized by some $3.35 per barrel. Alberta (Redwater) oil prices are $9.25 per barrel, some $3.45 per barrel below world parity.[44] The situation for producers and consumers of Canadian oil is illustrated in Figure 3 below.[45] The Figure is only illustrative because the precise location of the supply and demand curves for Canadian oil is not known. Moreover, the Figure abstracts from the timing of adjustments in supply and demand to price changes. Both adjustments tend to be stronger over the long term. Demand is strongly influenced by the current 'stock' of oil using equipment: changes in the stock take place gradually rather than rapidly.[46] Supply responses reflect substantial lead times required for the development of new sources of supply.

In Figure 3, line D_d represents demand for Canadian oil within Canada. The line S_d represents the upward sloping supply curve for Canadian oil production. In addition, there is export demand for Canadian oil. For simplicity, the United States demand for Canadian oil even at world price levels is assumed to be sufficiently large as to be represented by a horizontal line at the equivalent world price level. If the tax on exports levied by the Canadian government were e_t, then the price of Canadian oil to producers of Canadian oil and to Canadian consumers would be $P_c = P_w - e_t$. The point of intersection of the D_d and S_d lines in Figure 3 suggests that in the absence of export demand, current domestic demand for Canadian oil could be met at a price less than P_c.[47] In a free market, a single price would prevail for both domestically consumed and exported oil, namely P_w. Canadian oil production would be OD, of which AD would be exported and OA consumed in domestic markets. The export tax, e_t, reduces the price received by producers and paid by domestic consumers. Also Canadian production is reduced from OD to OC, of which BC would be exported.[48]

The areas designated 1 to 5 in Figure 3 identify the prime impact of the export tax. The sum of areas 1, 2, 3 and 4 represents the reduction in 'economic rent'[49] which producers or resource owners would suffer from the lower price and the associated lower rate of production; area 5 represents economic rent on the additional production forthcoming at the higher price, P_w.

FIGURE 3
The Impact of Subsidies and Export Taxes
on Producers and Consumers of Canadian Oil

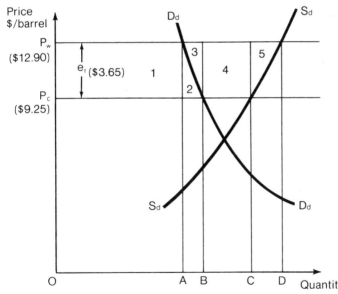

The Canadian price of oil is $3.65 per barrel lower than the world price. At the lower price Canadian production is lower than it would have been by CD, consumption is higher by the amount AB. Canadian producers and resource owners suffer a loss equal to the sum of areas 1, 2, 3, 4. Consumers of oil receive gains equal to the sum of areas 1 and 2, the government receives export tax receipts equal to area 4, and areas 3 and 5 represent deadweight losses.

107

Some of these losses to producers and resource owners appear as gains to other parties. Thus, areas 1 and 2 are the gain to domestic consumers of Canadian oil, of which area 1 is the consumer expenditure savings on the amount of oil which would have been bought at the higher price, P_w; area 2 is the consumer surplus on the increased amount of oil bought at the lower price. Area 4 represents Government export tax receipts.[50] However, areas 3 and 5 are 'deadweight' losses, since they are not offset by gains to other parties. Area 3 represents the difference between the value of exporting the volume of production AB and the value of consuming it domestically. Area 5 is a resource allocation loss: less is produced than could be sold at the opportunity price (P_w).[51]

An estimate of the current order of magnitude of these various transfers and losses can be made if some simplifying assumptions are made about the degree of response of supply and demand to changes in price - the price 'elasticity' of supply and demand.

Area 1 is a loss to domestic producers of Canadian oil but a gain to Canadian consumers of Canadian oil. Total annual value at present is around $1.4 billion.[52]

Area 2 is the consumer 'surplus'[53] on the additional amount of oil bought at the lower price, P_c (compared with P_w). It is in the same category as area 1: a gain to consumers but a loss to producers. Current annual value is about $110 million.[54]

Area 4, annual government tax receipts, is estimated as $560 million.[55] This amount will decline rapidly with the expected phasing out of exports over the next 5 years.

Area 3, the 'deadweight' loss from additional domestic consumption of oil rather than exporting it at a higher price is estimated as an annual value of some $130 million.[56]

Area 5, the deadweight loss from not selling additional domestic production forthcoming at the world price is estimated as some $200 million.[57]

In summary, then, the annual impact of the current regime of export taxes on transfers of income between the producing sector (gross of taxes and royalties) and the Canadian consumers of Canadian oil is in the region of $2.3

billion. Efficiency or deadweight losses are some $330 million.[58]

Figure 3 only relates to the production of Canadian oil and the markets it serves, both domestic (west of the Ottawa Valley) and export (United States). The impact of the price subsidy on that portion of the Canadian market served by imported oil (east of the Ottawa Valley) is shown in Figure 4. Here, the curve D_m is the Canadian demand for imported oil. Since Canada is a relatively small market, all required imports are assumed to be available at the going price[59] and therefore can be designated by the horizontal line P_w.

FIGURE 4
Price Subsidies and Imports

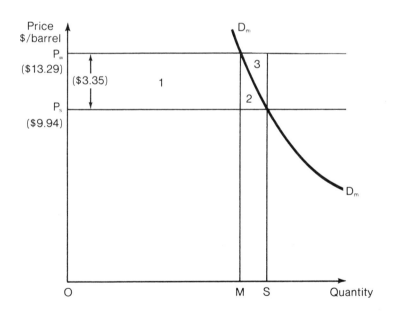

A subsidy of $3.35 per barrel is paid to domestic consumers of imported oil. This causes domestic consumers to use more oil than they would have if they had to pay the full world price (P_w). The cost of the subsidy is the sum of areas 1, 2, and 3 and amounts to $880 million per year. Of this, only areas 1 and 2 are transmitted to consumers in benefits and area 3 represents a deadweight loss.

If the full import price were charged consumers, consumption would have been OM. But at the subsidized price of P_s, consumption is OS. The cost of the subsidy is the sum of areas 1, 2 and 3, of which areas 1 and 2 are transmitted into off-setting benefits to consumers. Area 3, however, is a deadweight loss, since it represents a transfer to the foreign countries supplying the crude oil in excess of the valuation consumers place on the incremental volume of consumption, MS.

Estimates of current magnitudes of these income transfers are as follows. Area 1, the cost of the subsidy relating to the volume of oil consumption that would be demanded by Canadian consumers of imported oil at the world price (P_w), is about $880 million.[60]

Area 2 is the consumer's surplus on the additional consumption of oil at the subsidized price, P_c. Its current annual value is estimated at some $65 million.[61]

Area 3, the difference between value to consumers of the additional consumption induced by the subsidized price and its import cost is estimated at some $74 million. This is a deadweight loss not offset by gains elsewhere.

In broad terms, then, Figures 3 and 4 show the groups affected by the imposition of export taxes and subsidies. The nature of some of these components is examined in more detail below, starting with producer and resource owner rents. These consist of four components: royalties, income taxes, net returns to domestically-owned producers and net returns to foreign-owned producers. If benefits be considered as changes in national income, producer rents should be reduced by that portion accruing to and repatriated by foreign owners.[62] Foreign ownership is substantial in the producing sector,[63] and hence this consideration is not trivial. However, at present the majority of such earnings are reinvested rather than distributed.[64]

The export tax revenue is straightforward, but administration costs by both the government and companies need to be subtracted, assuming such resources could be utilized elsewhere in the economy. Benefits to consumers apparently represent a gain to the domestic economy. However, an adjustment is required here as well for foreign ownership and direct flows of benefits leaving Canada. This is because Canadian consumer benefits are reduced to the extent that savings on fuel costs in the industrial sector augment profits, and such profits accrue to foreign-owned corporations and are distributed outside Canada. To the extent that fuel cost savings are passed on to export buyers in the form of lower export prices, benefits accrue to foreigners rather than domestic consumers.

Two further aspects of the export tax-subsidy arrangements require comment. These are income distribution effects and effects on other energy sectors.

Income distribution effects follow from the changes in taxation flows and fuel prices induced by the export tax-subsidy policy. A distinction is made between vertical and horizontal income distribution effects. Horizontal effects refer to income between provinces, vertical effects to income within provinces. The mix of taxation flows is not assumed of itself to induce vertical income distribution effects. In other words, a dollar of tax revenue from the export tax and a dollar of the revenue from corporation tax are presumed neutral in terms of vertical income distribution.[65] However, the mix of tax flows has important implications for the horizontal distribution of income, both between provinces and between the federal and provincial governments. The main oil producing provinces view an export tax as an appropriation of revenues which would otherwise remain taxable in the provinces' hands or on which provincial royalties would be payable. The federal government regards substantial royalties, and in particular progressive royalties, as an erosion of its tax base. Enough heat has been generated on this issue as to not require further discussion here.

Vertical income distribution effects arise from the subsidization of oil consumers. Of interest is the degree to which this type of subsidy is progressive. Work by Waverman[66] suggests the subsidy is progressive: pro rata savings for the poor are greater than for the rich, although his results vary by area. However, as a method for income redistribution a subsidy for all consumers is inefficient, since all enjoy the benefits irrespective of income strata, and the more intensive the user the greater his absolute benefit. To the extent that higher oil prices are regressive, any subsidy policy should be specific by granting relief to low income groups rather than to all consumers.[67] That is, where it is desirable to cushion the reduction in real income caused by higher oil prices, this should be performed by transfer payments, rather than by introducing inefficiencies and granting subsidies to consumers who can adapt without hardship.

The second aspect is the impact of a subsidized oil price on other energy markets. In space heating and industrial energy markets, oil and natural gas are close substitutes. Hence subsidized oil prices would attract energy demand to oil, primarily at the expense of natural gas, unless gas prices were also held below levels they would otherwise reach. Consequently, when changes in oil demand resulting from subsidized prices entail changes in the production of other energy sources - for example, electricity and coal - the induced impacts require examination.

At present in Canada gas prices are held equivalent to subsidized oil prices[68] while gas exports are made at prices equivalent to world oil prices, thus the same sort of analysis as for oil would also be applicable to gas. Deadweight losses would exist unless mitigated by deductions representing foreign ownership transfers.

The Figures and preceding discussion have centred on the static effects of pricing subsidies. The longer such subsidies prevail, the more pervasive the effects. Setting oil and natural gas prices at levels below opportunity cost will tend to encourage more energy-intensive output than would otherwise be the case, much of which may be exported.[69] It is not clear why energy-intensive industries should be so favoured at a time when indigenous supplies of lower cost energy are dwindling. Energy resource suppliers do not receive proper price signals to encourage energy development, at least up to the level of costs represented by the cost of the alternative source of supply - world oil. Given an expected world price of oil, it is inefficient not to develop domestic resources with costs less than or equivalent to that level.[70] Pricing subsidies also obscure the evaluation of energy projects such as Syncrude, where the necessity to resort to pricing exceptions masks whether the investment is socially desirable or not.

To summarize: the ramifications of subsidizing one set of prices is complex. The policy gives to some groups at the expense of others. The effects are difficult to disentangle, especially where foreign ownership and commodity exports are involved. The use of price subsidies to satisfy other broad objectives, such as a more equal distribution of income or ensuring publicly-owned resources receive an appropriate share of resource rents, is inefficient.

In the same vein, if the main purpose of export taxes were to collect a share of economic rents, a better solution lies in adjusting the income tax and royalty system itself, not by introducing further distortions and inefficiency. In a broader context, more equitable distribution of the costs and benefits resulting from higher oil prices across the country should be sought through fiscal mechanisms, not by incurring efficiency losses through the price mechanism.[71]

The primary justification for a policy of export taxes and subsidies on domestic oil consumption is where the higher world oil price is expected to be no more than temporary. Here, the dislocation costs to consumers and the economy as a whole of adapting to what may be a short lived change justify a protective policy. However, once the new level of oil prices ceases to appear ephemeral and becomes well-established, price subsidies thwart proper planning by domestic producers and consumers and tend to prevent governments from coming to grips with the problems posed by high prices.

'Vintage' oil pricing and public utility pricing regulation

Rising supply curves with prices set at long-run marginal exploration and development costs imply substantial economic rents for producers with costs substantially below current price levels. Typically, these are enjoyed by reservoirs developed several years ago. One method suggested for capturing such rents - or a portion of them - from publicly-owned resources while not interfering with the amount of oil or gas produced is to hold down prices for intra-marginal volumes. Thus, while oil as a commodity may be homogeneous,[72] different prices would apply to different reservoirs. Such a system prevails at present in the United States, where different prices apply to 'new' oil and 'old' oil. Prices for refiners reflect the average of new and old oil prices.

In this kind of situation, the world oil price may be presumed to set the price of 'new' oil. Hence the marginal unit of supply has a cost equivalent to the world oil price. Units of supply costing less than the world oil price are paid their costs (supply prices).[73] The oil is assumed to be sold on the domestic market at an average price representing average production costs (supply prices). At this average price, excess demand would be generated, because the point of intersection of supply and demand is at the world price, not the average (lower) price. At the latter price, domestic oil demand and supply are not in equilibrium. Losses in producer and resource owner rents on domestic production by virtue of paying producers only their production costs on 'old' oil are offset by corresponding gains by consumers. However, a deadweight loss remains, consisting of the difference between the cost of satisfying the excess demand by imports at the world price and the (lesser) value attributed to the incremental demand by consumers. If imports were not available, total demand (including excess demand) would have to be rationed or otherwise constrained to meet the actual level of domestic production.[74]

Additional costs of imposing such a scheme relate to administration. These are not likely to be negligible. Perhaps more important is the fact that price controls in 'old' reservoirs will discourage the recovery of additional oil which would be economically attractive at higher prices.[75]

Another method of price regulation similar to vintage pricing is the application of public utility pricing concepts to oil and gas. In many sectors of the energy industry - especially pipelines and gas and electricity distribution systems - avoidance of duplication of facilities where economies of scale are prevalent leads to the provision of service by one supplier, on a public utility basis. In turn, to prevent monopoly pricing behaviour such activities are frequently subject to actual or overt regulation. The common technique employed is cost of service regulation to set approved prices.

An attempt has been made to apply this type of procedure to the natural gas industry in the United States, but the nature of the gas industry (and the oil industry) does not lend itself easily to this kind of regulation.[76] The problems primarily revolve around the substantial degree of cost differentiation between different sources of supply serving the same market, and the difficulty of defining costs with sufficient precision where joint costs exist.[77] Cost differentials require decisions as to which users should purchase the expensive oil or gas and which should enjoy the cheap oil or gas, if cost of service concepts are employed. Marketing at average prices creates the same problems as discussed beforehand for vintage pricing. The administrative burdens of regulation of this character for the exploration and producing sectors of the oil and gas industry are formidable, if not intractable. Even in simplified form, for example in United States area gas pricing, inefficiency and eventual consumer burdens are difficult to avoid.[78]

Natural gas pricing: "Commodity value"

Section II outlined the circumstances by which competition among gas buyers for Canadian gas supplies was effectively curtailed by the closure of additional export markets and a concentration of substantial buying power in one purchaser: TransCanada PipeLines Limited. It is in these circumstances that the Alberta Government's preoccupation with achieving "commodity value" (defined below) for Alberta natural gas can be interpreted as an attempt to simulate the impact that normal competition would have on gas prices. Commodity value was defined by the Alberta Government as:

> "the thermal value of gas determined by reference to the volume-weighted average prices of substitutable

energy sources competing with gas for the various end uses of gas in the consuming markets served, directly or through exchange, by the buyer of gas under a gas purchase contract" and "the premium value of gas determined by reference to its inherent special qualities when compared with competing energy sources."[79]

Elaborate calculations have been performed[80] to determine gas net backs to Alberta on this basis.[81] More recently (Nov. 1975), the Federal and Alberta governments agreed to set the price of gas at Toronto at a level of $1.25/MCF, which is about 85 per cent of the BTU equivalent value of crude oil.[82] Since natural gas and fuel oil derived from crude oil are close substitutes in many end uses, especially in space heating and industrial boiler markets, substantial gaps between the price of the two fuels expressed on a BTU equivalent basis (and after adjustment for any differentials in capital and operating costs) would not arise in a competitive market, except where supply conditions for the two fuels were quite different. Correspondingly, to avoid potential rationing problems any regulated price levels for oil and gas should not be too far apart.

If natural gas prices do not rise in sympathy with oil prices, demand for gas will become excessive and reserves will be increasingly unable to meet requirements. Therefore, during a period when crude oil prices have increased substantially (although still subsidized), natural gas prices should be allowed to respond to demand pressures, to avoid market distortion. As an interim measure, then, defining natural gas prices on the basis of commodity value or BTU equivalence of crude oil has merit.

Over the longer term, and in particular if subsidies on crude oil prices were removed, setting gas prices by a formula such as the definition of commodity value cited beforehand, or by a more simple relationship such as crude oil BTU equivalence, is not valid. If natural gas supplies were not as abundant as crude oil, an appropriate market price for gas might well be in excess of 'commodity value'. If gas supplies were more abundant, then domestic gas prices at levels below commodity value would encourage the desired degree of market penetration. Moreover, pricing on the basis of BTU equivalence does not express the nature of the markets involved. When people buy natural gas and electricity or oil products they do not buy BTU's per se: they buy a particular fuel. Only if the alternative energy forms were totally substitutable would BTU market price equivalence, or some other common numeraire, be appropriate.[83]

The answer to whether natural gas prices should be greater than, equivalent to, or less than oil prices can be provided by allowing market competition to set such prices. This would hold for domestic markets even when prices of exports or imports are set by other mechanisms. Adherence to formulae such as commodity value can be appropriate under certain conditions and as a substitute for buyer competition, but in general would result in inefficiency and market distortion. Such formulae are superfluous if market conditions allow the operation of competitive pricing.

V. CONCLUDING REMARKS

Generally, prices set under competitive circumstances avoid the intrusion of regulation. The latter may be arbitrary, paternalistic or complex. Prices which readily respond to changing circumstances induce appropriate changes in behaviour by both producers and consumers.

At least until the early 1960's, the pattern of oil and gas pricing in Canada which developed was consistent in most respects with the pattern which would be predicted under a competitive model. The main factors detracting from competition were provincial government regulations on the output of crude oil in Alberta and provincial and federal government regulation of natural gas marketing.

The period beyond 1961 has been characterized by increasing government involvement in setting oil and gas prices, culminating in direct government control of such prices by the mid 1970's at levels in the domestic market below world prices and at levels in the export market which approximate world prices. The current situation primarily reflects: the dramatic increase in the world price of oil; the effect of government pricing controls on the United States market for Canadian oil and gas; prospective dwindling supplies of oil and gas from traditional areas of production in Canada; and the problem of internal fiscal balance within Canada between producing and consuming regions.

This paper has argued that setting domestic prices of oil and gas below world prices can only be justified on temporary or expedient grounds. The identification of eventual gainers and losers under a subsidization policy is complex, and at any rate some losses are not offset by gains elsewhere in the economy. Such efficiency losses are likely to grow the longer the period the subsidy is maintained, as both consumers and producers continue to act upon distorted price information.

The application of public utility pricing and vintage oil pricing concepts to oil and gas have been examined and found wanting on the grounds of efficiency and administrative complexity. The pricing of natural gas by formulae such as commodity value or BTU equivalence may be suitable as an interim measure, and as a substitute for lack of buying competition. It cannot be justified on a long-term basis, since underlying supply and demand conditions may make gas prices either in excess of or below commodity value appropriate. Government involvement in the pricing and regulation of flows of exports of oil and gas will continue to be required, both to ensure distortions in United States markets do not adversely affect Canada and to prevent contractual rigidities reducing returns on Canadian resources from levels which might prevail under more flexible marketing conditions.

Appendix

This Appendix provides a diagrammatic treatment of the effects of 'vintage' pricing discussed in the text, Section III.

Figure A relates to the impact of 'vintage' pricing on consumers, producers and economic efficiency. The curves designated S and D are domestic oil supply and demand curves, respectively.[84] The world oil price which sets the price of 'new' oil is P_w, hence the marginal unit of supply has a cost equal to P_w. Units with supply prices less than P_w are paid their supply prices. The oil is assumed to be sold on the domestic market at an average price of P_a. Hence excess demand of AB is generated. The loss in producer and resource owner rents of areas 1 and 2 is offset by the gain in consumer surplus (areas 2, 3 and 4).[85] Domestic production, however, is OA and there is a deadweight loss corresponding to the excess demand, represented by area 5: the difference between the cost of satisfying the additional demand by imports and the value attributed by consumers. If imports were not available, the demand of OB would be rationed or constrained to the level OA.

FIGURE A
Effects of Vintage Pricing

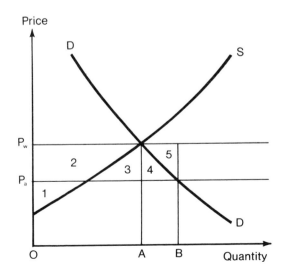

Notes

[1]Reference is made to crude oil throughout this section. The same sort of analysis applies equally to natural gas.

[2]Except for the possible burning of crude oil directly in certain industrial boiler uses, the demand for crude oil is derived from the demand for the products into which it is refined - primarily gasoline and fuel oils.

[3]See E.R. Berndt, "Canadian Energy Demand and Economic Growth" in this volume.

[4]More detail is included in the essay by R.S. Uhler in this volume.

[5]The price to which supply is related is before taxes and royalties.

[6]For details on incremental returns, see the essay by G.D. Quirin and B.A. Kalymon.

[7]For some theoretical background, see M.A. Adelman, *The World Petroleum Market,* Johns Hopkins, 1972, Chapter V.

[8]In effect, what was known as "Gulf Plus" pricing prevailed in Canada. 'Gulf' referred to the price of United States crude oil at the Gulf of Mexico; 'plus' referred to transportation costs therefrom.

[9]For simplicity, Figure 2 assumes unit transportation costs are the same for both United States and Alberta oil.

[10]Note that compatability does not mean that all aspects of the structure of the industry were competitive. After 1950 oil production quotas (called proration) were imposed on Alberta oil producers. This precluded the determination of the same level of output as would the equation of price and marginal cost under 'perfect' competition.

[11]A recent article by F.J. Anderson suggests that Canada might have benefited from allowing domestic crude oil prices to be set on the basis of world oil prices while imposing a modest tax on exports to the United States. See F.J. Anderson "Price Formation in the Canadian Crude Oil Sector", *Canadian Public Policy,* Winter, 1976.

[12]Comparison of Redwater crude oil and Saudi Arabian 'light' delivered prices laid down in Toronto (Source: AERCB).

[13]The delivered price of Canadian oil at Chicago was about $4.45/barrel (Canadian dollars) (Source: AERCB). Chicago displaced Detroit-Toledo as the competitive interface for Canadian oil with the extension of the Interprovincial pipeline network to reach Chicago refineries.

[14]These relationships concern 'new' oil in the United States, the price of which is governed by the delivered price of overseas supplies.

[15]Redwater 35° crude; the price at Edmonton is $9.25 per barrel.

[16]Estimated by AERCB for Arabian light crude oil (July 1976). The equivalent price in Alberta, using a Montreal basing point, is $12.69 per barrel. (Montreal price *less* transportation cost to Alberta.)

[17]But to repeat an earlier comment: while the pattern of movements may be consistent with competition, it does not follow that absolute levels of output and price are those which would be generated under full competition, given the impact of government policies, such as proration.

[18]AERCB data.

[19]The Gas Resources Preservation Act (1950).

[20]In the vernacular, called 'trend' gas.

[21]Source of data: AERCB and Canadian Petroleum Association *Statistical Year Book 1974.*

[22]Source: AERCB. This trend in prices partly reflected falling unit costs of pipeline transportation as throughput expanded.

[23]The BTU equivalent price of Alberta crude oil in 1967 was some 45-/MCF.

[24]The NEB's regulation of gas exports utilized an 'exportable surplus' concept similar to Alberta's policy. See National Energy Board Report "Reasons for Decision in the Matter of the Applications under the Natural Energy Board Act of Alberta and Southern Gas Co. Ltd., et al." November 1971.

[25]AERCB, *Report on Field Pricing of Gas in Alberta,* August 1972, p. 1-11.

[26]See *The Arbitration Amendment Act, 1973,* Statutes of Alberta, Chapter 88, 1973.

[27]Given the assessment of gas prices under the concept of 'commodity value' - see Section III below.

[28]Deemed to be equivalent to nearly 85 per cent of crude oil equivalent BTU value. As of July 1976, the Toronto city gate price for gas was $1.405/MCF and the export price was $1.80/MCF.

[29]Source: AERCB, *Alberta Oil and Gas Industry Annual and Cumulative Statistics,* 1974, p. 20 and *Summary of Monthly Statistics,* December 1975, p. 3 and June 1976.

[30]Statistics Canada Cat. 57-002.

[31]An approximation for the economic rent.

[32]Source: Canadian Petroleum Association *Statistical Year Book* and Westcoast Transmission Ltd.

[33]Such an examination can only be partial. Detailed research on the competitive structure of the Canadian petroleum industry is sparse.

[34]Source: *Oilweek,* May 12, 1975, p. 13.

[35]Nevertheless, even with proration, trends in the price of Alberta oil were consistent with the pattern of competitive responses, until the imposition of the National Oil Policy in 1961.

[36]In January 1976, 50 companies 'nominated' for Alberta oil.

[37]Exports of crude oil are now set by the NEB.

[38]See F.J. Anderson, *op. cit.,* for data west of the Ottawa Valley.

[39]A recent Royal Commission on petroleum product pricing in Ontario (the Isbister report) concluded that the oil industry in Ontario was competitive. A report of the British Columbia Energy Commission on gasoline marketing in British Columbia advanced some contrary views. See *Oilweek,* June 28, 1976.

121

[40]See G.P. Jenkins "Rates of Return and Taxation from Private Capital in Canada", *Ontario Economic Review*, Nov./Dec. 1972.

[41]Although the level of profit might be reduced to normal levels by the channeling of above average profits into protective or possibly inefficient investment. Where taxation regimes allow an industry to retain a portion of economic rent generated by higher prices, returns may rise even where competition prevails. More recent data for oil and gas industry profitability may demonstrate this effect.

[42]To a large extent, the intention of regulation is to simulate the competitive solution.

[43]More specifically, the $3.65 export tax applies to light and medium gravity crudes. A somewhat lower tax applies to heavy oils.

[44]Using a Montreal 'basing point'.

[45]For a similar figure, see T.L. Powrie and W.D. Gainer "Static Redistributive and Welfare Effects of an Export Tax: A Simple Model Related to Crude Oil in Canada." Paper presented to the Victoria Conference on Natural Resource Revenues, June 5-7, 1975.

[46]See also the article by E.R. Berndt, *op. cit.*

[47]This is reasonable at present.

[48]At the present time, the Canadian government also imposes quantitative restrictions on exports.

[49]Economic rent is any return over the relevant costs of production where such costs include the normal return of capital employed.

[50]From which should be deducted costs of administering the tax.

[51]Recall that Figure 2 is static, but still valid over time if the supply curve reflects 'user' costs: the discounted value of returns foregone by producing now rather than later.

[52]Export tax ($3.65) times estimated domestic consumption of Canadian oil (372 million barrels) at the world price (consumption at present prices, 436 million barrels).

[53]Consumer's surplus is the excess of the amount consumers would be willing to pay to consume the extra amount of oil (AB) over the amount they have to pay.

[54]This calculation assumes a price elasticity of demand of -0.5. The price elasticity of demand for crude oil reflects the weighted average price elasticity of demand of the products into which crude oil is refined. No definitive estimate of this elasticity has been made. The 0.5 figure approximates assumptions made in recent analysis by the Federal Department of Energy, Mines and Resources.

[55]Exports of 153 million barrels per year times the export tax of $3.65/barrel.

[56]Again, assuming a price elasticity of demand of -0.5.

[57]Assuming a supply elasticity of 0.5.

[58]These estimates of efficiency losses tend to represent an upper bound, since they do not take into account the possibility of future absorption of such production in the domestic market at actual or implicit (import displacement) prices in excess of extant prices. Such calculations are complex and would depend on the future time trajectory of prices, demand and supply.

[59]In the jargon, the import supply curve is perfectly elastic.

[60]Consumption of 262 million barrels per year times import subsidy of $3.35 per barrel (derived from actual consumption of 303 million barrels).

[61]Assuming a price elasticity of demand of -0.5.

[62]Repatriation may take place now or in the future.

[63]It is about 60 per cent (Source: Statistics Canada).

[64]If returns to foreign equity be reinvested in perpetuity, then the need for a distinction between foreign and domestically owned operations tends to disappear.

[65]Where the revenue from the export tax is allocated to a specific use, such as the oil subsidy, this assumption is less tenable.

[66]See Leonard Waverman "The Two Price System in Energy: Subsidies Forgotten", *Canadian Public Policy*, Winter 1974.

[67]One suggestion is through sales tax reductions. See Judith Maxwell "Policy Review and Outlook, 1976", C.D. Howe Research Institute, p. 64.

[68]See Section II beforehand. On a straightforward BTU basis, gas prices are less than oil prices.

[69]This is a bizarre result when at the same time steps are being taken by the Federal Government to cut back exports of oil and, to the extent permit commitments allow, of natural gas. It can be justified on the basis of 'value added' - embellishing the energy product - but not on the basis of conserving indigenous supplies, a current government policy objective.

[70]This is the deadweight resource allocation loss represented by area 5 in Figure 3.

[71]Conflicting objectives between provinces and between Provincial and Federal Governments make such agreements difficult, but resort to artifical prices as a palliative is a second (or third) best solution.

[72]Apart from quality differences, for example, gravity and sulphur content.

[73]The cost (or supply price) includes sufficient return on capital.

[74]For a diagrammatic treatment. see the Appendix to this paper.

[75]It might be possible to circumvent this by awarding the new oil price to such incremental production, but the administrative problems of identification would be intimidating.

[76]For an analysis of these problems, see Stephen Breyer and Paul W. MacAvoy "The Natural Gas Shortage and the Regulation of Natural Gas Producers", *Harvard Law Review*, Vol. 86, April 1973.

[77]Joint costs mean that an indivisible expenditure (input) may result in more than one product (outputs). For example, an exploratory well may discover a reservoir containing both oil and gas.

[78]See Breyer and MacAvoy, *op. cit.*, pp. 981-985. Moreover, where competition is prevalent, cost of service regulation is superfluous.

[79]Province of Alberta, "The Arbitration Amendment Act", Chapter 88, RSA.

[80]For instance, see Stanford Research Institute, *The Field Price of Alberta Natural Gas, 1972* and Foster Associates Inc. and Foster Economic Consultants Ltd., *The Current and Prospective Commodity Value of Natural Gas in North American Markets, 1972-1982.*

[81]However, some problems exist with these calculations: transporters of natural gas are assumed to be able to act as discriminating monopolists; relationships between distributor margins and market growth rates under alternative price regimes tend to be ignored; and calculations of premia are difficult.

[82]Subsequently increased to $1.40/MCF (August 1976).

[83]Over some market sectors, for instance when heavy fuel oil competes with natural gas in industrial boiler markets, BTU price equivalence of alternative fuels is suitable. In other markets, BTU equivalence would not express the different characteristics of the energy sources.

[84]For simplicity, these curves are shown intersecting at the world oil price, P_w. Assuming imported oil is readily available at the world price (i.e. infinitely elastic supply), the case where domestic supply is insufficient to meet domestic demand at the world price would require modifications to Figure A-2.

[85]Since output is assumed to be sold at average cost, areas 1 and 3 are equal.

PART II
GOVERNMENT IN
THE MARKETPLACE

Editor's Introduction

In most developed countries the role of private enterprise in the energy sector is under review. A recent manifestation in Canada is the creation of a national oil company, Petro-Canada. Professor Mead's essay surveys the advantages and disadvantages of private enterprise and government operation. He points out the twin problems of monopoly and externalities which bedevil socially-beneficial operation by private enterprise. Externalities refer to effects of company operations which do not enter the calculus of the profit and loss account. Mainly in the context of United States data, Mead finds no evidence of private monopoly power or of important externalities not already compensated for by regulation. Why, then, is the demand for more government control and ownership so insistent? Mead suggests the prime factor is the dramatic rise in energy prices since 1972. But, like Erickson and Winokur in this volume, he finds no justification for the theory that oil companies have conspired to increase prices: world inflation and the success of OPEC in elevating prices provide sufficient explanation. Mead then asks the important and oft-ignored question — is there evidence of net social gain from additional government control of the energy sector? There is a record of government control, and his examination of it provides little comfort for those desiring to extend government activity. The latter would only be appropriate when private enterprise is unable to perform the required functions. In short, private enterprise is imperfect, but wholescale replacement by government enterprise and regulation is worse, in the long run.

Private Enterprise, Regulation and Government Enterprise in the Energy Sector

WALTER J. MEAD

Professor of Economics
University of California, Santa Barbara

THE AUTHOR

Professor Walter J. Mead was born in Oregon in 1921; he received his A.B. degree in 1948 from the University of Oregon, his M.A. at Columbia University in 1950 and his Ph.D. at Oregon, 1952. He has been Professor in the Department of Economics, University of California, Santa Barbara, since 1966. Dr. Mead has been extensively involved in administration at his university and has chaired many U.C.S.B. committees.

The distinguished career of Dr. Mead has included associations with the Ford Foundation (1972-1973, the Energy Policy Project); Public Land Law Review Commission; Federal Energy Administration; and with corporations in the pulp and paper, lumber, plywood, electronics and electric power industries. He has served as consultant on economic development with Stanford Research Institute, U.S. Department of Agriculture (Forest Service), U.S. Department of the Interior (Bureau of Land Management), U.S. Bureau of the Budget, U.S. Federal Trade Commission, U.S. Office of Technology Assessment, Naval Petroleum and Oil Shale Reserve, and State of Alaska Legislature Resources Committee.

Dr. Mead's research activities have been sponsored by federal government agencies and important foundations. Among his studies are: "Resource Control as a Basis for Market Power: The Case of Timber," *Extractive Resources and Taxation*, Mason Gaffney, ed., University of Wisconsin Press, 1967; "Log Sales versus Timber Sales Policy," William McKillop and Walter J. Mead (eds.), *Timber Policy Issues in British Columbia*, University of British Columbia Press, 1976; "Petroleum: An Unregulated Industry?", R.J. Kalter and W.A. Vogely (eds.), *Energy Supply and Government Policy*, Cornell University Press, 1976.

Private Enterprise, Regulation and Government Enterprise in the Energy Sector

WALTER J. MEAD

Professor of Economics
University of California, Santa Barbara

I. INTRODUCTION

Throughout the world, national governments commonly have jurisdiction over most, if not all, energy reserves and resources. In Canada, the British North America Act gave provinces powers to make laws regarding natural resources located within provincial boundaries. In the United States, ownership of energy reserves and resources is divided between the federal government, Indian tribes (with the federal government having jurisdiction), state governments and private ownership. In both Canada and the United States, energy resources under government jurisdiction are transferred to private enterprise in exchange for payments approximating the economic rent. Payments are made in a variety of forms including bonus, royalty, annual rent, and even profit-share payments.

In both Canada and the United States as well as world wide, past institutional arrangements for producing energy from publicly-owned reserves are being re-examined. Important public policy decisions must be made concerning the role of private enterprise in extracting and processing publicly-owned energy resources. Specifically, should exploration for, production of, and distribution of natural resources continue to be primarily or exclusively undertaken by private enterprise? Should energy research be both financed and carried out exclusively by private enterprise, or exclusively by government, or by some combination of the two? Should government increase its present degree of regulation over private firms in the energy industry? The regulation issue includes the question of price control over energy resources and products.

The purpose of this paper is to explore the pros and cons of relatively unregulated private enterprise, closely regulated private enterprise, and government operation of energy production and distribution.

In Section II, we will identify two possible problems that may prevent private enterprise from serving the public interest. In Section III, one of these problems, the presence of major externalities, will be analyzed and corrective action discussed. Section IV analyzes the second potential problem, the extent of monopoly in the energy industry. Section V examines the record of price inflation in the energy industry and in general economic activity, explores the causes of inflation and suggests corrective action. In Section VI the record of government enterprise and government regulation of private enterprise is reviewed. Then in Section VII, a similar analysis of private enterprise in the energy sector is provided. Conclusions are drawn in Section VIII.

II. PROBLEMS OF PRIVATE ENTERPRISE

There is widespread agreement among professional economists that profit maximization by private enterprise produces results which closely approximate a maximization of the general welfare except when *(A)* individual industries are monopolized instead of competitive, or *(B)* important externalities exist.

(A) Perfect competition exists only in economists' conceptual models. The real question is whether or not the energy industry is, on one hand, effectively competitive, or on the other, sufficiently concentrated so that it is able to reduce output and thereby achieve prices above competitive levels. In this event consumers would be denied some of the "consumer surplus" to which they are entitled and resource

allocation would not be optimal. Where competition is inadequate, public policy solutions may call for either antitrust policy to break up monopoly firms, regulation in order to impose public determination of investment, output and price decisions, or public ownership of the monopolized industry. The extent of competition or monopoly in the energy industry will be analyzed below.

(B) An externality exists when private decision-makers do not bear all of the costs flowing from their actions, or do not receive all of the benefits from investments which they make. A classic illustration of an external *cost* is environmental pollution. An oil spill may kill fish life, destroy plant life, pollute beaches, and interfere with recreational opportunities. These involve real costs for society at large. If such costs are not entirely borne by the enterprise responsible for them, then an external cost is said to exist. A classic illustration of an external *benefit* occurs when a new technology is developed as a result of investments made by an individual or firm but patent protection is insufficient to prevent others from copying and benefiting from the same invention. In this event, benefits accrue to individuals other than the inventor-investor and spread to society at large.

III. COMPENSATION FOR EXTERNALITIES
Where important externalities exist public policy solutions may take one of four forms:

1. Net external costs may lead to government action which imposes a tax on the offending industry approximately equal to the value of the net external cost.[1]

2. In the event of net external benefits, a subsidy may be paid to firms responsible for producing the uncompensated social benefits. Ideally, the amount of such subsidy should equal the value of the net external benefit. These first two approaches are called "internalizing external costs or benefits."

3. External costs may be controlled through regulations which limit or eliminate the activity producing such costs.

4. Finally, where there are either net external costs or benefits, government owned and operated enterprise may substitute for private ownership.

Conceptually, the idea of compensating for and internalizing externalities may sound simple. However, in practice extremely difficult administrative problems are encountered. Methodologies for evaluating externalities are primitive and inexact. Furthermore, economic life is dynamic. Technological and economic conditions are constantly changing. Therefore the net value of externalities is constantly changing and any tax or subsidy designed to compensate for such externalities must be constantly reappraised. The administration of compensation for externalities is difficult, bordering on the impossible. Conceptually, in the case of an external benefit, the burden of paying a subsidy should be borne only by those who benefit from the externality while the subsidy should flow only to those who create external benefits. Similarly, in the case of external costs, taxes should be levied upon those responsible for creating externalities while those suffering losses should receive the proceeds. Obviously identification of all relevant parties, levying charges and paying benefits would pose difficult and expensive administrative problems. In view of these considerable difficulties, except where the external costs and benefits are large, society might be better off in a welfare sense, to simply let the matter pass.

Regulation as a solution to the externalities problem has its own set of problems. Evaluation of the externality is still necessary in order to determine the need for and extent of regulation. Regulations that impose costs in excess of their corresponding benefits should be avoided. Regulations should change as dynamic conditions increase or decrease the burden of the externality to be regulated. Finally, as will be discussed in more detail later, regulation is administratively imperfect and may, throughout its life cycle, impose even greater costs on society.

In the absence of any government action to "internalize externalities" by imposing taxes or granting compensating subsidies, the market itself and political-economic institutions may correct for externalities. In simple cases involving few people, mutually acceptable solutions may be bargained between parties involved. Private suits may involve payments between the two parties or prohibitions on certain actions. Where many people are involved, class-action suits may internalize external costs. This happened after-the-fact in the case of the Santa Barbara oil spill. Payments were made from oil companies to some injured parties including owners of pleasure boats and commercial fishing boats. In the future, buyers of off-shore oil and gas leases will undoubtedly consider the social costs via a contingent liability from a possible oil spill as they calculate their private costs and benefits from buying and subsequently operating off-shore oil leases.

The extent of remaining external costs not subject to regulatory constraint or market adjustments such as described above may not be significant. Increasingly, governments are mandating land reclamation in the case of strip mining or deep mining of coal, oil shale, uranium and tar sands. Institutional arrangements have been imposed which require compensation to injured parties from coal mining accidents or such health hazards as black lung disease. All of these actions may improve and perfect the private decision-making system. They may also over-compensate for external social costs. In this event resource allocation again becomes imperfect, but is then the result of excessive compensatory action by government or legal institutions.

IV. COMPETITION IN THE ENERGY INDUSTRY

If the energy industry and its sub-sectors are monopolistic and competition is ineffective then government action is called for. Thus an analysis of the role of private enterprise in energy production and distribution requires an appraisal of the extent of competition.

(A) Competition in the international oil industry has been subject to frequent economic analysis. A 1952 study by the U.S. Federal Trade Commission concluded that competition was ineffective. The FTC found that "Control over the

international oil industry is largely in the hands of seven integrated companies. Outside the United States and the Soviet Union, they control the bulk of production and marketing of oil moving in international commerce."[2] The "seven sisters" were made up of five American oil companies (Exxon, Texaco, Standard Oil Company of California, Mobil, and Gulf) plus two foreign companies (British Petroleum and Royal Dutch/Shell). Professor Adelman found that, as recently as 1950, the seven sisters plus a French company partially owned by the French government, Compagnie Française de Petroles, accounted for 100 per cent of world oil production, excluding production in Communist countries and North America.[3]

Observed monopolistic behavior of world oil by a private cartel was eroded away by the entry of new firms beginning about 1950. A recent staff report for the Committee on Banking and Currency of the U.S. House of Representatives outlined the entry of new firms as follows:

> "In 1940, the seven sisters and the CFP were the only significant presence in the Middle East. By 1950, ten U.S. independents were present though their production was miniscule. By 1955, seven more U.S. firms were active, the majority of them brought in through the Iranian consortium. Two more U.S. firms, and two Japanese companies had entered by 1960, to be joined in the next five years by eight more U.S. firms and seven other foreign companies. Between 1965 and 1970, thirty-one companies entered, leaving (after mergers) a total of the big seven, twenty-four U.S. independents, thirty-one foreign companies, and thirteen government entities. The seventy-five companies had grown to almost one hundred by 1974."[4]

The entry into international oil production outlined above is impressive and probably sufficient to introduce effective competition into world oil markets. However, in the late 1960's a new cartel was in the process of establishing its own dominance — the Organization of Petroleum Exporting Countries (OPEC). By the early 1970's, control of production abroad was entirely in the hands of host governments. Adelman observed as early as 1972 that "The multinational oil companies have no control of supply, no power to cut off anybody or to protect them from cutoff. Nobody owns oil at the wellhead or underground reserves anymore except the governments who have the physical force above-ground."[5]

In describing the energy crisis, Adelman testified in 1974 that "The world-wide crisis is the work of a world-wide monopoly, but it is a monopoly of the producing nations. The multinational corporations are now merely collection agents."[6] Thus, the international oil industry probably has a sufficient number of individual firms operating in it such that its performance would be competitive in the absence of the multi-government cartel. Private monopoly is no longer the problem.

(B) Given the fact of a multi-government crude oil producing cartel, governments of consuming nations have very little choice but to take the state of competition in international oil as a datum in determining their own policies. If their own domestic oil industries are monopolized then again there is a role for government in either anti-trust, regulation or government ownership and operation. In appraising the extent of competition in the domestic oil industry, we will look first at competition among oil companies as bidders for new oil and gas resources and second at competition among oil companies as sellers of petroleum products.

In appraising the extent of competition in competitive bidding for certain Alberta petroleum reservoirs in the 1960's,Watkins concluded that "All, or at least a significant portion, of the foreseeable economic rent was obtained (by the government of Alberta) under the system of competitive bidding. It follows that actual or potential lease competition was at high levels for these tracts. This suggests that competition in the industry for acquiring leases was generally keen during this period."[7]

In the United States a similar analysis was made of 184 leases purchased by competitive bidding from the Federal Government in the Gulf of Mexico during the years 1954 and 1955. The analysis concluded that the internal rate of return earned by the successful bidders was 7.5 per cent before taxes.[8] This evidence indicates that on the basis of the tracts studied competition for Federal oil and gas leases in the United States was intense and competition was overly effective.[9] The observed 7.5 per cent rate of return before taxes is substantially below the average competitive return on investments indicating that bonus bidding was excessively high.

The extent of competition at the output level in the petroleum industry must also be appraised. Most of the studies of petroleum industry concentrations have concerned the U.S. rather than the Canadian industry. However, entry into the Canadian petroleum market appears to be free except for barriers imposed by the Canadian government. This analysis will be limited to studies of competition in the U.S. petroleum industry. The paper by G.C. Watkins in this volume presents data on the Canadian oil industry indicating that the structure of the producing sector is "sufficiently competitive."

There is a widespread impression that the U.S. domestic oil industry is monopolistic. For example, Congressman and presidential candidate Morris Udall stated that "By any reasonable criteria of what constitutes a concentrated industry . . . the energy industry qualifies and is in clear violation of the intent of the anti-trust laws."[10] Most professional economists who have examined in detail the structure of the domestic petroleum industry in the United States reach conclusions directly opposite to that of Congressman Udall. Johnson found that the big 4 producers of crude oil in 1972 accounted for only 29.4 per cent of total U.S. crude oil production and the big 8 firms accounted for 46.9 per cent.[11] These levels of concentration are low relative to concentration ratios for U.S. manufacturing industries in general where average 4-firm concentration in 1970 was found to be 41.2 per cent and of 8-firm concentration 54.2 per cent.[12]

Concentration in petroleum refining is similarly low among the big 4 firms relative to other manufacturing. In 1972 the big 4 concentration ratio in petroleum refining was 31.0 per cent and the big 8 concentration ratio was 56.0 per cent.[13]

A degree of uncertainty hangs over the use of concentration ratios to appraise the competitive structure of the oil industry. This is due to the fact that joint ventures link major oil companies as partners in the same industry. The oil industry is the most joint venture prone industry in the entire economy. An examination of the 32 largest American oil companies revealed that Exxon Corporation had 302 joint ventures with 27 other oil companies out of 31 possibilities. Mobil was found to have 300 joint ventures with 28 other companies out of 31 possibilities. All of the big 8 oil companies have joint ventures with all 7 of their large competitors. In fact one must go down the list of big firms to Sun Oil Company as the 12th largest firm in the oil industry before one finds a blank in all possible combinations of big firms. Thus, of the 11 largest oil companies there are joint ventures uniting as partners all possible combinations among these 11 firms.[14] While much is known about the structure of joint ventures, economists have not found evidence that collusive behavior or poor performance follows from joint venture relationships.

The most conclusive evidence of monopoly power in the oil industry that any objective research has been able to establish is due to market restrictions imposed by the Federal government. These take the forms of market demand prorationing and oil import quotas primarily. These devices became ineffective in 1972 and 1973 respectively. Erickson examined the extent of competition and concluded that "The U.S. petroleum industry is effectively competitive. In the absence of constraints (tax subsidies, prorationing and import quotas) the free market forces of supply and demand could be expected to provide us with an efficient allocation of resources."[15] Similarly the staff report to the Committee on Banking and Currency, U.S. House of Representatives concluded that "Crude oil production in the United States is basically a competitive enterprise."[16]

With respect to the vertical integration structural characteristics of the oil industry, de Chazeau and Kahn wrote that "All it really says is that companies have sought managerial control over their raw material supplies and product distribution because they wanted the greater

137

assurance that financial control brings. Attempts to supply narrower and more precise interpretations invariably lack conviction."[17] More recently, Professor Kahn reviewed the structure and performance of the oil industry and concluded that:

> "The most serious and anti-competitive element in our domestic petroleum industry has been the complicated network of government controls on the production and crude oil market. If that market had been effectively competitive, I believe the performance of the industry would have been far better during the last two decades, with no other changes in its organization. But with the crude oil market rigged as it was, I believe the vertical integration of the major oil companies — their combining under one financial control operations and production, transportation, refining, and marketing — has been a second aggravating monopolistic factor, which has in turn created serious distortions and impediments to effective competition at the refining and marketing level."[18]

Professor Kahn's conclusion is similar to that of Erickson and other researchers. The monopoly element has been introduced by the Federal government and except for this rigging of the market the industry would be effectively competitive. Of course, such government rigging came about as a result of petitions from the oil industry. These government constraints have been removed effective in 1972 and 1973. But, they have been replaced by government price controls over some industry opposition. In their absence one must conclude that the industry would be effectively competitive.

Strong charges have been levied against the petroleum industry by Professors Allvine and Patterson stating that "The major integrated oil companies cannot and will not, as a general rule, compete with one another by discounting prices."[19] Allvine and Patterson elaborate their charge as follows:

"Competition is not functioning as an effective regulator of the (petroleum) industry and ... the principal companies in the industry have insulated themselves from the guiding influence of the marketplace. By whatever criteria one chooses to judge the marketing of gasoline — market structure, economic performance, or business conduct — the result is less than the public has a right to expect. Both prices and costs are higher than they would be if competition were working effectively. The entry of new firms and the emergence of new ideas and new methods are clearly restricted by the present structure of the industry. Predatory and exclusionary tactics to discipline innovators and to focus market and financial power on the smaller independents abound."[20]

The source of monopoly power which Allvine and Patterson find is identified not as the customary monopolizing practices but rather intervention originating with the Federal government.

"The system of state and federal oil laws has become a mechanism for permitting the administration of high noncompetitive crude-oil prices and for insulating crude-oil production from the normal competitive forces of the market. The artificial control of crude-oil production thus emerges as the crux of the perplexing problem posed by vertical integration in the petroleum industry."[21]

Another challenge to the competitive thesis comes from the Federal Trade Commission. A staff report to the Commission concluded that "The major oil firms have considerable market power. The industry operates much like a cartel with 15 to 20 integrated firms being the beneficiaries of much Federal and State policy. Thus, the Federal and State governments with the force of law do for the major companies that which would be illegal for the companies to do for themselves."[22]

In a highly unusual procedure the Department of the Treasury, Office of the Energy Advisor, produced a point by point rebuttal of the Federal Trade Commission's Staff Report. The Treasury analysis stated:

> "It should be very clear from the discussion of this analysis that the FTC has misinterpreted many actions and motives of the petroleum industry. These misinterpretations have caused the FTC to incorrectly conclude that the present shortage is a result of sinister, anti-competitive actions on the part of the major oil companies. As discussed throughout this analysis, the shortage has been caused by a variety of factors, mostly governmental laws and policies."[23]

According to the Treasury analysis "The solution to the shortage, therefore, is not divestiture, but rather a change in (government) policies."[24]

Johnson's conclusion to his 1976 study is that "The oil industry is one of the least concentrated in the United States. There is no evidence that the major oil companies have expanded their share of the market place at the expense of independents. Indeed, the evidence, if anything, suggests the opposite. Nor, as a rule, does it seem that the majors have used vertical and horizontal integration, joint ventures, exchange and processing agreements, or interlocking directorates to engage in anti-competitive practices. Finally, oil industry profits, when viewed in their historical perspective, have not been excessive; nor were recent short-lived increases in profits 'unconscionable'."[25]

Monopoly power in any industry cannot be effective for long unless entry into that industry is blockaded. Where entry is relatively free, but not necessarily inexpensive, competition is normally effective.

The critical point at which entry must be appraised in the petroleum industry is entry into crude oil exploration and production. If entry is free at this point and crude oil production responds to market forces then restrictions on output at the refining or marketing level become unworkable. Restrictions at these later points in production would require product storage. But storage of crude oil and petroleum products is expensive such that long-term restrictions on output are probably not economically feasible.

Entry into crude oil exploration and production appears to be relatively free due to the ownership structure of potential crude oil reserves. Crude oil as well as natural gas prospects are owned by the Federal government, Indian tribes with leases administered by the Federal government, state governments and individuals. Lands in public ownership are subject to periodic auction sales. Entry into these periodic auctions is free. If there are restrictions on the quantity of new leases being offered for sale, then the restrictions come from government rather than from private firms. A 1950 study by McKie concluded that "The exploratory stage of the industry considered by itself, exhibits no artificial impediments to the optimum adjustment of discovery to demand in the long run."[26] The record of bidding for OCS leases clearly supports the 1950 McKie hypothesis indicating relatively free entry conditions. In the twenty year period from 1954 through 1973, 128 firms have won OCS oil and gas leases in the Federal government auctions.[27] In addition, a large number of other firms performed a useful competitive function by submitting bids although they were not among the winners. Large size is not a necessary condition of entry into the OCS lease market. Joint bidding has enabled smaller firms to combine into effective bidding entities.

On the basis of data on market structure, including conditions of entry into crude oil exploration and production, and appraisals conducted by others, the evidence tends to support the conclusion that the oil industry is effectively competitive. Evidence to the contrary is lacking.

(C) There is little question but that the coal industry is among the more highly competitive sectors of the American economy. During the 1960's several major oil company acquisitions of coal firms were consummated. For example, Continental Oil Company purchased Consolidation Coal Company, the second largest coal producer in the United States. Occidental Petroleum Company acquired Island Creek Coal Company, the third largest producer. Standard Oil Company of Indiana acquired Old Ben Coal Corporation, the tenth largest coal company. Gulf Oil Company acquired Pittsburgh and Midway Coal Company, the thir-

teenth largest coal firm. The largest coal company, Peabody Coal, was acquired not by an oil company, but by Kennecott Copper Corporation. These acquisitions, however, did not increase concentration since the firms involved were either not in the business of producing coal or were unimportant factors in the industry. As of 1972 the four largest coal producers produced only 30.4 per cent of the total coal output of the nation and the top eight companies produced only 40.4 per cent. These are again relatively low concentration ratios.

In addition, entry is relatively free into the coal industry. Coal reserves available in the United States are extremely large (about 42.9 per cent of estimated world coal reserves[28]) and are owned primarily by the federal government. As of January, 1976, a five year lease-sale moratorium was lifted by the federal government and the Interior Secretary announced that new lease-sales would be offered on a competitive bid basis effective in 1977.[29]

Duchesneau has computed concentration ratios for the energy industry through the medium of BTU content of oil, gas, coal and uranium output by firm. He found that, as of 1970, the big four producers of energy in the United States accounted for only 21 per cent of the nation's primary energy output. The big eight firms accounted for 35 per cent.[30] These concentration ratios are very low relative to other major sectors of American industry. On the basis of this concentration data, one must conclude that the energy industry is among the more competitive industries in the economy.

Evidence has now been presented indicating that the energy industry in total and its major sectors is probably effectively competitive. The evidence indicates no structural impediments to competition, apart from those imposed by government regulation. Monopoly power is found only in the international oil industry where a multi-government cartel (OPEC) is apparent. Other evidence of monopoly power has been introduced by government through such devices as market demand prorationing and import quotas.

The counter-productive role of government in the problems associated with the energy crisis has been a consistent element in the conclusions reached by nearly all professional analyses of competition whether by those who find private market power (the Federal Trade Commission and Allvine and Patterson), or by the larger number of researchers who find none. Erickson and Spann addressed this issue directly as follows: "The energy crisis has been policy induced and is not the result of market power."[31] Nearly identical conclusions attributing energy problems to public policy are to be found in Johnson[32] and Duchesneau,[33] in addition to those already cited.

This analysis started with the argument that if important externalities existed or if monopoly power was apparent then there was an important role for government to perform in either anti-trust policy, regulation, or government ownership and operation. No such evidence has been found.

V. ENERGY PRICE TRENDS

In spite of the evidence introduced above, there are substantial demands voiced in the press and in legislative circles for more government control of the energy industry or outright government ownership. The primary factor leading to such demands appears to be the fact that energy prices have risen dramatically since 1972. If energy price inflation is the result of private monopoly power then the call for more regulation or government ownership might be justified. We have found no such evidence. What then, is the cause of the dramatic energy price increases?

The answer to this question comes in two parts. First, inflation has not been restricted to energy but rather has been economy-wide and world-wide. In Canada, "double digit" inflation occurred for the first time in 1974 when, on an annual basis, the consumer price index increased at a 10.9 per cent annual rate. A similar record was established in the United States where the consumer price index increased at an 11.0 per cent annual rate in 1974.

The explanation for widespread inflation should be sought, however, in corresponding increases in the money supply rather than a sudden increase in monopoly power. For the ten years from 1955 through 1964 the historic rate of inflation in Canada was 1.7 per cent. This modest rate of inflation corresponded with a modest 3.5 per cent annual rate of increase in Canada's money supply. Then in the next ten years from 1965 through 1974 the consumer price index in Canada increased at a 5 per cent compound annual rate, corresponding to a 9 per cent annual increase in the Canadian money supply. From 1970 through 1974 price inflation accelerated to 6.5 per cent while the money supply growth rate accelerated to 12.7 per cent.

A similar and almost identical record is recorded in the United States. Relatively modest inflation from 1955 through 1964 corresponded with a modest growth in the money supply. Then both price inflation and monetary expansion occurred beginning in 1965 and extending through 1974. The record is shown in Table 1:

TABLE 1
Annual Rates of Change in the Money Supply (M_1) and the Consumer Price Index, Canada and the United States, 1955-1974

	Canada		United States	
	M_1	CPI	M_1	CPI
1955-1964	3.5%	1.7%	2.0%	1.6%
1965-1974	9.0%	5.0%	5.8%	5.1%
1970-1974	12.7%	6.5%	6.6%	6.2%

Note: M_1 is defined as coin, currency and demand deposits held by commercial banks.
Source: Federal Reserve Bank of St. Louis, *Rates of Change in Economic Data for Ten Countries,* Annual Data, 1955-1974, September 1975, p. B-1 and J-1.

Thus general inflation is closely related to corresponding changes in the money supply.[†]

[†]Editor's Note: For a more complete discussion of the relationship between the printing of money and inflation, see M. Walker, Editor, *The Illusion of Wage and Price Control: Essays on Inflation, its Causes and its Cures* (Vancouver: Fraser Institute, 1976) ISBN 0-88975-001-7 and M. Walker, Editor, *Which Way Ahead? Canada After Wage and Price Control,* (Vancouver: Fraser Institute, 1977) ISBN 0-88975-010-6.

The second important element in the price inflation problem is the rapid increase in energy prices. In 1972 the price of crude oil at the wellhead in the United States, averaged $3.45 per barrel. Three years later the free market price was about $13.00 per barrel, nearly four times its 1972 level.

The cause of this rapid increase in crude oil prices is found, first, in the Arab-Israeli war of 1972-1973 and the associated five-month Arab oil embargo, and second, in the successful cartel behavior of OPEC in setting oil prices and then accepting output reductions necessary to achieve cartel price policy. Supply reductions, interacting with a highly inelastic demand for crude oil, were sufficient to sustain major oil price increases.

The OPEC cartel policy was facilitated by a corresponding decline of the United States as a world oil producer. Apart from the Prudhoe Bay discovery, which is not scheduled for production until 1977, U.S. crude oil reserves reached a peak in 1961. Production from declining reserves continued to expand through November 1971 when production reached a peak slightly in excess of 10 million barrels per day. By the first week in May 1976, U.S. crude oil production had declined to 8.08 million barrels per day, a decline of 19 per cent. The United States has fallen from first to third place among world oil producing nations. The hard fact of life is that oil production in the United States has been artificially stimulated by tax subsidies such as the fifty years of depletion allowance and by thirteen years of import quotas which restricted foreign supplies, with the result that we have simply exhausted our easy-to-find, low-cost domestic crude oil.

The facts cited above appear to be sufficient explanations for the nearly four-fold increase in crude oil prices since 1972. There is no need for a conspiracy theory holding that oil companies have conspired to reduce output and increase prices.

An important element in the nationwide (both Canada and the United States) and world-wide march toward increased government regulation and government ownership in the energy sector has been consumer resentment against the rapid price inflation. Yet we find that price inflation, as one of the important problems to be solved, is the result of government mismanagement of the money supply, government energy policy, and successful operation of a multi-national government petroleum cartel.

If government policy is to be rational then prior to additional government regulation or ownership and management of the energy sector, evidence should be presented showing that there would be a net social gain accruing from such government activity. There is a record of government regulation and there is a record of government ownership that may be examined. What is there in this record that might demonstrate superior efficiency where resources are allocated through government regulation or decision-making, compared to private decision-making? We now turn to an examination of this record.

VI. THE RECORD OF GOVERNMENT ENTERPRISE AND GOVERNMENT REGULATION OF PRIVATE ENTERPRISE

A. Government Enterprise. Empirical studies of government enterprise performance are surprisingly scarce. Some government enterprises are too young to evaluate. Petro-Canada, Ltd., the new 100 per cent Canadian government owned oil corporation, was created in 1975. Panarctic, as a partially-owned Canadian corporation, in conjunction with a consortium of oil companies, has produced no net income to date. The West German firms, Deminex and Veba Chemie have existed only since 1968.

In France the ELF group is 100 per cent owned by the French government and was created by a merger of several national petroleum companies after World War II. The ELF group includes Aquitaine, which is the largest producer of natural gas in France, and is also deeply involved in chemical production. Also in France the TOTAL group with Compaignie Francaise de Petroles (CFP) the parent company, was created in 1924. The French government owns 35 per cent of the stock of CFP and controls 40 per cent of the voting power. In spite of its majority private ownership, it was organized to manage and develop the petroleum rights granted to France in the Middle East after World War I and "to create a vehicle for realizing a national oil policy."

In Italy, the dominant petroleum enterprise is Ente Nazionale Idrocarburi (ENI), formed in 1953 by the Italian government for the purpose of promoting and carrying out programs of national interest in the hydrocarbons sector and is 100 per cent owned by the Italian government. Currently ENI has approximately 100 subsidiaries and affiliates to which it provides overall policy and direction along with planning, coordination and financial assistance. Its three major subsidiaries and affiliates are (1) SNAM, a wholly-owned subsidiary engaged in transportation of petroleum products and natural gas by pipelines and tankers, (2) AGIP, engaged in oil exploration, production and marketing, and (3) ANIC, 66 per cent owned by ENI and active in refining and petrochemical operations.[34]

In the United Kingdom the Anglo-Persian Oil Company was registered on April 14, 1909 to develop newly-discovered oil resources in Iran. The name was changed to Anglo-Iranian Oil Company, Limited, in 1934, and then to British Petroleum, Ltd., in 1954. Entry of the British government into stock ownership in what is now British Petroleum (BP) occurred in 1914. The British government has been a minority stock holder holding 48.2 per cent of the "ordinary capital" of the company. The other major stockholder in BP has been a private company, the Burmah Oil Company, which owned 21.5 per cent of the "ordinary capital". Burmah has recently encountered financial difficulties which forced it to transfer its shares in BP to the British government. Hence, the British government now owns a controlling share (about 70%) of the BP stock.

While the British government has been the dominant stockholder in BP and, under ordinary conditions, would easily obtain effective voting control, such control has never been exercised. Frankel noted this political independence as follows:

"The board members nominated by the government have never been known to interfere in the business of the company — although there were some rumblings of mutual discontent when the Labour Cabinet under Wilson came to power. The experience of what is now British Petroleum has, however, only limited general relevance: Firstly, because the innate discipline of the British made it possible for the government to rely on the ordinary directors of their company to take overall national interests as fully into account as they knew how; secondly — and this is infinitely more relevant — that company, due to its endowment but also to the continuing and outstanding buoyancy of the oil industry, never needed any actual help, to which strings would have been attached, nor did it ever need government-borne finance of any kind."[35]

The record of the public enterprises identified above has been evaluated in a 1975 report to the Federal Energy Administration. This evaluation drew the following conclusions: "Overall, the comparative performances analysis provides no basis for concluding that public corporations will be more efficiently operated than private corporations, and evidence is available from this record to suggest the opposite, that public control produces less efficiency."[36]

As a sub-heading under this conclusion, it should be pointed out that the social need for a public corporation operating in the energy industry depends largely on the willingness of private capital to undertake energy development projects and the availability of private funding. The report to the FEA elaborated this point as follows:

"The advantages of a government oil company pertain mainly to countries in a relatively early stage of development. If private capital will not flow from investors in a given country into the international oil business, and if such a flow is desired by the government, then creation of a government enterprise would appear to be a relatively attractive solution. If some private capital is available, then a partially-owned government enterprise would appear to be preferable to a wholly-owned enterprise. These conditions, however, do not pertain to the United States where there are already many existing private international oil companies and private capital readily flows to international oil investments."[37]

The distinction made in the quotation above between 100% and partial government ownership, is based on the report's analysis which indicates that the performance of partially government-owned companies such as British Petroleum shows a performance superior to that of the 100 per cent government-owned companies where management decisions are largely determined by political rather than economic factors.

In addition to the analyses of government enterprises in the energy industry, there are some useful studies of government enterprise performance in other industries. For example, in a study of Australian airline efficiency between two domestic airlines, the Trans-Australian Airlines (TAA) which is owned by the Australian government and the privately-owned ANSETT Australian National Airways, the author wrote that "Except for type of ownership, these two firms have a remarkable number of similar characteristics. The two-airline situation in Australia is probably as near to a laboratory experiment as an economist ever comes."[38] The author evaluated these two firms on the basis of (1) tonnage of freight and mail carried per employee, (2) number of paying passengers carried per employee, and (3) revenue earned per employee. The author concluded that "The data support the contention that the private company is economically more efficient than the public firm."[39]

Another series of studies analyzed the relative efficiency of private versus nationalized industry in England. After evaluating performance on the basis of ten factors, the authors reached the following conclusions: (1) "The record of nationalised industries compared with that of private industries, measured by any of the usually accepted indicators of efficiency, shows generally inferior performance, and (2) there are no aspects of this performance which provide evidence of the inherent superiority of public ownership."[40]

Other studies of public versus private industry performance in rubber production, helium production, and electric power, have been made. While the conclusions of such studies almost universally support the hypothesis that private enterprise is more efficient than public enterprise, the conclusions are almost always ambiguous. Comparability is rarely achieved. In the public utility area, the picture is clouded by government regulation.

Apart from the record of performance there are problems inherent in decision-making within a framework of government ownership. In a prior section we indicated that private decision-making motivated by the profit maximization goal is socially efficient only where (1) effective competition prevails and (2) where there are no important externalities present. We now point out similar basic problems of decision-making in government.

First, a management incentive to operate efficiently appears to be relatively weak in government enterprises. The operating goals of public enterprise may not give first priority or even high priority to profit maximization.[41] If government enterprise is to maximize profit, then there is no clear reason for having government enterprise. This is true if private capital is available as pointed out above. Given the availability of private capital, the existence of government enterprise is in itself testimony to the point that profit maximization is secondary to other considerations. These other considerations might be to conduct operations in areas that do not yield an attractive rate of return or may even involve net losses. If there are no externalities involved as discussed above then from a social point of view one must ask why society's scarce resources would be invested where the yields are low or negative when those same resources can be invested in such areas as medical research, education, etc. where the social rate of return may be attractively high. If any society is to maximize its standards of living, its scarce resources, whether under private control or public control, should be allocated in those areas yielding the highest rates of return. Unless the goals of public enterprise are consistent with this principle the performance of public enterprise will be relatively unattractive.

Within a private enterprise system, management rewards normally consist of salaries that are indirectly related to a profit performance standard, bonuses directly related to profit performance, and stock options indirectly related to profit performance through stock market evaluations. In a publicly-owned enterprise management rewards are rarely if ever a direct function of enterprise profitability and therefore efficiency of resource allocation. The U.S. Postal System which never earns a profit, and the new Amtrak System which has not yet earned a profit, are cases in point. The reward system for management is unclear in government enterprises. In those instances where members of a public enterprise management team are fired, it is usually because of incurring the wrath of the political establishment, either the Congress or the Administration, and rarely because of failure to operate efficiently or at costs less than revenue.

Second, a government enterprise is frequently a monopoly and hence is not subject to any check from competition. This is true in the case of the U.S. Post Office[42] and the Mexican National Oil Company, PEMEX, as illustrations. Evaluation of the performance of the PEMEX management is virtually impossible since no Mexican standard exists by which their performance may be compared. Without the check of competition, a monopoly guarantees inefficiency and perhaps social irresponsibility as well.

Third, where a public corporation is not a monopoly but rather competes with private firms it may have a preferred relationship conferred by the power of government. This is currently an issue of great importance in the newly-created Petrocan. The chairman of Petrocan recently announced that this federal oil company will receive preferential but not exclusive use of exploration permits on lands subject to Federal jurisdiction.[43] In the United States the proposed but not yet enacted Federal Oil and Gas Corporation (FOGCO) was to receive preference rights on Outercontinental Shelf oil and gas leases under the jurisdiction of the Federal government. The existence of preference rights in any important form makes evaluation of public enterprise performance extremely difficult. Preference rights, whether they provide access to the best oil and gas prospects, low interest or zero interest Federal loans, immunity from Federal taxation as in the case of the Tennessee Valley Authority (TVA) in the U.S. and publicly-owned telephone companies in Canada, or immunity from certain types of Federal regulation, permit inefficiency to be offset and hidden from public view and lead to resource misallocation. This issue merges into the "yardstick" concept wherein a public corporation is to serve as a standard by which private corporation performance in the same industry may be judged. The "yardstick" concept is valid only if all important rules of the game are essentially identical. If the government corporation has preference rights not available to the private enterprise with which its performance may be compared, then the yardstick role cannot be performed.[44]

B. Government Regulation of Private Enterprise. The record of government regulation of private enterprise has been subject to more empirical study than has the record of government enterprise. The classic problem of government regulation is that the regulatory agency quickly becomes dominated by the economic interest that it is intended to regulate. As cases in point, the records of the U.S. Securities and Exchange Commission, Civil Aeronautics Board, and Interstate Commerce Commission are often cited. Currently in the United States there is a revival of political interest in reducing the economic powers of regulatory commissions. Congress recently approved a move by the Securities and Exchange Commission to abandon authority to fix brokerage rates on corporate security transactions and to require instead that brokerage rates be market determined. The dominant opposition to this reduction in government price fixing authority came from the brokerage industry itself. Currently, hearings are being held in Congress to reduce the regulatory authority of the Civil Aeronautics Board. Again, major resistance in the hearings is coming from the airline industry, suggesting that it is a beneficiary of such regulation.

In the energy industry the major area of regulation since the 1930's has included market demand prorationing, rationalized in terms of resource conservation. Market demand prorationing evolved into a system whereby the authority of government was used to reduce crude oil output in order to attain a market price above competitive levels. Similarly, regulation in the oil industry included import quotas instituted in 1959. Import quotas again reduced oil supply in order to attain domestic price levels above that which competition would permit.

Why would government wish to undertake regulation in the energy industry? In terms of economics, the answers are in two areas elaborated above. Regulation would be justified if there are important externalities involved in private decision-making or competition is inadequate and regulation is deemed to be the preferred means of correcting for these market failures. If regulation is instituted, then presumably government has come to the conclusion that performance under regulation would be superior to imperfect performance under free market conditions.

Regulation of the wellhead price of natural gas provides an excellent case study of regulation in the energy industry market. Government regulation has received Congressional support primarily out of a belief that competition between producers of natural gas as sellers, and pipeline companies as buyers, was inadequate and required government protection on behalf of ultimate consumers. The wellhead price of gas flowing in interstate commerce was introduced haphazardly as a result of a Supreme Court decision in 1954. Gas flowing only within the borders of the producing state has not been subject to price control by the Federal Government.

The dominant interest group calling the tune in natural gas price regulation has been natural gas utilities as buyers and distributors, and consumers in non-producing states.

The result of 22 years of field price control of natural gas is fairly clear. The wellhead price has been set at levels below prices which would have been determined by free market conditions. The proof of this point is that demand clearly exceeds supply at prevailing prices. At these artificially low prices, consumers who currently have natural gas hookups and are receiving gas are getting an impressive bargain relative to the cost of oil or other heat sources, while others who cannot obtain new hookups or have been cut off from past supplies cannot buy natural gas at any price. At artificially low prices, consumers receiving uninterruptable supplies are free to consume gas lavishly as if it were a cheap and abundantly available energy source.

There is a strong consensus among professional economists that natural gas price control has been a mistake and that deregulation should take place. One of the most authoritative analyses of natural gas price regulation drew three conclusions as follows:

"First, Commission activity benefited the consumer very little if at all. The administrative costs of operating the Commission, including the costs to litigants . . . is small when compared with gas and electricity revenues, it did not buy much. Measures of the effectiveness of gas pipeline price regulation indicate that pipeline prices were not lower than they would have been without regulation. Gas producer price regulation, which accounted for the largest portion of the administrative expense attributable to commission operation, caused more harm than good. Ceiling prices at the wellhead were set too low, creating a reserve shortage and a production shortage . . .

Second, the study adds support to the growing suspicion that regulation by commission is at best a clumsy tool for achieving economic goals. In each instance, the FPC responded slowly and inefficiently to changing conditions. Once the Commission set ceilings on pipeline profit, it maintained them for months or years, despite changing economic conditions; it reversed them only after hearing numerous conflicting expert views in lengthy adjudicatory proceedings; and the profit ceilings it set only very generally approximated the actual economic costs of capital . . .

Third, the study shows the serious risks that flow from an agency's single-minded pursuit of lower prices. An important strain of regulatory thought views low prices as good in themselves and brushes aside any inefficiencies they may cause on the ground that such inefficiencies are simply the price paid for an improved income distribution."[45]

The solution recommended by Breyer and MacAvoy is, "efforts to regulate the prices charged by natural gas producers should be abandoned."[46] The Breyer-MacAvoy conclusions and recommendations are widely shared by other professional economists.[47]

C. Regulation in Public Utilities. Regulation in the public utilities area has been justified on the basis of inadequate competition. Utilities have characteristically been termed "natural monopolies." The long-run average cost for electric power and natural gas distribution in particular is believed to decline persistently until any relevant market has been served by one distributor. Therefore, competition by two or more firms in any single market would be inefficient. This line of reasoning therefore rules out an anti-trust approach to this problem and leaves only a choice between regulation or government ownership and operation. Both approaches have been used.

Professor Thomas Gale Moore has studied the effectiveness of the regulatory process in reducing electric power prices to residential customers. He examined cost and demand functions for sixty-two private and municipal electric power companies and concluded that "Regulation has not reduced prices more than 5 per cent and probably less than that."[48] The standard for Moore's comparison was a monopoly profit maximization price. Moore further concluded that "Regulation is not performing one of its main functions and some major changes in regulation are due."[49]

A highly-regarded public utility economist, currently serving as Chairman of the New York State Public Service Commission, has indicated that public utility regulation inherently is unable to produce efficient solutions. Alfred E. Kahn wrote:

"It is a commonplace observation that public utility regulation is inherently incapable of supplying the kind of continuous pressure and incentive for efficient operation that we rely on competition to supply in non-regulated industries. The regulation of rates almost inevitably takes on the characteristics of cost-plus contracts, with all their familiar problems and limitations. Paradoxically, the only systematic way in which regulation escapes these pitfalls is by being less than continuously effective; it is only regulatory lag — lapse of time between rate cases — that imposes on the regulated monopolist a stimulus to reduce costs, because it will, in the interim between rate cases, bear the burden of increasing costs and reap the rewards from holding them down."[50]

D. Regulation by the Federal Energy Administration. More recently the major center of government regulation of the energy industry has become the Federal Energy Administration (FEA). Its predecessor organization, the Federal Energy Office (FEO), has been subjected to an economic evaluation for efficiency. Professor Mancke concluded that "On balance the measures taken by FEO actually exacerbated the nation's oil supply problems."[51] The primary criticism levied by Mancke is that the FEA over-reacted in its allocation system. It underestimated the consumer response to higher prices and its action actually resulted in a build-up of inventories during the embargo by about 80 million barrels compared to year-earlier inventory levels.

More recently Johnson has examined the successive phases of crude oil price control through both FEO and FEA and concluded that controls were counterproductive in 12 different ways.[52]

Another analysis of the present oil price control program evaluated performance in terms of the stated goal of price control — cushioning the domestic impact of sharply higher external oil prices. This analysis concluded "The controls will (1) become ineffective, over time, with respect to the . . . intention, and (2) will enhance the ability of external suppliers to manipulate prices."[53] The report further stated that "Controls provide both disincentives to produce oil domestically and incentives to import oil. As imported oil becomes an increasing proportion of total domestic consumption, the effective domestic price of oil will increase also. The greater U.S. reliance on foreign sources of supply, in turn, enhances the unity of the foreign oil cartel such that the United States becomes increasingly vulnerable to external pricing and producing decisions. A situation has been fostered which would perpetuate rising world oil prices in the future."[54]

More generally price and wage controls both within and beyond the energy industry have generally been unsuccessful. Ulman and Flanagan examined the history of price and wage controls in the United Kingdom, The Netherlands, Sweden, Denmark, France, West Germany and Italy and concluded that "Incomes policy, to generalize from the experience of the countries studied in this account, has not been very successful."[55] The authors go on to specify that "In none of the variations so far turned up has incomes policy succeeded in its fundamental objective, as stated, of making full employment consistent with a reasonable degree of price stability."[56]

E. The Costs of Regulation. Roger Noll observed that "Strangely enough the costs of regulation were largely ignored by economists until recently, despite their characteristic concern for economic efficiency."[57] Regulations are frequently advocated and often enacted by Congress without a question ever being raised as to their costs and benefits. Weidenbaum has estimated that in the fiscal year 1976 Federal expenditures for business regulation amounted to $2.9 billion. This estimate, however, is conservative. For example, Weidenbaum allocated only $50 million of the Federal Energy Administration's $142 million budget to regulation.[58] Weidenbaum goes on to say that this estimate "is only the tip of the iceberg. It is the costs imposed on the private sector that are really large, the added expenses – which inevitably are passed on to customers – of complying with government directives."[59] He also noted that "Another hidden cost of federal regulation is the reduced rate of technological innovation. The longer it takes for some change to be approved by a federal regulatory agency – a new product or a more efficient production process – the less likely it is that the change will be made."[60] We have no estimate of the total cost of regulation. It is quite possible, however, that regulation in total may not be worth the costs imposed and that regulation is counterproductive. Empirical evidence is lacking.

It is unclear whether the problems of regulation are problems of administration or are inherent in the nature of regulation itself. After a detailed review of government regulation, Weiss and Strickland emphasized the inherent problems of regulation. They wrote as follows:

> "Altogether, regulators face enormously complex problems that no one has to solve in competitive markets. They must determine what costs are and what prices will cover them — issues that are settled automatically when competitive forces are strong. The regulators must also decide among contending suppliers, something the customers do for themselves in competitive markets. And finally, regulators must decide on the right degree of price discrimination, something that cannot occur in unregulated industries if markets are fully competitive."[61]

The more detailed regulation becomes, the greater the problems. The output of one industry is the input of another. Thus price regulations of one industry determine costs or revenues of another. Further, the economic world is dynamic while regulations tend to be static and inflexible. Any change in technology and any change in costs and demands should bring forth adjustments in regulations. But changes in regulation require prior studies and often hearings, in order to give all interest groups an opportunity to be heard. This requires the passage of time. As the Federal Power Commission learned, detailed regulation of gas prices resulted in the build-up of a tremendous backlog of cases forcing the Commission to move away from detailed regulation toward more and more generalized controls.

Yet another inherent problem is that individuals and business firms always have the final word. A regulatory agency can set prices and rules. Firms and individuals always have the right to react to them. Regulations have a built-in incentive leading clever buyers and sellers to search for loopholes and other devices to circumvent regulation. A major function of astute management is to overcome roadblocks and bottlenecks in the way of profitability. This includes roadblocks and bottlenecks set up by regulatory agencies. Further, regulation normally controls only one or a few elements of competition. Regulation of price leaves open compensatory and off-setting behaviour in other dimensions of competition. The high price set on some commodity, creating attractive profits in the producing industry, opens the way for competition in that industry to offer expanded services in lieu of, and equal to, lower competitive prices. An empirical study of the stockbrokerage industry has demonstrated this point. Since 1935 (until 1975) brokerage rates on securities transactions have been endorsed and enforced by the Securities and Exchange Commission. These government approved brokerage rates have been high relative to what competition would determine. But the brokerage industry is nevertheless effectively competitive. Shepard has found that monopolistic commission rates have simply caused brokerage houses to emphasize non-price competition in the form of more "back office" services for which no charge is levied.[62]

Finally, regulation may be doomed by its own life cycle. Regulation is normally inspired by an observation of some kind of injustice where the solution is found to lie in government regulation. In this early phase of the regulatory life cycle there is great enthusiasm for solving a pressing social-economic problem. But what is proposed to Congress and what comes out of Congress after hearings have been held and all interest groups have been heard is not likely to be the ideal solution that was proposed by its enthusiastic initial supporters. Another phase in the regulatory cycle begins with the establishment of the new regulatory agency. The initial staff may very well be composed of enthusiastic people who believe that they now hold the solution to an important problem. But with the passage of years the enthusiastic initial staff goes on to greener pastures and the dull day-to-day routine of the regulatory commission must be carried out. Experts who know the industry to be regulated must be hired. These people often come from the industry to be regulated. Within a decade it is quite likely that the regulatory agency has taken on a life of its own which may bear only a partial resemblance to what Congress has authorized and no resemblance at all to what the initial proponents had in mind. Finally, in order for a regulatory agency to survive the annual budgetary process it must have a constituency. The constituency that is reliable year-after-year, willing to pressure Congress in support of the agency budget, turns out to be the same group that it is supposed to regulate. The mature regulatory agency is then characterized as a bureaucracy captured by the group which it is supposed to regulate and the agency is now mature.

In sum, the record as well as the future of government regulation does not appear to be rewarding in terms of serving the public interest in the long run. Even if administration is improved through legislating a new set of administrative practices, regulation may still be counterproductive due to its inherent problems. In spite of its poor record of performance, where external costs are extremely large as in the case of nuclear electric power generation, regulation appears to be a necessity. Where natural monopoly exists, public utility type regulation will undoubtedly continue. Studies might be undertaken to determine whether the social benefits of regulation exceed the social costs.

VII. THE RECORD OF PRIVATE ENTERPRISE IN THE ENERGY SECTOR

In the foregoing section we have found government enterprise a mixed blessing and appropriate mainly when private enterprise is unable or unwilling to perform essential functions. We have also found government regulation of private industry to be unsatisfactory. We now turn to an evaluation of private enterprise performance in the energy industry.

By what criteria should we evaluate the performance of private firms in the energy sector? The basic role of private enterprise is to supply reliable products, in a variety of forms, in response to consumer demand, at prices that are equal to real cost including a competitive profit. Satisfactory performance also requires innovation. This includes new

160

product and a new process innovation. The aforementioned goals might be expanded to include other points. However, we are constrained by the need to evaluate performance. Generalized goals not subject to empirical testing are not very helpful in an attempt to evaluate the performance of an industry. Accordingly, we will limit this evaluation of performance to points that are testable given the limited data available.

A. Is there any evidence that the private sector has failed to supply energy as demanded by consumers? Until the late 1960's, apart from shortages induced by major wars, there were no significant periods when private firms in the energy industry failed to supply energy markets. Energy shortages in any form were unknown. However, beginning in the 1960's shortages appeared in natural gas. Today the demand for natural gas is far in excess of its supply at prevailing prices and there is clearly a shortage. But the explanation for the shortage has already been given. The field price of natural gas flowing in interstate commerce has been controlled since 1954 by the federal government. This price control is fully responsible for the shortage. There would be no shortage in the absence of government controls. The price system would perform its usual function of clearing the market. The price of gas at the wellhead would approximate the cost of substitute fuels. Currently this would require a price of approximately $2.15 per Mcf.

A shortage of crude oil, gasoline and other petroleum products developed in 1972 and intensified in late 1973. This shortage however was due, first, to import quotas in existence since 1959 through May 1, 1973. Quotas artificially restricted crude oil and product imports. As U.S. domestic supplies declined, a shortage developed. But again this is the result of Federal government policy.

The intensification of shortages in crude oil and products occurred suddenly with the Arab oil embargo in October 1973. This shortage was further intensified by inept government controls composed of price control, allocation and entitlements. Responsibility for the shortage lies with the embargo and with government policy.

B. Have prices been excessively high for energy products? An evaluation of price levels and trends is extremely difficult and often misleading. We have no clear standard by which we can judge the price record. We can examine the trend in energy prices relative to the trend of non-energy prices. However, oil, gas and coal as well as uranium are all non-renewable resources and hence the comparison may not be valid. As a persistent problem of evaluation, we have no way of knowing what would have been the trend of prices under different but hypothetically ideal conditions. Given these problems we will briefly examine only the record of wholesale gasoline prices.

Beginning in 1950, the average price of gasoline (regular) at retail in the United States, excluding all taxes, was $0.201 per gallon. By 1972 gasoline prices had risen to $0.245 per gallon. However the slight increase in the nominal price of gasoline is less than the average increase in all consumer prices. If we correct for the effects of inflation by dividing by the consumer price index we find that, in terms of 1950 constant dollars, the real price of gasoline declined from $0.201 in 1950 to $0.172 in 1972. Thus the real price of gasoline declined 29.7 per cent over this 22 year period.[63]

From 1972 to July 1974 the real price of gasoline increased 50 per cent. But again, this reflects the five months embargo which ended in February 1974 plus OPEC cartel behavior. From July 1974 through January 1976 the real price of gasoline has actually declined 9.5 per cent. This record of price trends over a long period prior to the embargo and prior to the present system of Federal price controls on the petroleum industry suggests but does not prove a satisfactory competitive performance.

C. Has the petroleum industry shown progressiveness in its rate of innovation? If an industry is innovative and continuously introduces better and cheaper ways to produce products, then evidence should appear in the form of relatively rapid increases in the output per man hour and output per unit of capital and other resources employed.

Kendrick has compared the productivity record of major industries in the U.S. economy over much of the post World War II period. The several measures utilized by Kendrick all show an outstanding innovative performance by the petroleum industry. From 1948 through 1966, the average annual percentage rate of change in output per unit of labor input for petroleum refining was 5.5 per cent. For all manufacturing in the United States, the comparable annual rate was only 2.9 per cent and for the private domestic business economy in total, including farming, mining, transportation and other sectors, the rate was 3.1 per cent.[64]

A broader measure of productivity that includes not only labor input but "total factor productivity" shows that petroleum refining increased output 3.0 per cent per year whereas all manufacturing recorded 2.5 per cent and the total private domestic business economy, 2.5 per cent.[65]

As a consequence of this record of rapid productivity gains, wage rates have been very high in the petroleum industry. Kendrick's analysis of average hourly compensation in 34 industry groups showed that throughout the period from 1948 through 1966, petroleum refining wage rates were the highest of all 34 industries analyzed.[66]

D. Have profits been excessive in the energy industry? We will analyze only the record of profitability in the petroleum industry. Profit rates in public utilities are regulated. The only area of controversy on profitability concerns the petroleum industry. There are several ways to examine the profitability record in the petroleum industry and the record has been analyzed by a large number of separate studies. Using First National City Bank data, which extends back to 1937 on an annual basis, we find that the rate of return on net worth for leading U.S. petroleum industry corporations averaged 12.2 per cent from 1937 through 1973. For other manufacturing, excluding petroleum, the comparable rate of return was 12.5 per cent.[67]

Comparing the oil companies listed in the *Fortune* magazine annual list of 500 largest industrial corporations with all non-oil industrial corporations we find that over the decade ending in 1972 the oil industry was "typically a just-below-average performer. In seven out of ten years . . . the median return for the 20 to 25 petroleum refining companies in the 500 was below the median for the entire 500."[68]

Using Federal Trade Commission data for the big 8 oil companies only and for the 21 years from 1951 through 1971 we find that the big 8 oil companies earned an average of 11.9 per cent rate of return on stockholder equity compared to 10.9 per cent for all manufacturing.

Oil company profitability increased with the substantially higher crude oil prices brought on by the Arab oil embargo and the successful monopolizing behavior of the OPEC cartel. In 1974 the 28 largest U.S. oil companies earned a very high 17.2 rate of return on stockholder equity. However, the rate of return returned to an approximately normal 12.3 per cent in 1975.[69]

Consumers have been shocked by higher petroleum product prices. High oil company profits, particularly 1973 and 1974, led to widespread public suspicion of monopoly power. Political figures have responded by reference to "obscene profits" in the oil industry. Professional economists examining the data have almost universally reached the conclusion that profits over the long term in the oil industry are approximately normal and reflect competitive conditions. For example, Erickson and Spann concluded their evaluation of competition in the U.S. petroleum industry with the statement: "The record of long-run profitability in the U.S. petroleum industry indicates that the firms in this industry do not enjoy substantial, systematic market power. This index of effective competition yields positive results whether the comparison is to all U.S. manufacturing, Moody's 125 Industrials, Moody's 24 Public Utilities, or a group of industrial firms known to possess market power, or the cost of equity capital for the petroleum industry."[70]

VIII. CONCLUSION

Because of the shortages that have occurred in petroleum products and the sharply rising energy price levels since 1972, consumers are unhappy with various segments of the energy industry. Given this general dissatisfaction, political appeals for increased regulation and even public ownership are more frequently voiced and welcomed by an irate public. However, this survey of performance of government ownership and regulation does not suggest that either is a satisfactory approach to observed problems.

We have surveyed concentration ratios and performance of private firms in the petroleum industry and have reviewed structural conditions in various segments of the energy industry. We found no evidence that the industry in total or separate sectors possessed monopoly power or earned monopoly profit. Our survey of performance suggests a relatively satisfactory record.

We have shown that the problems that increased regulation of the energy industry and even government ownership might possibly solve are not the real problems. Instead, the primary cause of general inflation is shown to be a corresponding rapid increase in money supplies since 1965. Rapid price increases in petroleum products are due to the Arab oil embargo and to a multi-government oil cartel known as OPEC. The ability of OPEC to control prices of crude oil was enhanced by the increasing exhaustion of easy-to-find and low-cost crude oil in the United States. United States production increased steadily until 1971 when a persistent decline of output set in. Crude oil production in the United States in April 1976 was approximately 20 per cent below its October 1971 peak. But this is due not to private restrictions in the United States but to the fact that after many years of subsidies to the oil industry stimulating domestic production, low-cost new crude oil reserves within the United States no longer exist. The same is true for Canada. Energy resources are non-renewable resources and the large reserves of low-cost crude oil are no longer to be found in North America.

Private enterprise is imperfect. It suffers from market failure when external costs or benefits are present.

However, many of these externalities have been internalized either by government regulation or by the market. Also competition is not perfect. However, we have seen that in the energy industry competition appears to be reasonably effective. The comparison of private enterprise performance with government enterprise performance or government regulation leads us to a Churchillian conclusion. Allocation of scarce energy resources by private decision-making is probably the worst economic system, except that the next best alternative, government enterprise and government regulation, is an intolerable second best. Government decision-making, where resources are allocated to serve the general welfare directly, sounds good as a proposition. But Kenneth Boulding goes one step beyond Churchill and argues, "Everything you do to hurt people, helps them; and everything you do to help them, hurts them."[71]

Notes

[1] Alternatively, a payment might be made to firms in the offending industry to induce them to reduce or cease their action which creates external costs. Payments to polluters may not be politically acceptable, however.

[2] U.S. Federal Trade Commission, "The International Petroleum Cartel", a Staff Report submitted to the Committee on Monopoly of the Select Committee on Small Business, U.S. Senate, 82nd Congress, Second Session, 1952, p. 32.

[3] M.A. Adelman. *The World Petroleum Market.* Baltimore: Johns Hopkins University Press, 1972, p. 81.

[4] "Oil Imports and Energy Security: An Analysis of the Current Situation and Future Prospects", Report of the Ad Hoc Committee on the Domestic and International Monetary Effect of Energy and Other Natural Resource Pricing, Committee on Banking.

[5] M.A. Adelman, "Is the Oil Shortage Real?" *Foreign Policy,* Winter, 1972-73, p. 101.

[6]M.A. Adelman, Testimony before the U.S. Senate Committee on Interior and Insular Affairs, 93rd Congress, First Session, p. 1333.

[7]G.C. Watkins, "Competitive Bidding and Alberta Petroleum Rents", *Journal of Industrial Economics,* June 1975, 23(4), p. 308.

[8]W.J. Mead, "Evidence from the Rate of Return on Outercontinental Shelf Investments," in R.B. Krueger (Editor), *Study of the Outercontinental Shelf Lands of the United States,* a report to the Public Land Law Review Commission, Vol. 1, 1968, pp. 521-527.

[9]This internal rate of return study is currently being updated by the author to include production data through 1975 and is being extended to include six more lease sales in the Gulf of Mexico through the year 1962.

[10]Quoted in William A. Johnson. *Competition in the Oil Industry.* Washington, D.C.: George Washington University, Energy Policy Research Project, 1976, p. 1.

[11]*Ibid.,* p. 3.

[12]W.F. Mueller, and L.G. Hamm, "Trends in Industrial Market Concentration, 1947 to 1970", *Review of Economics and Statistics,* Nov. 1974, 56(4), p. 512.

[13]Johnson, *op. cit.,* p. 3.

[14]See testimony by W.J. Mead before the Special Sub-committee on Integrated Oil Operations, Committee on Interior and Insular Affairs, U.S. Senate, 93rd Congress, First Session, Part 3, December 12, 1973, p. 1008. For an additional analysis of joint ventures see testimony of John W. Wilson before the Sub-committee on Anti-trust and Monopoly, Committee on the Judiciary, U.S. Senate, 93rd Congress, First Session, June 27, 1973.

[15]Edward Erickson, Testimony before the Committee on Interior and Insular Affairs, U.S. Senate, 93rd Congress, First Session, Part 1, 1974, p. 364.

[16]*Op. cit.,* p. 62.

[17]Melvin G. de Chazeau and Alfred E. Kahn. *Integration and Competition in the Petroleum Industry.* New Haven: Yale University Press, 1959, p. 104.

[18]Hearings before the U.S. Committee on Interior and Insular Affairs, U.S. Senate, 93rd Congress, First Session, Part 1, 1974, p. 317.

[19]F.C. Allvine and J.M. Patterson. *Competition Ltd.: The Marketing of Gasoline.* Bloomington, Indiana: Indiana University Press, 1972, p. 273.

[20]*Ibid.,* pp. 271-272.

[21]*Ibid.,* p. 247.

[22]U.S. Federal Trade Commission. *Preliminary Federal Trade Commission Staff Report on its Investigation of the Petroleum Industry.* Committee on Interior and Insular Affairs, U.S. Senate, 93rd Congress, First Session, 1973, p. 27.

[23]U.S. Department of the Treasury, Staff Analysis of the Preliminary Federal Trade Commission Staff Report on its Investigation of the Petroleum Industry, July 2, 1973, p. 65.

[24]*Ibid.,* p. 67.

[25]Johnson, *op. cit.,* p. 113.

[26]James W. McKie, "Market Structure and Uncertainty in Oil and Gas Exploration", *Quarterly Journal of Economics,* November 1960, p. 543.

[27]Susan M. Wilcox, "Joint Venture Bidding and Entry in the Market for Off-Shore Petroleum Leases", unpublished Ph.D. dissertation, University of California, Santa Barbara, March 1975, p. 92.

[28]National Coal Association, *World Coal Trade*, 1972 edition, p. 37.

[29]U.S. Department of the Interior, "News Release, January 26, 1976".

[30]Thomas D. Duchesneau. *Competition in the U.S. Energy Industry*. Cambridge, Mass.: Ballinger Publishing Co., 1975, p. 96.

[31]*Op. cit.*, p. 7.

[32]"The Impact of Price Controls on the Oil Industry: How to Intensify an Energy Crisis", *op. cit.*, p. 1.

[33]*Op. cit.*, p. 183.

[34]Moody's *Industrial and Government Manual*, 1968, p. 3521.

[35]P.H. Frankel. *Mattei: Oil and Power Politics*. New York: Praeger, 1966, p. 157.

[36]*An Evaluation of the Options of the U.S. Government in its Relationship to U.S. Firms in International Petroleum Affairs*, a Report prepared for the Federal Energy Administration, by Nossaman, Waters, Krueger, Marsh and Riordan, February 1975, p. A-47.

[37]*Ibid.*, p. A-46.

[38]Donald G. Davies, "The Efficiency of Public Versus Private Firms, the Case of Australia's Two Airlines", *Journal of Law and Economics*, April 1971, 14(1), p. 154.

[39]*Ibid.*, p. 71.

[40]George Polanyi and Priscilla Polanyi. *Failing the Nation, The Record of the Nationalised Industries*. September 1974, p. 6.

[41]It should be pointed out that profit maximization depends upon minimization of costs for any given level of revenues. Careful attention to cost minimization simply means that resources are conserved and are managed effectively.

[42]For a study of the motivations that led to the postal monopoly and the factors that have enabled it to survive, see George L. Priest, "The History of the Postal Monopoly in the United States", *Journal of Law and Economics*, April 1975, 18(1), pp. 33-80.

[43]Reported in the *Oil and Gas Journal*, Feb. 2, 1976, p. 32.

[44]For a further discussion of economic and political problems of public enterprise see Arlon R. Tussing, "The Role of Public Enterprise", a paper delivered at the British Columbia Institute for Economic Policy Analysis, Conference on Mineral Leasing, Victoria, B.C., Sept. 18-20, 1974.

[45]Stephen G. Breyer, and Paul W. MacAvoy. *Energy Regulation by the Federal Power Commission*. Washington, D.C.: The Brookings Institution, 1974, pp. 122-124.

[46]*Ibid.*, p. 132.

[47]See for example, Robert B. Helms. *Natural Gas Regulation, An Evaluation of the FPC Price Controls*. Washington, D.C.: American Enterprise Institute, 1974; Patricia E. Starratt. *The Natural Gas Shortage and the Congress*. Washington, D.C.: American Enterprise Institute, 1974, and Keith C. Brown. *Regulation of the Natural Gas Producing Industry*. Baltimore: Johns Hopkins University Press, 1972.

[48]Thomas Gale Moore, "The Effectiveness of Regulation of Electric Utility Prices", *Southern Economic Journal*, April 1970, 36(4), p. 374.

[49]*Ibid.*

[50]Alfred E. Kahn, "Foreword" to *Public Utility Productivity*, Albany, N.Y.: New York State Department of Public Service, 1975, p. iii.

[51]Richard B. Mancke. *Performance of the Federal Energy Office*. Washington, D.C.: American Enterprise Institute, 1975, p. 6.

[52]William A. Johnson, "The Impact of Price Controls on the Oil Industry: How to Intensify an Energy Crisis", unpublished manuscript, July 16, 1974, pp. 48-50.

[53]Hans H. Helbling and James E. Turley, "Oil Price Controls: A Counterproductive Effort", *Federal Reserve Bank of St. Louis, Review*, November, 1975, 57(11), p. 2.

[54]*Ibid.,* p. 6.

[55]Lloyd Ulman and R.J. Flanagan. *Wage Restraint: A Study of Incomes Policies in Western Europe*. Berkeley: University of California Press, 1971, p. 216.

[56]*Ibid.*

[57]Roger G. Noll, "The Social Costs of Government Intervention", in *The Business-Government Relationship: A Reassessment*, Neil H. Jacoby (ed.), Pacific Palisades, California: Goodyear Publishing Company, 1975, p. 58.

[58]M.L. Weidenbaum. *The New Way of Government Regulation of Business*. Washington, D.C.: American Enterprise Institute, 1976, p. 5.

[59]*Ibid.,* p. 4.

[60]*Ibid.*

[61]Leonard W. Weiss and A.D. Strickland. *Regulation: A Case Approach*. New York: McGraw-Hill, 1976, p. 32.

[62]Lawrence Shepard, *The Securities Brokerage Industry*. Toronto: Lexington Books, 1975, p. 82.

[63]Data have been developed from U.S. Department of Commerce, *Survey of Current Business*, biennial editions.

[64]John W. Kendrick. *Postwar Productivity Trends in the United States, 1948-1969*. New York: National Bureau of Economic Research, 1973, pp. 94-95.

[65]*Ibid.,* pp. 78-79.

[66]*Ibid.,* p. 118.

[67]First National City Bank, Petroleum Department, mimeographed reports.

[68]Carol J. Loomis, "How to Think about Oil Company Profits", *Fortune*, April 1974, p. 99.

[69]*Oil and Gas Journal*, May 3, 1976, p. 117.

[70]Edward W. Erickson and Robert M. Spann, "The U.S. Petroleum Industry", in *The Energy Question: An International Failure of Policy*, E.W. Erickson and L. Waverman, (eds.), Toronto: University of Toronto Press, 1974, p. 6.

[71]*The Business-Government Relationship: A Reassessment*. N.H. Jacoby (ed.), Pacific Palisades, California: Goodyear Publishing Company, 1975, p. 151.

Editor's Introduction

An understanding of the manner in which world crude oil prices are determined is crucial to the formulation of energy policy. The essay by Erickson and Winokur focuses on the relationship between the major oil companies, the OPEC countries and world oil prices. They confront four alternative explanations of the world oil market. The first is what they refer to as the Cassandra theory: distortions preclude prediction. The second is that the world oil price is set collusively (and clandestinely) by the major oil companies. Third, OPEC is a cartel for which the major companies 'manage' world oil supplies. Fourth, OPEC is an association with a dominant price leader - Saudi Arabia. Erickson and Winokur find the first two explanations lacking in perception. The third is rejected on two grounds: OPEC is not a cartel and the major oil companies' role in crude oil supply is technical rather than managerial. The fourth explanation is the one which Erickson and Winokur believe accords best with known facts. They suggest Saudi Arabia will continue its dominant role for quite some time to come, that the world price of oil will be steady in nominal terms and that it may be indexed to compensate for inflation. These findings are especially important: the dramatic increases in world oil prices are not ephemeral. They are likely to be sustained and even increased. 'High' cost oil is here to stay. Erickson and Winokur also examine the debate in the United States on breaking up large oil companies into smaller independent units (horizontal and vertical divestiture). They conclude such policies are irrelevant to the energy problems with which we are confronted.

Nations, Companies and Markets: International Oil and Multinational Corporations

Professor of Economics and Business
North Carolina State University

and

HERBERT S. WINOKUR , Jr.

Associate Lecturer
John Fitzgerald Kennedy School of Government
Harvard University

THE AUTHORS

Edward W. Erickson is Professor of Economics and Business at North Carolina State University. He was educated at Pennsylvania State University where he took his B.A. in 1959 and Vanderbilt University, where he received his Ph.D. in 1968. His teaching career has included instructorships at the University of Tennesse and at Vanderbilt University as well as posts at N.C.S.U.

Born in 1936 in Pennsylvania, Dr. Erickson has served on the National Petroleum Council, 1975-76; the North Carolina Energy Policy Council, 1975-76; as Chairman, Technical-Supply Advisory Committee on Exploration, Development and New Reserves Additions for the Federal Power Commission Natural Gas Survey, 1975-76.

Dr. Erickson was a delegate to the Economic Commission for Europe Symposium on Mathematical Models of Sectors of the Energy Economy, Alma-Ata, U.S.S.R., 1973.

Among the extensive number of publications by Dr. Erickson are: *The Energy Question: An International Failure of Policy, Volume 1, The World,* and *Volume 2, North America,* (Toronto, University of Toronto Press, 1974), (co-editor with L. Waverman).

Herbert S. Winokur, Jr. was born in 1943. He is presently Associate Lecturer, John Fitzgerald Kennedy School of Government, Harvard University. He received his B.A. and then his M.A. in Applied Mathematics at Harvard University in 1965. In 1967 he received his Ph.D., also at Harvard.

From 1967 to 1969, Dr. Winokur was associated with the office of the Secretary of Defense (U.S.). He is a co-founder of ICF, Inc., a Washington-based management consulting firm and was Principal and Director from 1969 to 1974. From 1974 to 1976 Dr. Winokur was Vice-President (Business Development) and Treasurer of Buckeye Pipe Line Company, a Pennsylvania firm. Since 1976, he has been Vice-President (Energy Planning and Development) of Pennsylvania Company, in Arlington, Virginia, as well as a director of several other firms.

In May 1974, with T. Grennes, Dr. Winokur published "Oil and the U.S. Balance of Payments," in Erickson and Waverman, *The Energy Question,* University of Toronto Press. His work is also included in the January 1970, U.S. Government Printing Office Publication, *The Oil Import Question,* President's Cabinet Task Force on Oil Import Control. He has published numerous other scholarly papers.

Nations, Companies and Markets: International Oil and Multinational Corporations

EDWARD W. ERICKSON

Professor of Economics and Business
North Carolina State University

and

HERBERT S. WINOKUR , Jr.

Associate Lecturer
John Fitzgerald Kennedy School of Government
Harvard University

I. INTRODUCTION

Controversy is no stranger to discussions of energy policy. Current North American energy policy controversies include: the roles of alternative sources of energy in satisfying the prospective North American demand; the economic and philosophical bases supporting trade relationships between the United States and Canada; alternative North American oil and gas pipeline routes; the extent and kind of Federal, provincial/regional and state governmental participation in U.S. and Canadian energy supply development and demand management; the continued vertical and horizontal organization of the major energy companies in the United States; and the relationship between the major oil companies, the OPEC countries and the world price of oil. We focus upon this last question. Our perspective is admittedly

173

one of "United Statesians", but the view from the United States is not irrelevant to Canadians — who share with the United States the same general resource base, imbalance in relative regional import dependency, and geographic location relative to the rest of the world.

Many of the large energy companies which operate in Canada are subsidiaries of companies based in the United States. The most highly-charged energy policy controversy in the United States is the question of legislative action to divest vertically and disintegrate horizontally the major oil companies. Now, the summer of 1976, a bill is pending before the full U.S. Senate, the enactment of which would break the major oil companies into component parts. Under this bill, each part would be limited by law to specialization in either production, transportation or refining and marketing.[1] In addition, Senate hearings have been held on proposed legislation which would disintegrate the energy industry horizontally, prohibiting oil companies from participating in coal, uranium, geothermal, solar and other forms of energy development.

The announced purpose of the proposed legislation is to improve competition in the U.S. energy industries. The effect of divestiture on competition has been extensively debated. We believe that the weight of the evidence strongly supports the contention that the oil industry in particular, and the energy industries in general, already are effectively competitive in the present environment.[2]

Competition among companies with or without divestiture, in our view, will have little effect on prices of oil which consumers face, relative to other factors discussed below. It is our belief that the price of oil in international markets will be determined by world demand, the special position and interest of Saudi Arabia, and the availability (or lack thereof) of alternative supplies. These factors are treated in turn; first we wish to set oil at center stage.

The world is now primarily a fossil fuel economy and is likely to remain so throughout the lifetimes of readers of this volume.[3] Of the fossil fuels, oil is the premier fuel. The importance of oil can be measured in volumetric terms or in BTU's, but its dominance results from its ready availability, flexibility of use, transportability, and relatively low cost of production. Relative to the demands placed upon it, the supply of oil on a worldwide basis is and will remain plentiful for the foreseeable future. This is not to say that oil will be "cheap". Rather, there is no imminent or longer-run danger of physically "running out".[4] Contrary to the "doomsayers" propounding limits to growth, there appears to be sufficient oil, gas and coal resources in the world to support the progress of human society, in the 21st century and beyond, in ways that we may only dimly imagine.

The immediate primacy of oil also stems from the fact that existing price relationships, economic conditions and technology have made oil a more flexible fuel than natural gas or coal. It is possible to use oil, natural gas or coal in transportation, space and process heating, petrochemical feedstocks and electrical generation. In some applications, coal and natural gas have clear economic or technical advantages over oil. As relative prices and availability change, old relationships will alter and new technology will be developed. But no fuel has had the kind of flexibility across the broad spectrum of energy uses that has been enjoyed by oil. This flexibility is apt to continue. As a result, oil markets may be viewed as a bellwether for energy markets in general. If oil markets have fallen out of equilibrium due to structural changes or policy failures in important countries,[5] it can be expected that substantial spillover effects will be felt in other energy markets as well.

The purpose of this paper is to explore alternative explanations of the workings of the world oil market — in particular, the setting of the equilibrium price. Four alternatives are discussed. First, we deal with the "Cassandra" theory, which contends that the 1973 "oil shock" so distorted the world supply and demand picture that we today are following a totally unforeseen — and unpredictable — course.

One of the first official governmental recognitions of the shift in world oil supply and demand balances was embodied in the 1969-1970 work of the U.S. Cabinet Task Force on Oil Import Control (CTF). The beginning of the deterioration in Canadian-U.S. energy relations came out of that evaluation of U.S. import policy, although the CTF actively sought closer ties between the two countries.[6] We find that, somewhat surprisingly, U.S. oil supply and demand in 1975 is much as forecast in 1969 — despite a several-fold unforeseen increase in price. (While the gross accuracy of the CTF forecasts is fortuitously high, the national security implications of oil trade flows were only partially predicted.)

A second possible explanation for the workings of the world oil market is that the major multinational oil companies clandestinely and collusively determine the world oil price. We critically examine the view of two recent commentaries on the world oil market and the role of the major international oil companies. Public hostility toward the oil industry in general and the major oil companies in particular has been very real. The widely-circulated views of Anthony Sampson and Christopher Rand require consideration as both reflection of and reinforcement for the public opinion from which policy may be made. We find lacking in perception their explanations for both the recent oil price and their models for future country-company behavior.

Third, we develop what we believe to be a basic fact underlying the current world oil market — OPEC is not a cartel, because the prerequisite conditions for a cartel are not met. The major international oil companies do not "manage" the world supply of oil on OPEC's behalf.

Fourth, we discuss the dominant price leadership model as it applies to the world oil market, and conclude that it closely represents the facts as we now know them — with Saudi Arabia playing the dominant role. Finally, we discuss the implications of all of the above for future world energy prices.

Before the fall: a review of the import question
Operations of the future world oil market can be projected more readily with an understanding of the world oil market in the late 1960's. The United States President's Cabinet Task Force on Oil Import Controls (CTF), in its 1970 report,[7] described the market's operations in 1968 and projected future supply, demand and price through 1980. We describe here the reasoning and forecasts presented by the CTF, and relate them in rough terms to current supply, demand and price.

The worldwide market in 1969

Worldwide, there was a substantial surplus of productive capacity in 1969. Crude oil prices, then averaging $2.00 per barrel for Middle East crude landed in North America (or slightly over $3.50 in today's dollars), had declined in real terms over the previous decade. World demand and supply by region are shown in Table 1 below. The U.S. accounted for about one-third of "free world" supply, and a slightly higher proportion of demand. It is also interesting to note that the Western Hemisphere was largely self-sufficient.

TABLE 1
1968 Free World Oil Supply and Demand
(Million b/d)

	U.S.	Canada	Other Western Hemisphere	Eastern Hemisphere	Total Demand
U.S.	10.5	0.5	1.8	0.6	13.4
Canada	—	0.7	0.7	—	1.4
Other	—	—	2.5	15.1	17.6
Total Production	10.5	1.2	5.0	15.7	32.4

Notes: U.S. supply includes natural gas liquids. Production and demand data from *Basic Petroleum Data Book*, American Petroleum Institute, Washington, D.C.; trade flow estimated from CTF Report and *Basic Petroleum Data Book*.

The U.S. oil market

In 1968, the U.S. consumed 13.4 million barrels per day, produced 10.5 million barrels per day, and imported 2.9 million barrels per day, or 21.6 per cent of consumption. Of the 2.9 million barrels per day imported, 0.5 million barrels per day were imported from Canada, 1.8 million barrels per day were imported from other Western Hemisphere sources (primarily residual fuel oil from Venezuela), and only 0.6 million barrels per day were imported from the Eastern Hemisphere. (These relationships held true generally during the 1960's.) The wellhead price of U.S. crude oil in 1968 averaged approximately $3.00 per barrel, about 50 per cent higher than the cost of world oil landed in North America, due to the effect of U.S. oil import controls.

The imports to the U.S. were subject to an oil import quota program established in 1959. Imports into states east of the Rocky Mountains were set at 12.2 per cent of crude oil production within those districts; imports to states west of the Rockies were set annually to fill the gap between domestic production and demand at the then-market price, and residual fuel imports generally were uncontrolled. Imports were allocated to refiners as a percentage of their crude oil inputs, with special treatment provided to small refiners, petrochemical processors, and other special interest groups. The import quota program had been established in March 1959 by Presidential proclamation on the basis that national security might be impaired by the increase in oil imports projected through the 1960's. Gasoline and heating oil prices faced by consumers had declined in real terms for at least the preceding 15 years, as the following table shows. (This decline tracks closely the decline in the real price of crude oil in international markets.)

TABLE 2
Real U.S. Gasoline and Heating Oil Prices

	Retail Price of Regular Gasoline in 1967 ¢/U.S. Gal.	Retail Price of Home Heating Oil in 1967 ¢/U.S. Gal.
1950	37	N.A.
1955	36	19
1960	35	17
1965	33	17
1969	32	16

Source: Retail prices, consumer price index taken from *Basic Petroleum Data Book*, American Petroleum Institute, Washington, D.C., Section VI, Tables 4 and 5. Heating oil price shown for 1955 represents 1956 data.

The Canadian-U.S. oil trade

As noted above, Canada exported 0.5 million barrels per day of crude oil to the U.S. in 1968. These U.S. imports from Canada were exempt from oil import quotas, under an "overland" exemption which included Mexican imports as well. (A 1967 agreement between Canada and the U.S. established volume limits on Canadian imports to the U.S., but provided no enforcement mechanism. In fact, imports from Canada were included within the overall U.S. import quota ceiling, thereby diminishing the quota available to other producing countries.)

Canada produced about 1.2 million barrels per day of crude oil in 1968, and consumed about 1.4 million barrels per day. Because most of the Canadian production was (and is) located in western Canada, while population is centered in eastern Canada, transportation economics and the disparity between the higher U.S. price and the lower world price led to Canadian exports of 0.5 million barrels per day (to the U.S. midwest and far west), offset by Canadian imports of 0.7 million barrels per day (primarily from Venezuela).[8]

The Cabinet Task Force view of the mandatory oil import quota system

The CTF study was requested by the President because U.S. supply was seen to be declining (excluding potential production from Alaska, which was just being developed), and a substantial increase in imports into the U.S. was expected. The CTF completed the first analytical study of the world oil market by a U.S. government agency since the inception in 1959 of the mandatory oil import quota program. It sought and obtained from the public forecasts of future supplies and demand for oil, both with and without quotas or other protective programs, through 1980. The CTF's principal stated concerns were the United States' national security needs: to protect essential demand for oil and to prevent severe weakening of the national economy. Other considerations were: to achieve the above criteria at minimum cost to consumers; to maintain maximum flexibility of operation of the free market system; and to avoid negative foreign relations impacts of changes to the quota system.

The CTF report reached the following major conclusions:[9] while total abandonment of all oil import controls might threaten the U.S.'s security of supply, the CTF felt that some liberalization of import controls, phased in over a reasonable time period, would neither weaken the national security nor weaken the national economy substantially. Based on their assumptions about supply, demand and price, the CTF estimated that, even with substantial weakening of import controls, the U.S. could at that time withstand a one-year supply interruption of all imports from Eastern Hemisphere and Latin American producing countries. (The CTF presumed that Canadian supply was essentially as secure as U.S. production.)[10] They forecast even under this extreme circumstance only a modest deficit between supply and demand, which they felt could be met with some tolerable (10 per cent or less) level of rationing, or could be counterbalanced by maintenance of security storage.

Because of the change in the volume and sources of U.S. oil imports, the complete elimination of U.S. excess producing capacity and the lack of strategic security storage, the vulnerability of the U.S. to supply interruptions is now much greater. In addition, old assumptions about the security of Canadian supply of U.S. imports may no longer be appropriate.

Expectations of future supply embargoes and price changes

The CTF report assigned little probability of (political) upheaval in all or most of the exporting countries simultaneously. They noted that: "the growing number and diversity of their (the exporting countries) locations and interests also make it more difficult to achieve a prolonged concerted boycott for political or economic ends."[11] However, the CTF recognized that growth in oil production concentrated in the Arab states would require special attention. They noted that:

> "the Arab states might band together as they did briefly in 1967 to ban oil shipments to specified Western coun-

tries. . . .The probable duration of any such concerted action may, however, be limited by the difficulty of maintaining political cohesion in the face of sacrifice of immediately needed revenues and the risk of losing market share to exporters not participating in the boycott. Still, given the tensions in the area, the possibility of a prolonged and virtually total boycott cannot be ignored. We will focus our planning hypotheses on a 12-month Arab supply interruption, while also considering the effects of a longer and broader denial."[12]

The CTF did address and dismiss the establishment of an effective cartel. They further noted that the possibility of being forced to pay monopoly prices in the future did not appear to be a persuasive reason for paying an enhanced price — in the form of import quotas — at present. The CTF did not predict a "substantial price rise in world oil markets over the foreseeable future" for two reasons. [13] First, there was a decline in real costs predicted for tanker, domestic terminal, and refinery capacity. Declines in these costs presumably would offset any rise in real production costs that did occur. The CTF further noted that:

"whether (the producing countries) succeed in creating an effective price-raising cartel will, however, be largely independent of our import policy. No projected change in our imports over the next decade will be large enough in proportion to total world demand to affect significantly the incentive or ability to raise world prices."[14]

They further pointed out that exporting countries increased production taxes over the last eight years prior to 1969, and that the world oil market seemed likely to become more competitive in the future, as the growing number and diversity of producing countries made a cartel more difficult to organize and enforce.[15] The CTF concluded by noting that "a substantial increase in the price of foreign oil would tend to reduce both (1) the savings and (2) the decrease in domestic production-exploration that would otherwise attend the relaxation or abandonment of import restrictions."[16]

U.S. supply, demand and import forecasts

The demand and supply forecasts in terms of barrels per day of production and consumption which were made by the CTF were the central basis of its evaluation of the effect of embargoes on the U.S. national security and economy. As the following section will show, their forecasts appear to have been surprisingly accurate, given the length of time and the uncertainties which have resulted in the intervening six years.[17] (On the other hand, it is probably true that the forecasts turned out to be relatively right for the wrong reasons.)

U.S. demand in 1980 was projected to approximate 19 million barrels per day, trending upward from about 16 million barrels per day in 1975 (and compared with 13 million barrels per day in 1968). In fact, demand in 1975 approximated 15.9 million barrels per day — almost exactly on forecast.[18]

U.S. production in 1980 was estimated at 11-13.5 million barrels per day, depending on the 1980 price of crude oil. In 1975, production was estimated to range from 11.6-12.4 million barrels per day, including about one million barrels per day of Alaskan oil. Excluding Alaskan oil, production was expected to approximate 1968 production of 10.6 million barrels per day. Actual 1975 production (November 1975) approximated 9.8 million barrels per day, or about 0.8-1.6 million barrels per day below that forecast for 1975 (excluding Alaskan output). The CTF forecasts were based on prices of oil in 1975 of $2.50 to $3.30 in 1969 dollars, which translate to approximately $3.60 to $5.80 in today's dollars, based on adjustments for the loss of tax depletion benefits and for inflation.[19] Therefore, it appears that U.S. production has fallen only about 10 per cent below the forecasts for 1975, excluding Alaskan output — delays in which seem to be directly attributable to U.S. government decisions.[20]

Import forecasts for 1975 of 4.7 million barrels per day averaged only 0.1 million barrels per day below actual imports, excluding about 1.0 million barrels per day due to changes in the timing of Alaskan crude deliveries.[21] However, the source of actual 1975 U.S. imports has changed substantially from that forecast. The CTF forecast about 2.0 million barrels per day imports from Canada, the same from other Western Hemisphere sources, and the balance from the Eastern Hemisphere. In fact, through November 1975, Canadian imports averaged only about 0.6 million barrels per day.[22] Other Western Hemisphere imports approximated forecast levels. The shortfall in Canadian exports to the U.S. of 1.4 million barrels per day has been supplanted by an increase in U.S. imports of Middle East and African oil.

Conclusions from the above

It appears in retrospect that the Cabinet Task Force did propose reasonable forecasts of supply, demand, and imports for the price levels assumed. Further, actual supply, demand and imports have not differed substantially from those forecast, especially when allowance is made for changes in the timing of Alaskan crude production, and the effects and changes in tax laws and general price controls — unforeseen in 1969 — on exploration and development activity. Therefore, in volume terms current U.S. supply and demand was roughly foreseen in 1969, but not on the basis of accurate price assumptions. In particular, the CTF thought the emergence and continuing strength of a cartel unlikely. But the dominant fact in world energy markets has been the oil price revolution engineered by the OPEC countries. The Cabinet Task Force was not alone in misreading the future. The multinational companies and government agencies which made submissions to it, academics, and the general public were also taken by surprise. We suspect, from the vantage point of their expectations in 1970, that the OPEC countries themselves have also been surprised. Although the basic underpinnings are still economic, oil is now also a political variable. And, as evidenced by the divestiture debate in the United States, the companies have been caught up in the middle of the political controversy.

II. THE COMPANIES AND THE WORLD PRICE OF OIL

Of those large, vertically-integrated oil companies frequently designated as the "seven sisters," five — Exxon, Gulf, Texaco, Mobil and Standard of California — are U.S. firms. These companies — together with the other two "sisters" (Royal Dutch/Shell and British Petroleum) and a host of other companies of U.S. and other origins — are prominent in the world oil market. The world oil market has recently undergone substantial changes. The price of crude oil has risen by approximately five-fold since 1970.

The increase in the price of oil has been achieved as a result of the formation of what appears superficially to be an effective cartel of the OPEC countries. The mechanism which initially was used by the OPEC countries to increase price was the tax rate levied on oil produced in the member countries. Taxes determined prices and prices determined rents. Rents are now more directly determined by the price of the Saudi Arabian marker crude. Host country rents on oil have risen by a larger degree than have oil prices and constitute more than 100 per cent of the increment in prices. Perhaps even more importantly, the equity ownership in OPEC countries of oil reserves by multinational companies has been expropriated, leaving those companies basically service agents (albeit with a continuing small economic advantage).

Despite the obvious role of the OPEC countries in establishing world oil prices, and despite the contribution of public policy failures in the consuming countries which permitted OPEC to obtain – and maintain – the leverage it now enjoys,[23] some commentators have attempted to place the responsibility for the dramatic increase in the world price of oil directly upon the major international oil companies. In the United States, these charges have been likened even by industry critics to the vituperation suffered by some hapless souls during the McCarthy era when the real agents of our frustration were beyond our reach.[24] In addition, the major companies have been criticized for being poor diplomats, for being run by engineers, for being insensitive to the cultures of the host countries, and for caring more about their own profits and market success than about the price-determined rents of the host countries.[25] Whether true or not, these factors will have little effect upon the future of world oil prices.

Private diplomacy

The line of reasoning which attributes responsibility for the upheaval in the world price of oil to the companies follows two threads. First, the companies are accused of being inadequate negotiators and unskilled in the arts of diplomacy. Throughout *The Seven Sisters*, Sampson characterizes oil company executives in terms such as, "He was not a man of great international sensitivity,"[26] or "he had a sailor's internationalism, but without any real political sensitivity: the world was a market with no barriers or taboos,"[27] or "Exxon's dealings. . .revealed a good deal of the political naivete and arrogance of the oilmen,"[28] or "As it was, Exxon like most of the others remained ruled by Texas engineers with a sadly limited political vision."[29] This theme is echoed by Rand: "Hand in hand with the obduracy and deafness of the industry representatives went a real absence of diplomatic creativity,"[30] or ". . .the industry's innate weakness in communication and diplomacy."[31]

The thrust of these observations is that the companies, had they been more skilful, could have done something to prevent OPEC from realizing the market position it now enjoys. This implication is most directly stated by Rand: "The oil price and supply problems which have been visited upon the Western consumer in the 1970's owe much, in their distant inspiration, to the industry's failure to take uniform measures in the 1950's which would update and upgrade agreements which prevailed in the 1930's."[32] This is a conclusion with some impact. It may be true. But it suffers from a lack of specificity. There is not even speculation as to the steps to upgrade and update, how they would have worked, and how the results would have been better. The countries have shown themselves willing to break agreements when it was in their interest and power to do so. Absent alternative supplies, the companies' scope for negotiation was severely restricted.

The emphasis upon diplomatic failure is curious for at least two reasons. First, Sampson tells us that the United States had two conflicting Middle Eastern foreign policies during the quarter century which followed World War II — one with respect to Israel and one with respect to the Arabs.[33] He claims that the companies provided the buffer which made this dual policy possible. If the companies provided a quarter of a century of private negotiations which helped maintain an otherwise less tenable public posture, they would seem to have made a diplomatic success.

The second curious aspect of Sampson's criticism — which holds failure of the companies' private diplomatic skills as the key to the success of OPEC — is that it ignores the effect of a major intrusion of U.S. governmental diplomacy into the negotiations between the multinational companies and producing countries.[34] It is possible, even likely, that the changing balance of circumstances which resulted in the exercise of effective OPEC price policies was inevitable.[35] We will never know. What is certain, however, is that the confusion introduced into the negotiations by the public diplomats of the United States did not make things any less easy for OPEC.[36]

The companies as agents of OPEC?

The second thread in the attribution of responsibility to the companies for the surge in world oil prices is the assertion that the companies act as agents of OPEC. This assertion has itself two aspects. The first is undeniable: that the companies are tax collectors for OPEC. (The "taxes" are the rents determined by the price of oil.) As long as OPEC is successful in maintaining the world price of oil above "free market" levels, someone will be the tax collector. This is true whether the specific producing arrangements in the OPEC countries rely upon the present (mainly U.S.-based) international oil companies; companies from Japan, France or elsewhere; or national oil companies of the OPEC countries themselves. As long as the existing major oil companies provide the principal conduits through which OPEC oil reaches the consuming nations, they will be the principal tax collectors for the host governments. But the OPEC countries are the beneficiaries — substance rather than form is critical.

The second aspect of the assertion that the companies are agents of OPEC and hence responsible for the prevailing world oil prices is that the companies serve as the "prorationing" device for OPEC production.[37] For example, Sampson asserts: "To maintain this favoured status (with respect to access to OPEC oil), the international companies help proration the product on cutbacks among OPEC members,"[38] and "...the oil companies were really doing the countries' rationing for them."[39] Sampson's attribution of responsibility for cementing OPEC together, which helps maintain the world price of oil, has been reinforced by the statements (not impartial) of the Shah of Iran: "With the sisters controlling everything, once they accepted, everything went smoothly."[40] These are strong statements, but they are incorrect.

The "sisters" do not control everything. They now control relatively little. In the past the companies owned substantial interests in oil production in the OPEC countries. Their equity interests resulted from the traditional concession, royalty and tax arrangement which then existed. These relationships have changed. First royalties and then taxes began to take larger and larger fractions of the per-barrel price of crude oil. In addition the old concession agreements were replaced by nationalization and participation arrangements.[41] The companies now in general act simply as service contractors and are paid a modest fee per barrel for their technical contribution. It is in the countries' interest to acquire technical services at the lowest possible cost and to earn the highest possible net price on the crude oil production which is demanded of them. It is in the companies' interest to receive the highest possible remuneration for the services they provide and, in order to be more competitive in final product markets, to satisfy their crude oil requirements at the lowest possible laid in, tax paid price. Rather than a convergence of interests in which the companies act as agents of the OPEC countries, the changes in the country-company relations which have developed over recent years have replaced one set of tensions between the companies and the countries with another.[42]

The price system

The restrictive mechanism is not a prorationing system administered by the companies. The restrictive mechanism is the price system. The countries determine price. Price rations demand. The OPEC countries have established prices which are an approximation of the monopoly price. All the oil which the consuming nations desire is available at the present price. As a result of price-induced reductions in quantity demanded and temporary negative shifts in demand caused by the world recession, idle tankers have been laid up all over the world — including the Persian Gulf.[43] There is no evidence that any potential buyer who wishes today to load a tanker with oil at the going OPEC price is denied access to oil. The notion of a company-operated prorationing system is false.

High prices, given general economic conditions, restrict the quantity of oil demanded from the OPEC countries — individually and in aggregate. This restrictive mechanism has not been perfect, but it has been adequate for the job it had to do. Changes in freight rates due to the tanker surplus and price differentials reflecting the quality of oil available from various countries have shifted demand across countries, as companies searched for the minimum net cost of their oil supplies.[44] But mutual self-interest among the OPEC countries, together with the threat of and capacity for Saudi Arabian retaliation in the case of a price break, have been sufficient to maintain discipline.[45] Now, as the world recession ends and industrial recovery proceeds, world oil demand growth — for which the major OPEC producing countries are the residual suppliers — appears sufficient to maintain the world price structure.

The lack of alternative sources of supply is the fact which permits the OPEC countries to maintain price. Anyone who firmly predicts world oil prices is treading a very slippery limb. But if there is to be a break in nominal prices, or continued erosion of real prices, non-OPEC supplies must become available. Critical to the availability of alternative supplies is the time required to turn resources and reserves into realized productive capacity.

Alternative supplies

The development of crude oil producing capacity is expensive and time-intensive. These characteristics are accentuated as incremental sources of supply are provided increasingly from more and more hostile and formidable environments. Deep water exploration and sea bottom well completions in the Gulf of Mexico and offshore California are two of the technical problems the industry faces. Severe weather, operating and logistic problems in onshore Alaska and the Canadian Arctic are others. The Canadian Arctic islands, the Gulf of Alaska and the North Sea combine offshore, deep water and hostile conditions in an often multiplicative fashion. The U.S. Atlantic Outer Continental Shelf is an unproven area with no readily-available base of logistic support. The offshore areas of Southeast Asia are politically risky. Increased output through application of enhanced recovery techniques to known producing areas is technically immature and complicated by price controls in the United States and tax policies in Canada. The best current examples of the cost and time-intensiveness required to develop alternative, non-OPEC sources of supply are Prudhoe Bay and the North Sea.[46]

If alternative supplies of crude oil can be made available from non-OPEC sources which have a lower long-term laid-in cost than OPEC crude oil, the companies would have an incentive to find, develop and produce such supplies.[47] OPEC in general and Saudi Arabia in particular appear to have the greatest potential to add to world crude oil supply at little cost.[48] In addition, the OPEC countries have the advantage that the cost to the companies of OPEC oil, on average, is primarily economic rent accruing to the countries — which can be adjusted administratively to meet changing competitive conditions. The typical cost of non-OPEC oil has on average a much higher component of real resource costs — which are not amenable to administrative modification.[49]

Such a juxtaposition of real resource and administratively-determined costs creates risks in the event of a break in the world price of oil.[50] Nevertheless, conditional on their expectations concerning the stability of the OPEC price, the companies appear to be allocating relative world-wide investment expenditures for exploration and production on the basis of the potential for greater margins in non-OPEC areas. In the years prior to 1971, when OPEC sources of incremental production were relatively more attractive on a cost basis, the share of company total worldwide exploration and production investment expenditures allocated to increasing capacity in primarily OPEC countries increased by over 50 per cent, from 20 to 33 per cent.[51] The share of worldwide new crude oil capacity investment of the U.S., Canada and Europe fell from 80 per cent to 67 per cent. Since 1971, the pendulum has swung the other way. The share of worldwide investments to increase crude oil capacity expended in primarily OPEC countries fell from 33 per cent in 1971 to 23 per cent in 1974, while investments in the U.S., Canada and Europe have increased correspondingly.[52]

It is too early to predict with confidence the effect of this reallocation of relative effort on the world price of oil. Investments outside of the Persian Gulf typically have lower productivity (in terms of the increment to capacity per unit of expenditure) than do investments in the Persian Gulf. For reasons to be discussed below, we do not expect a near-term break in the world price of oil. But the allocation of capital investment supports the contention that the international companies[53] — rather than being agents of OPEC — are searching actively worldwide for those circumstances which generate the maximum advantage. Because these circumstances involve the creation of alternative, non-OPEC supplies, and because the creation of such supplies is in conflict with the interests of OPEC, the companies' exploration activity adds to country-company tension. Even if new, non-OPEC oil is found in substantial quantities, its effect on world oil prices will depend on the growth of world demand,[54] and the economic structure of OPEC. To this latter we now turn.

III. THE ECONOMIC STRUCTURE AND BEHAVIOR OF OPEC

OPEC is commonly thought of as a cartel. OPEC talks like a cartel and the world price of oil has taken the same kind of jump that it would have if an effective OPEC cartel were in operation. But OPEC is not a cartel. In our opinion, the economic structure and behavior of OPEC is best described as that typified by a dominant price leadership model and the dominant price leader is Saudi Arabia.[55]

Cartelization

A cartel raises price by restricting output. The restriction of output is a result of concerted and coordinated action on the part of the cartel members. Price determines total demand for the product, but price does not act as the rationing mechanism which allocates sales among the cartel members. Sales are allocated among cartel members on the basis of a quota or prorationing system which is agreed upon by the cartel members. The quota system may be specified in terms of percentage market shares, physical units of output, assignment of particular customers or regional markets, or some combination of all of these arrangements. The basis for the quota system is usually historical market share of the producing capacity of the individual cartel members. Historical market share and producing capacity are, of course, usually closely related.

Because the cartelized price exceeds the marginal cost of production for the members of a cartel, there is a strong incentive for the members of a cartel to cheat on the cartel price. The cartel price is maintained (in a stable cartel) as a result of the restriction of total cartel output which the quota system creates. Cheating by one of the cartel members initially increases that cartel member's market share at the expense of the other members of the cartel. The ability of any cartel member to increase market share is limited by that member's production capacity. The cheating may take the form of secret price concessions, enhancement of product quality, delivery or credit terms, service arrangements, etc. But as cheating, particularly price cheating, is detected, other cartel members retaliate in kind to protect their market shares. The result is a breakdown in the quota system, a scramble for market position and a collapse of the cartel.

Even when the price remains stable, there are internal dynamics at work which affect the behavior of individual cartel members. Of particular interest is the case in which the quota system is based upon physical production capacity or investment in plant and equipment. Because price exceeds the long-run marginal cost of adding production capacity, and because each cartel member's quota is a lagged function of capacity, there are strong incentives to add capacity. These incentives operate in two ways. First, if no other members of the cartel increase capacity, and if the capacity-based determination of individual members' quotas is enforced, then that member which adds capacity increases market share at the expense of the other members, but without cheating on price. Second, if each cartel member expects every other cartel member to behave in the manner just described, then all cartel members have a defensive motive to add capacity to maintain market share. The result of such behavior is growth in total cartel capacity relative to demand at the cartel price. Greater total excess capacity contributes to potential instability because it results in greater potential for and fear of cheating.

Because the quota system may be at best a fragile thing, the redetermination of quotas based upon changes in capacity may introduce considerable tension into the internal operation and decision-making processes of the cartel. In addition, when there are differences in marginal costs among cartel members, various cartel members may desire different cartel prices. Different cartel prices result in different restrictions of output and more or less restrictive quota systems. The problem of determining jointly a cartel price and a system to ration output is further complicated if the members of the cartel do not produce exactly the same product — perceptions of the response of market demand to price changes may vary among cartel members. All of these factors contribute to internal tension within the cartel and may result in long-run cartel instability.

The hallmarks of an effective cartel are a price which exceeds the competitive price, a quota system to ration output, and relatively stable market shares. OPEC meets only one of these criteria — a price in excess of the competitive price. It has been correctly observed by Sampson and others that OPEC has no quota or prorationing system.[56] The OPEC countries do not assign rates of output among themselves based upon historical market shares, capacity or any other criterion. In addition, market shares among the OPEC countries are quite volatile. Table 3 shows the pattern of year to year percentage changes in output for prominent OPEC countries with production in excess of one million barrels per day. These countries account for about 90 per cent of OPEC output, nearly half of world output, and still larger fractions of both OPEC and world capacity. Because total world output did not vary a great deal for the period in question,[57] these percentage changes in actual output may be regarded as close proxies for percentage changes in market shares.

TABLE 3
Percentage Changes in Annual Rates of Output
for Prominent OPEC Countries

	1974/1973	1975/1974	1976/1975*
Venezuela	-11.3%	-21.2%	-19.2%
Abu Dhabi	7.9	-0.3	48.5
Iran	3.3	-11.1	-5.3
Iraq	-6.0	19.9	-5.8
Kuwait	-16.3	-19.3	-13.7
Saudi Arabia	10.7	-16.6	19.5
Indonesia	5.2	-5.8	17.6
Algeria	-5.6	-7.3	10.3
Libya	-30.9	-2.2	79.0
Nigeria	12.0	-20.8	11.3

Source: *Oil and Gas Journal, loc. cit.*
  *First four months only.

One conclusion is clear from Table 3. Over the period since the revolution in the world price of oil, the market shares of the prominent OPEC countries have not been stable. For all but Kuwait and Venezuela there have been swings in both directions. These are the kinds of market share swings one would expect without an explicit quota system to allocate total output among countries. But the world price of oil has been very stable. The swings in market shares have not destabilized the price.

The absence of a quota system administered by OPEC, and the resulting wide swings in market shares, make the cartel model for the economic organization of OPEC highly dubious. Sampson and others have argued that the companies do the prorationing for OPEC and operate an implicit quota system. But it seems highly unlikely that the countries would tolerate a company-administered quota system which involved such instability and wide swings in market shares. We believe that there is a much simpler explanation for the success of OPEC. This explanation is that the structure and behavior of OPEC is best characterized by the dominant price leadership model; Saudi Arabia is the balance wheel of the system.

Dominant firm price leadership[58]

Dominant firm price leadership, as with a cartel, also results in a restriction of output. But unlike a cartel, the restriction is passive rather than active. No quota system is required. There is no explicit allocation of market shares among firms. Concerted and coordinated action to prorate output is not a part of the behavior pattern because it is unnecessary. The dominant firm, or balance wheel of the system, takes up the slack.

In the classic textbook treatment of the dominant price leadership model, the dominant firm is usually assumed for convenience to be both the lowest cost and largest firm. This assumption is true for Saudi Arabia — Saudi Arabia is both the largest and lowest cost OPEC producer.[59] The mode of operation of the dominant price leader is to estimate total market demand at various prices, calculate what will be supplied by other firms at those prices, and then derive a residual demand schedule which it (the dominant price leader) faces at the various alternative prices considered. This residual demand schedule is the difference between total demand and what is supplied by others at each price. In the classic textbook example, the dominant price leader chooses a price upon the basis of a formal equation of marginal costs and the marginal revenue function derived from the residual demand schedule.

Because turmoil and trauma have characterized the world oil market over the past few years, the pure formalism of the dominant price leader model is less relevant than is its underlying rationale. This rationale has two important aspects. First, the dominant price leader is just what the name implies. By virtue of low production cost and high excess capacity, the dominant price leader is able to make stick that price which it desires. Second, and closely related to the first, the dominant price leader is the supplier of last resort. In choosing to act as the passive balance wheel, the dominant price leader must be willing to absorb substantial decreases in output when the others supply more. And, if the dominant price leader is to make the chosen price stick, it must also be prepared to meet market demands which others are unable or unwilling to meet at the established price.

Between 1974 and 1975, total world oil output fell by just under 2.9 million barrels per day as a result of the world recession and in response to higher prices. This was a net reduction. Output from some countries increased, while that of other countries decreased. The most significant increases were the U.S.S.R., Iraq, Communist China, Mexico and Norway.[60] Total OPEC output decreased by about 3.4 million barrels per day. Saudi Arabian output decreased by just over 1.4 million barrels per day. The decrease in Saudi output accounted for just over 40 per cent of the net OPEC reduction in output, just under half of the total net world reduction in output, and nearly three-quarters of the non-Communist world net output reduction.[61]

Over the first four months of 1976, total world oil output increased by 2.5 million barrels per day, compared to the same period in 1975. OPEC output increased by approximately 2.0 million barrels per day, and non-Communist world output increased by about 1.7 million barrels per day.[62] Saudi Arabian output increased by almost 1.3 million barrels per day during the first four months of 1976. The

Saudi increase in output accounted for over three-quarters of the non-Communist world increase in output, about two-thirds of the OPEC increase in output and over half of the total world increase in output.

There is a great deal of "jitter" in the country by country changes in output rates. (See, for example, Table 3.) This "jitter" is associated partly with the political and economic trauma and turmoil which accompanied the embargo and the establishment of a new world oil price regime and partly with quality differences associated with shifts in products demand. But we believe that the overall pattern is what is important. The overall pattern is that Saudi Arabia is the balance wheel. If Norway, Mexico, Iraq, the U.S.S.R. and Communist China increase output by an aggregate total of over 1.6 million barrels per day during a period in which world demand is falling (1975), Saudi Arabia must be (and is) prepared to complement the natural decline in production in such established sources of supply as Canada, Venezuela and the United States by accepting a smaller demand for its output. If world demand increases, Saudi Arabia has shown itself willing to offset the natural decline in some areas, and supplement the increases from others, by providing a residual source of supply which allows total supply to meet demand at the going market price. And the going market price is determined by the Saudi price. Table 4 shows one projection of the swing in Saudi Arabian oil exports, in 1976 and 1980, under two assumptions: (1) 1974 market share is preserved and (2) the revenue needs of poorer OPEC countries are satisfied prior to setting Saudi output. The difference is severe. Of more interest, however, is the comparison between 1976 actual production and either of the hypothetical exports. (For most of the OPEC countries, local consumption is small.) There is "jitter". Although the first four months' results for 1976 are closer to the 1974 market share projection, neither of the scenarios precisely match actual behavior.[63] This is consistent with our feeling that there is no well-defined formula, quota or prorationing system which allocates production among OPEC countries. Saudi Arabia sets the price for the marker crude, world demand develops as a result of price and other factors, other countries offer output at the marker price, and Saudi Arabia makes up the difference.[64]

TABLE 4
OPEC Exports by Country
(Million b/d)

	Actual 4 Mos. 1976 (production)	Projected 1976		Projected 1980	
		1974 Market Share	Meet Poor Countries' Revenue Needs	1974 Market Share	Meet Poor Countries' Revenue Needs
Saudi Arabia	7.8	7.9	4.7	8.2	2.4
Venezuela	2.1	2.0	2.1	1.1	2.0
Libya	1.8	1.3	1.3	1.1	1.1
Algeria	1.0	0.9	0.9	0.9	0.8
Kuwait	1.7	2.0	2.3	1.2	2.0
Nigeria	2.0	2.2	2.4	2.4	3.2
Iran	5.3	5.1	6.3	4.6	5.8
Iraq	2.0	1.7	2.3	1.9	2.6
Indonesia	1.5	1.3	1.6	1.7	3.3
Other	2.7	2.3	2.7	2.6	2.5
Total	27.9	26.7	26.6	25.7	25.7

Source: *Oil and Gas Journal*, June 28, 1976, p. 206, and Data Resources, Inc., *DRI Energy Outlook. Special Analysis: Trends in the World Price of Oil 1975-1980* (Lexington, Mass.: August 1975), Tables 7A and 7B, p. 14.

The balance wheel role of the Saudis as dominant price leader places them in a special position relative to world demand. The dominant price leader faces the residual demand schedule, and the residual demand schedule is much more sensitive to price than is the total world demand schedule. Increases in price affect the demand for Saudi oil — as the supplier of last resort — in two ways. First, at higher prices, world demand is less than at lower prices. Second, at higher prices, the supply of oil from other countries is higher than at lower prices. These two factors cut the demand for Saudi oil in a double-edged fashion. As a result, strictly on the basis of self-interest, one would expect to see the Saudis much more reluctant to raise prices than other OPEC countries. This is a direct behavioral prediction from the dominant price leader model. It is also what we have observed.[65] The internal OPEC price determination process may be summed up as: Amouzegar proposes, Yamani disposes. It is not by accident that the OPEC marker crude is Saudi Arabian light.

There is a final aspect of Saudi behavior which requires consideration — the recent drive of the Saudis to create considerable excess capacity. We believe that there are three reasons for this action. First, as dominant price leader, the Saudis must be willing and able to meet or accommodate swings in world demand in *both* directions. If the Saudis as price leader are going to make their decisions hold, they must be prepared not only to accept substantial reductions in output but be ready and able as well to satisfy increases in demand at the going price. This is what we have observed.

Second, the Saudis must also be prepared to retaliate if some OPEC country (no other countries today have enough in-place excess capacity even to consider it) significantly breaches the OPEC price. The Saudis must be prepared to finish what any other country may start — to the detriment of all. This is the oil equivalent of a "nuclear deterrent" strategy. The Saudis are in such a position, and presumably have carefully explained on a private basis what the consequences of rash action would be.

Third, history can be a great teacher. One of the motivating forces in the organization and cohesion of OPEC has been an abiding discontent that for years world oil policy was United States policy. This discontent was exacerbated by the fact that most of the international oil companies are American companies. The United States was able to make world oil policy its own policy. Competition among American oil companies, by playing off each company's alternative sources of supply against the others', reduced world oil prices in real terms as long as the United States had — or was perceived to have — substantial excess producing capacity in total. It is doubtful that this historical detail has been lost on the Saudis. The question is, at what price level do the Saudis wish to maintain sufficient excess capacity to exercise a dominant price leadership position. This depends upon what the actual residual demand for Saudi oil (and how the Saudis perceive that demand), but it is also a question with political implications — both within and without OPEC.

IV. CONCLUSIONS

The shift in supply sources and growth in demand which led to the current organization of the world oil market began to be recognized in the late 1960's. But such observers as the U.S. Cabinet Task Force on Oil Import Control did not anticipate the oil price revolution, despite their surprisingly accurate (in volume terms) predictions of present supply and demand. It is the relative insensitivity of oil demand to price, together with the absence of alternative non-OPEC supplies, which fostered and sustains the price revolution.

The absence of alternative supplies does not suggest that the world is running out of oil; there is no danger of that. But the price of world oil will change only as a function of the timing and magnitude of alternative supplies. The multinational companies are diversifying their worldwide search for oil, but the discovery and development of new sources of oil is uncertain, costly and time-intensive. (And we do not pass lightly over the potential for surprise.) The multinational companies are viewed by many as the agents of OPEC, but this is incorrect. It is true that the companies are the conduits through which pass the OPEC countries' price-determined rents, but the allegations that the companies somehow operate a prorationing system which allocates output by quota among the OPEC countries are wrong. The price determination process is much simpler.

In our opinion, the central fact in the world oil market is the position of Saudi Arabia as the dominant OPEC price leader. OPEC is a cartel in name only. The dominant price leadership model describes the general behavior of OPEC countries' market shares, the specific pattern of variation in Saudi output and market share, and the Saudi pricing strategy. In an ironic sense, the CTF dismissal of the possibility of an effective OPEC cartel was correct. A common statement is that the OPEC cartel has weathered the recent world recession and therefore can be expected to be stable for the foreseeable future. A more accurate statement is that Saudi leadership has been tempered in both political and economic fires and found equal to the test.

The Saudis' task was made easier by the behavior of some OPEC member countries, and complicated by the behavior of other countries — both members and nonmembers of OPEC. But in both retrospect and prospect, the Saudis occupy the pivotal position. Had the development of Alaska or the North Sea been accelerated, had U.S. oil and natural gas prices been allowed to reach market clearing levels so that U.S. demands for world oil were reduced and supplies increased, had Canadian potential lived up to expectations, or had various countries behaved differently, the Saudi task would have been more difficult. We will never know how far the Saudis would have been willing under different circumstances to see their output and market share decline to maintain the world price. What we do know is that, under the circumstances which did obtain, the Saudis accepted sufficient contraction to establish their leadership and prevent price erosion. And the Saudis appear to have sufficient capacity to meet incremental world demand.

The future price of oil depends upon the Saudis' ability to continue in their role of dominant price leader. This ability in turn depends upon the growth of world demand, potential Saudi producing capacity, the availability of alternative supplies of oil, and the development and adoption of substitutes for oil. In our opinion, the Saudis will remain in control for more than a few years. World demand is recovering and conservation even if successful will only slow the growth in demand. Alternative low-cost oil supplies do not appear to be available soon enough and in sufficient magnitude to test the Saudis more severely than they have already been tested, but predictions of new supplies of oil should be humbly made. The development and adoption of high-cost substitutes for oil are long-term phenomena and are likely to be a response to the price of oil rather than a major price–determining factor. Policy discussion in the United States is focused upon the irrelevant (in terms of increases in either energy supply or competition in the U.S. or world energy markets) vertical divestiture and horizontal disintegration debate. In this environment the world price of oil appears steady in at least nominal terms. The world price of oil may be indexed to reflect inflation, but effective indexing will be implemented only to the extent that it is in the Saudis' self-interest.

Notes

[1]S. 2387, "The Petroleum Industry Competition Act of 1975". Proponents of the vertical divestiture legislation often are not specific about the number of companies they expect to be affected, but 18 integrated companies are commonly cited. That the number is so large in itself is casual evidence concerning the competitiveness of the industry. Because so many refiners and producers own some pipelines, the actual number of companies potentially affected may be on the order of 50 or more.

The vertical divestiture proposal is often compared to the Supreme Court decree of 1911 which broke up the Standard Oil Trust and created so many of the corporate entities that now are the major oil companies. But there is a striking difference. The 1911 Court decision did not prohibit the severed companies from organizing themselves individually as they chose. Those companies which survived, prospered and grew generally did so on a vertically-integrated basis. (See Arthur M. Johnson, "Lessons of the Standard Oil Divestiture", in Edward J. Mitchell, editor, *Vertical Integration in the Oil Industry*, Washington: American Enterprise Institute, 1976), pp. 191-214). The proposed U.S. divestiture legislation, rather than breaking up a trust, dismembers a large number of companies — many of which have no historical Standard Oil origins — and prohibits them by statute from attempting to regain any efficiencies of their former vertically-integrated organization by regrouping *via* merger, acquisition, internal growth or contract.

[2]See, for example, the argument and data presented in *The Petroleum Industry-Vertical Integration*, Hearings before the Sub-committee on Anti-trust and Monopoly of the Committee on the Judiciary, United States Senate, Ninety-fourth Congress, first session (Washington: U.S. Government Printing Office, 1976); and E.W. Erickson and R.M. Spann, "The U.S. Petroleum Industry", *The Energy Question*, Vol. 2, pp. 5-24 (Toronto: University of Toronto, 1974).

This view seems gradually to be prevailing. The proponents of divestiture less and less seem to argue about domestic competition, and more and more contend that divestiture would operate to restrain further OPEC price increases or to reduce OPEC prices, as a result of increased buying pressures from the newly-created class of nonintegrated refiners who would bargain for the best crude oil purchase terms.

Given that "participation" and nationalization of crude oil reserves by most OPEC countries have effectively disintegrated a large portion of the majors' refinery capacity, if nonintegrated refiners are good bargainers, we should see the results of their buying without divestiture.

[3]It is likely that in 1976 the world will derive more useful energy from the combustion of wood, charcoal and animal dung than from nuclear fission. Even the most optimistic proponents of nuclear energy, solar and other alternative energy sources assign them relatively modest potential contributions even by the year 2000. Because oil, gas and coal are ultimately in finite supply, substitute forms must *sometime* replace them as our principal sources of energy. But the time at which we derive as much as 50 per cent of our energy from other than fossil fuels appears to us to be at least two generations away.

[4]In this regard, one must distinguish between resources and proved reserves. Proved reserves are the shelf inventory of developed resources which the industry finds it worthwhile to hold to support current production. Because proved reserves cost money to develop, there is always an incentive to hold as small a stock as feasible to facilitate actual output. Resources include undeveloped potentials such as the Athabasca tar sands, the Venezuelan heavy oil tar belt, undrilled areas in the Persian Gulf countries, and enhanced recovery from conventional fields.

[5]For a discussion of policy failures in the United States which contributed to the OPEC oil price revolution, see the editors' introductions to *The Energy Question, op. cit.* Shortly after the several-fold increase of world oil prices, U.S. coal and natural gas (intrastate) prices rose sharply to maintain inter-fuel competitiveness.

[6]J.W. McKie, Chief Economist to the CTF, refers to the needless discord in Canadian-U.S. energy relations fostered by the Nixon administration's treatment of import policy as "one of the great bonehead plays of history". See J.W. McKie, "Erickson and Waverman's *The Energy Question*", *Bell Journal of Economics*, Vol. 6, No. 2 (Autumn, 1975), pp. 720-723. Further, the failure of U.S. policymakers in 1971 to anticipate the demand for Alaskan oil in the U.S. Midwest, suggesting a trans-Canada rather than an Alaskan oil pipeline, may have been equally a "bonehead play". See statement of Herbert S. Winokur, Jr. in "Minutes of Proceedings and Evidence of the Special Committee on Environmental Pollution", House of Commons, Third Session, Twenty-eighth Parliament, May 18, 1971, Information Canada (Ottawa). The same issues are now being discussed relative to gas pipelines.

[7]Cabinet Task Force on Oil Import Control, *The Oil Import Question: A Report on the Relationship of Oil Imports to the National Security* (Washington: U.S. Government Printing Office, February 1970). Hereafter "CTF Report".

[8]This pattern of movement was bolstered by the Canadian National Oil Policy instituted in 1961. In its absence, Canadian prices could have been lower, and some sort of export tax might have been required on movements to the United States, whose prices were above world prices. See J.G. Debanne, "Oil and Canadian Policy", *The Energy Question, op. cit.* for a discussion of the history of and rationale for the Canadian "production-exports-imports triangle". Should Canadian Arctic exploration be successful, and should U.S. support of high-cost domestic production lead again to U.S. oil import quotas, we would not be surprised to see the triangle reappear.

[9]Other important conclusions of the CTF were the following. First, the program operated at a substantial annual cost to consumers — about $5 billion in 1969 dollars. (Consumers paid more money to domestic producers, landholders, etc., than they would have been required to pay to purchase the same volumes of crude oil from foreign producers at world prices.)

Second, if quotas were continued, as much as $1.5-2.0 billion annually in 1980 would be invested in domestic oil production which would not have been invested under a free market system, thereby creating "efficiency losses."

Third, the fixed quota program bore no reasonable relationship to requirements for protection either of the national economy or of essential oil consumption. Administrative inconsistencies, arbitrary restrictions, and many special arrangements imposed costs and inefficiencies without associated benefits to both consumers and the economy.

202

[10]"In each situation, we consider the U.S. and Canada together, because of the existence of an integrated transportation network and the likelihood that the two countries would consult closely during a crisis" and "On the other hand, there may be reason to consider Canada more reliable than any other foreign supplier - because of present and potential common energy policies...." (CTF Report, pp. 59 and 70.)

[11]*Ibid.*, p. 33.

[12]*Ibid.*, p. 34.

[13]*Ibid.*, p. 20.

[14]*Ibid.*, p. 21.

[15]The CTF, relying heavily on Canadian National Energy Board forecasts, felt that Canada's output could exceed 5 million barrels per day by 1980 (excluding tar sands production). The consensus now is quite different. See, for example, the forecasts presented in *Proceedings of the Conference on The Economics of Oil and Gas Self-Sufficiency in Canada*, The Department of Economics, University of Calgary, Calgary, Alberta, Oct. 8-9, 1975. Hereafter, "Proceedings".

[16]CTF, *op. cit.*, p. 21.

[17]The authors, having participated directly in the CTF work, may not have a totally unbiased view. The acid test is a comparison of what the CTF would have predicted had they anticipated the price increase in real terms and other factors. As is so often the case with acid tests, there is no way to know. As we note in more detail below, however, there seems to be a remarkable insensitivity across forecasts to price assumptions.

[18]The CTF forecasts represented simple extrapolations of the actual demand figures in 1968. The growth rate assumed was 3.0 per cent per year, the average of the growth rates of forecasts submitted to the CTF by major oil companies and other interested parties. It should be noted that the actual growth from 1968 through 1975 consisted of several years of very much higher than 3.0 per cent growth, coupled with two years of demand reductions and lower growth rates.

[19]The controlled lower tier, or "old oil" price in the United States represents a *decrease* in economic incentives to maintain production through investments for enhanced recovery relative to the economic incentives which existed in 1969. Without the unforeseen price rises for that oil which has qualified for them, actual production would have been lower. Therefore, the CTF estimates essentially are too high, but the degree of supply elasticity exhibited has been much less than expected, partly through price expectation distortions, lags and other possibly more fundamental geological and cost aspects.

[20]The CTF estimates of production were based on independent work, but were supported by estimates submitted by major oil companies. As the CTF noted, the dispersion among the estimates was not wide, and the estimates appear to have been based on careful structural analysis of geological facts, economic costs, and other factors. The CTF declined to forecast production levels past 1980, as well as to forecast additions to supply which might result from prices higher than the 1969 real price levels. But what is important about the above is that actual production in 1975 did not fall sharply outside the range forecast, especially given that price expectations in the U.S. probably have been severely depressed as a result of continu-

ing price controls and government policy uncertainty since 1971. The real ceiling price of price-controlled, lower-tier crude oil in the United States (net of the loss of percentage depletion) is about 20 per cent below the $3.30 reference price in 1969 dollars.

[21] Actual U.S. imports in 1975 averaged 5.8 million barrels per day. Had Alaskan oil been available in forecast quantities, U.S. imports would have averaged about 4.8 million barrels per day.

[22] The announced Canadian policy is to reduce oil exports to the U.S. to zero by 1981-82. The start-up of the Sarnia-Montreal extension of Interprovincial Pipeline facilitates achievement of this policy, although the policy may not be the most efficient in the context of North American energy needs. Because it changes U.S. and Canadian supply and demand interdependence, the Sarnia-Montreal extension also complicates diplomatic considerations concerning planning for potential supply interruptions and pipeline routes for Arctic oil and gas.

[23] See editors' introduction, pp. vi-xxv, *The Energy Question*, Vol. 1, *op. cit.*

[24] See M.A. Adelman, *Statement* before the Subcommittee on Multinational Corporations of the United States Senate Committee on Foreign Relations, January 29, 1975.

[25] See, for example, Anthony Sampson, *The Seven Sisters: The Great Oil Companies and the World They Shaped* (New York: Viking, 1975) and Christopher T. Rand, *Making Democracy Safe for Oil, Oilmen and the Islamic East* (Boston: Atlantic-Little, Brown, 1975). We will here use the Sampson and Rand books as typical examples of these arguments.

[26] Sampson, p. 156.

[27] Sampson, p. 81.

[28] Sampson, p. 69.

[29] Sampson, p. 310.

[30] Rand, p. 228.

[31] Rand, p. 331.

[32] Rand, pp. 341-2.

[33] Sampson, p. 100.

[34] See, for example, M.A. Adelman, *The World Petroleum Market*, Erickson and Waverman, *op. cit.*, p. 540, especially pp. 18-20.

[35] See, for example, Erickson and Waverman, *op. cit.*, pp. vii-xxv; James T. Jensen, "International Oil-Shortage, Cartel or Emerging Resource Monopoly?" *Vanderbilt Journal of Transnational Law*, Vol. 7 (Spring, 1974), pp. 335-81, and James Akins, "The Oil Crisis: This Time the Wolf is Here", *Foreign Affairs*, Vol. 51, No. 3 (April 1973), pp. 462-490.

[36] A good history of the confusion and "defeatism" introduced by U.S. public diplomats is presented in *Forbes*, April 15, 1976, pp. 69-85. *Forbes* concluded about James Akins, former U.S. Ambassador to Saudi Arabia and previously White House Staff Advisor on Energy, that "James E. Akins never seemed quite sure whether he was U.S. Ambassador to Saudi Arabia or Saudi Arabian Ambassador to the U.S."

[37]The term "prorationing" derives from a policy that was practiced in the United States by state conservation agencies in Texas, Louisiana, and several other states, and in Canada by Albertan authorities. This policy, called "market demand prorationing", restricted the output of the companies operating in these states and provinces. The rationale was to restrict supply to market demand at the going market price. Because the states and provinces which practiced market demand prorationing were the major producing areas, the restrictions were effective in supporting the North American market price. The U.S. price was further supported by the insulation which mandatory import quotas provided from the world market. In the United States, crude oil output was restricted by the establishment of "allowables" which determined permissible monthly production on a well-by-well basis. Because the practice of determining market demand and setting allowables was administered by the same agencies which were responsible for well-spacing and other regulations, it was called "conservation" regulation. But there is considerable evidence that the administrative mechanism of market demand prorationing actually resulted in considerable waste of other resources through excess drilling. See J.W. McKie and S.L. McDonald, "Petroleum Conservation in Theory and Practice", *Quarterly Journal of Economics*, Vol. LXXVI (February 1962), pp. 98-121; and M.A. Adelman, "Efficiency of Resource Use in Crude Petroleum", *Southern Economic Journal*, Vol. XXXI (October 1964), pp. 101-122. This waste resulted because in the major U.S. producing states, wells rather than reservoirs were regarded as the units of production for "conservation" purposes. Canadian reforms ended this form of waste in 1964. There was no explicit coordination of production rates between Texas and Louisiana, but the U.S. federal government cooperated in the restriction scheme by making it illegal to ship across state lines oil produced in excess of state allowables and delegated responsibility for regulation of offshore production in the Gulf of Mexico to the onshore states. In addition, there is also considerable evidence that one of the effects of the regulation was to discriminate against large, efficient fields typically owned by the major companies in favor of stripper production more often owned by local state interests. As we will later discuss, no such complicated set of production controls exists for OPEC.

[38]Sampson, p. 304.

[39]Sampson, p. 301.

[40]Sampson, p. 259.

[41]See "The International Implications of the Vertical Divestiture of U.S. Oil Companies", William A. Johnson and Richard E. Messick, forthcoming, *Law and Policy in International Business*.

[42]See Johnson and Messick, *Ibid.*, for a summary of the various country-company contractual relations as of April 1976. Some of these tensions, as in the case of Iraq, can be of a quite long-run nature. It is reasonable to wonder, if the "sisters" controlled everything, why the price of crude oil declined in real terms during the 1960's.

[43]The tension among producing countries is not all in terms of prices and output rates. We understand that Saudi Arabia prefers this area to be referred to as the Arabian Gulf. We here use the still more common designation of Persian Gulf for purposes of clarity.

[44]Sampson, pp. 301 and 303.

[45]The possibility that divestiture, within the U.S., of oil companies would affect either of these factors is remote. The immediate effect of divestiture would neither be to increase buying pressure for OPEC oil nor be to increase new supply. In the long run, even Sampson suggests that divestiture might lead to higher consumer prices and admits that new non-OPEC supply is the key to lower prices; "They (the companies) had, as they admitted, no leverage over prices; their concessions were rapidly being taken over or nationalized; and they were buffeted as never before between producers and consumers." (Sampson, p. 308.) On the selling side, even the severest industry critics acknowledge that: "Most serious students of the industry do not believe that a cartel has existed even among the seven major oil companies", (Rand, p. 349.) In this regard, it is worth noting the antipathy with which both Sampson and Rand regard the companies, the sympathy they extend to particularly the Arab members of OPEC, and Sampson's belief that high oil prices are good for the West. Sampson favors the picaresque language that the goal of the companies was to "screw" the producing countries (pp. 174 and 209), decries "gas guzzlers" (p. 296) and feels that in a free market "imported oil was not too expensive, but too cheap" (p. 305). Rand desires consideration of divestiture of the integrated international major oil companies so that: "The people of the United States have a chance to stay on reasonable terms with them (the Arab world) for a long time to come." (p. 350.) This last statement seems most odd, because the Arab countries themselves have already effectively divested the companies.

[46]See Francisco R. Parra, "The Pricing of Oil in International Markets", *Proceedings, op. cit.*, pp. 6-8.

[47]Were individual OPEC countries willing to shade prices significantly, companies would also have an incentive to shift liftings among OPEC countries. As a result of imperfect transportation and quality differentials, and some marginal price shadings, there have been swings in production rates among OPEC countries. (Recent warm winters in Europe. and economic conditions generally have reduced heavy fuel demand, thereby making heavy crudes less attractive.) But for reasons which we will discuss below, we do not believe that these factors are apt by themselves to cause a major break in the world price of oil.

[48]But the potential production from the Venezuelan tar belt — though of low quality — is enormous. Platt's *Oilgram*, September 8, 1975, noted the following:

"Venezuela should embark immediately on a moderate development program of about 100,000 barrels per day in the Orinoco heavy oil belt, according to Juan Jones Parra, director of Petroleum Institute of Simon Bolivar University....

"Based on low estimates of the belt's reserves, such a recovery rate would increase Venezuela's present 18.5 billion barrels of proven reserves by between 195-billion and 210-billion barrels, oil specialists say.

"Jones Parra said initial studies indicate production costs in the belt would be less than $2 per barrel, about twice the cost of producing conventional crude in Venezuela." (The difference between *a priori* cost expectations and *a posteriori* actual costs of U.S. oil shale and Canadian tar sands suggests that this estimate may be too low.)

206

[49]This is not to say that non-resource costs which are administratively-determined by public policy decisions are not important outside of OPEC. The mobility of drilling rigs into and out of Canada and the sensitivity of North Sea activity to tax policy effects are evidence that non-resource costs are important outside of OPEC, and that companies respond to price differentials which their variation causes. But the potential scope for such variation outside of OPEC, and particularly outside of the Persian Gulf, is much less.

[50]A document submitted by the U.S. to the Conference on International Economic Cooperation indicates that today's high prices are leading to inefficient investment in high-cost energy production by consuming countries. (April 26, 1976 *Oilgram*, p. 1.) This investment most likely will be protected should world prices fall — thereby reducing, perhaps substantially, market share of producing countries and increasing costs to consumers. No doubt these cost increases will be justified in the time-worn name of national security, but indigenous North American supplies do have a security premium which justifies a cost in excess of the landed price of OPEC oil. The arguments which led in 1959 and 1970 to affirmation of mandatory oil import controls in the U.S., and more recently to export controls in Canada, may reappear in the next decade.

[51]Shares of capital investment in recent years in OPEC countries have also been affected by takeovers of producing facilities and functions by host governments. Obviously, the scope now for the companies to make investments in these countries is less. See Johnson and Messick, *op. cit.*, Table 2. The source of the Johnson and Messick data is The Chase Manhattan Bank, Energy Economics Division, *Capital Investments of the World Petroleum Industry*. The years covered are 1967 through 1974. The figures discussed here refer to the non-communist world (other than the U.S., Canada and Europe), but these are primarily OPEC countries.

[52]Canada's ultimate potential still is open to question. To some extent, the improved political climate in Canada seems to be yielding increased exploration. *The New York Times* (1/25/76 International Economic Survey) stated the question as follows:

"Relief clearly lies with increased production. But the conventional oil sources in Alberta have yielded no new discoveries for more than a decade, and the exotic areas of the Athabasca tar sands and the Arctic region have consumed far more money, labor, time and effort in exploration than anyone expected.

"C.R. Hetherington, president of Panarctic Oils Ltd., a consortium of public and private interests, says Canada's self-sufficiency and export potential depend on 'the extent to which the Canadian Arctic is developed and the timing of that development.' "

There seems to be little question — dating even from 1969, in the CTF report — that the largest new potential is from frontier areas (Canadian Arctic and offshore Atlantic Coast). While expectations concerning the prospects of the latter have been revised downward, hopes remain high for the former. A field in the Prudhoe Bay class would do wonders for North American self-sufficiency, although any price effects would depend upon size and timing.

[53]The international companies have included many more companies than the seven sisters for many years. See Rene P. Manes, "Import Quotas, Prices and Profits in the Oil Industry", *Southern Economic Journal*, Vol. XXX (July 1963), pp. 13-24.

But even were the number of companies with international capability much smaller than it is, the effect of the search for maximum net advantage would still result in a highly competitive world oil market from the companies' perspective.

[54]Three U.S. demand forecasts which assume different prices and rely on differing methodology are summarized below and compared to the CTF 1969 forecast. None suggests major reductions in U.S. demand; the same conclusion is probably true for other consuming countries as well.

Projected/Actual U.S. Consumption Production and Imports (Million b/d)

	1975 Actual	1980 Data Resources, Inc. (Consensus Case)	1980 Stanford Research Institute	1980 Federal Energy Administration Reference Scenario	CTF
U.S. real price/bbl (1975 dollars)	$7.7	$12.0	$6.0-9.0	$8-16	$5.6
U.S. consumption	15.8	18.7	17.7	17.5-16.5	18.6
U.S. production	10.0	12.8	10.9	11.9-13.1	13.5
U.S. imports	5.8	5.9	6.8	7.6-3.4	5.1
Imports as a per cent of consumption	37%	32%	38%	39%-21%	27%

Sources: Data Resources, Inc., "DRI Energy Outlook. Special Analysis: Trends in the World Price of Oil, 1975-1980" (Lexington, Mass.: August 1975), Tables 3 and 5.

John P. Henry, Jr., "World Energy Prices and Their Impacts on New Technology", Stanford Research Institute (Palo Alto, Calif.: March 31, 1976).

Federal Energy Administration, *National Energy Outlook*, FEA-N-75/713 (Washington, D.C.: February 1976), p. G-22.

CTF Report

"Actual" from *Oil and Gas Journal*, January 26, 1976, p. 105.

These demand forecasts seem unusually insensitive to forecasts of real price. A difference of 100 per cent in assumed real price seems to have only a small effect on demand. While production appears to be responsive to price, its implicit supply elasticity appears to be very small, as well. As a result, U.S. import projections appear to be stable across all forecasts, and further, not too different from today's import levels. (However, since all the assumptions of the forecasts were not the same, one cannot conclude definitely that price elasticity is minimal. What is known, of course, is that short-term elasticities are small. Over the longer term, a more significant price effect will accrue.)

[55]In economic analysis, models are abstractions — schematic skeletons which capture the essentials of a situation. The appropriateness of the use of a particular model to analyze a particular situation depends less on whether all the descriptive details associated with the model are reproduced by the case at hand, than whether the behavior of the phenomenon under examination is close to that which the model would lead one to expect, and whether the model is useful for making predictions. One may use the competitive market model to analyze a particular industry without requiring that there be an infinite number of firms. Alternatively, the monopoly market model may be the most appropriate in some situations, even when there is not a complete absence of substitutes. The question is which market model, of the many which might be employed, leads to the best predictions.

[56]Sampson, pp. 259, 301, and 304.

[57]World production averaged 55.8 million barrels per day (b/d) in 1973, 55.9 million b/d in 1974, 53.1 million b/d in 1975, and 54.4 million b/d for the first four months of 1976. (*Oil and Gas Journal*, February 24, 1975, p. 110; February 23, 1976, p. 167; and June 28, 1976, p. 206.)

[58]In this discussion we refer to "firms", because the traditional treatment of this model in the economic literature is in terms of the dominant firm case. In the case of OPEC, the firms are countries. Everywhere that "firms" are mentioned, read *countries*. When we refer to the private international oil business firms, we will use the term "companies".

[59]While data on reserves, production and cost are only approximate, *International Petroleum Encyclopedia*, Petroleum Publishing Co. (Tulsa, Okla.: 1976), pp. 302-303, and M.A. Adelman, *The World Petroleum Market*, The Johns Hopkins University Press (Baltimore: 1972), provide good reference material. See also *Oil and Gas Journal*, August 16, 1976, pp. 52-53.

[60]Both the U.S.S.R. and Communist China are acting as classic free-riders on the OPEC price increase. See Arthur W. Wright, "The Soviet Union in World Energy Markets", and Thomas G. Rawski, "China and Japan in the World Energy Economy", in *The Energy Question, op. cit.*, pp. 85-100 and 121-146. Norway represents the first significant addition to world supply from the North Sea. Mexico is defining what may be one of the most significant additions to world oil reserves in this decade. Iraq, though a nominal hawk on higher prices, is an actual price shader vis-à-vis the OPEC price to redress what it regards as an inequitably low market share (based on reserve potential). Its low market share in part may be due to its acrimonious historical relations with the international companies. The point is, however, that Saudi output decreased sufficiently to make room in the market for these incremental supplies.

[61]Kuwait and Venezuela, the two countries with persistent decreases in output, accounted respectively for 13 per cent and 17 per cent of the non-U.S. (non-Communist) supply reduction. Venezuelan conventional production suffers from natural decline as well as political restriction. Kuwait is concerned about the longevity of its reserves and its future, as compared to current, revenue needs. The behavior of other OPEC countries has both complicated and facilitated the Saudis' situation. In some cases, the complicating and facilitating behavior comes from the

same country. See, for example, the swings in Libyan output in Table 3. The Saudis are presumably pleased when Libya restricts output, but neither Libyan restriction nor expansion is sufficient to destabilize the world price.

[62]U.S. and Canadian production declined by 500,000 b/d. *Oil and Gas Journal*, June 28, 1976, p. 206.

[63]Until more data are in, it will be impossible to tell conclusively whether there is any special significance to the 1974 market shares. Saudi production in May of 1976 averaged 8.3 million barrels per day. Between 1974 and May of 1976, U.S. and Canadian output fell a combined total of 1.1 million barrels per day. The magnitude of this decline was largely unforeseen and contributes to volatility in the Saudi rate of output and market share.

[64]See Parra, *op. cit.*, p. 8.

[65]Minister Yamani confirms this observation in *Oil and Gas Journal*, July 19, 1976, p. 102: "No action is taken in OPEC unless Saudi Arabia wants it". Before the recent OPEC meeting in Bali, Kuwaiti Ambassador Bishera said that world oil prices can't be raised without Saudi Arabian consent (*Oilgram*, May 7, 1976). The informal reports in the industry press since that conference have confirmed our views.

PART III
OIL IN THE SEVENTIES
POLICIES AND PROSPECTS

Editor's Introduction

Although oil and natural gas prices received by Canadian producers are not at world equivalent levels, nevertheless they have more than doubled since 1973. Ostensibly, one would expect such a price rise would stimulate investment in petroleum exploration and production and encourage an inflow of capital into the industry. The essay by Professor Quirin and Professor Kalymon shows this has not happened. No influx of capital into the Canadian petroleum and coal industry is indicated; the proportion of industry cash flow devoted to exploration and development fell, 1972 to 1975. These trends reflect insufficient average returns on investment in relation to higher replacement costs, and increasing government taxes. Quirin and Kalymon suggest the major factor inhibiting industry profitability is the share of cash flows garnered by royalties.

The key issue is the sufficiency of returns in the exploration and production sector. Determination of a required return on investment must recognize the relative riskiness of petroleum exploration. Quirin and Kalymon attempt to quantify this risk and find that with the inclusion of a risk premium the required after tax return to producers is around 19 per cent, which compares unfavourably with apparent available returns on new investment of about 14 per cent. Yet Quirin and Kalymon estimate the industry would have to rely on capital markets if it were to pursue the objective of self reliance recently suggested by the Canadian government. They conclude that a sufficiency of return on new investment requires a reduction in government royalty taxes, even if oil and gas prices escalate to world levels.

The Financial Position of the Petroleum Industry

GEORGE DAVID QUIRIN

Professor of Economics and Finance
University of Toronto

and

BASIL A. KALYMON

Professor, Faculty of Management Studies
University of Toronto

213

THE AUTHORS

George David Quirin was born in 1931 in Calgary and graduated M.A., 1958, University of Alberta. He received his A.M. in 1960 and his Ph.D. in 1961, both from Princeton University.

After consulting on petroleum economics with the Department of Northern Affairs and Natural Resources, Professor Quirin taught overseas, at the University of British Columbia, and at the University of Toronto before taking up his present post as Professor, Economics and Finance, School of Business, University of Toronto.

Professor Quirin has published widely on the subject of oil and gas resources, economics and policies. Included among his publications are: "Energy, Policy Choices Regarding Exploitation and Export," in *Proceedings of the Royal Society of Canada Symposium on Energy Resources*, (Ottawa: October, 1973); "Economics of Oil Transportation in the Arctic," (with R.N. Wolff) in L.M. Alexander and G.R.S. Hawkins, (eds.), *Canadian-U.S. Maritime Problems*, (Kingston, R.I., Law of the Sea Institute, 1972).

Basil A. Kalymon, born in 1944, is Professor, Faculty of Management Studies, University of Toronto, where he took his first degree (Honours Mathematics and Statistics) in 1966. Twice winner of Yale Fellowships and recipient of a Ford Foundation Fellowship, Professor Kalymon graduated from Yale, M.Phil., (Operations Research), 1968 and Ph.D., (Operations Research), 1970.

Before taking up his present post in 1975, Professor Kalymon taught at the University of California, the University of Toronto, and Harvard University.

He is the author, with G.D. Quirin, of "Changing Incentive Structures in Petroleum Exploration," a working paper prepared for the Canadian Tax Foundation. Professor Kalymon's other scholarly publications include "Economic Incentives in OPEC Oil Pricing Policy," *Journal of Development Economics*, 2, (1975).

The Financial Position of the Petroleum Industry

GEORGE DAVID QUIRIN

Professor of Economics and Finance
University of Toronto

and

BASIL A. KALYMON

Professor, Faculty of Management Studies
University of Toronto

I. INTRODUCTION

Much of the recent national debate on energy policy has centered on the fortunes and future prospects of the Canadian oil and gas industry. Such concern is well-founded in the case of an industry whose output represents approximately 65% of total national energy consumption and in which world prices have increased 400% since the Arab oil boycott in 1973. In response to the sudden jump in oil prices, both provincial and federal governments introduced measures to appropriate a substantial portion of the increased industry revenues for domestic consumers or the public purse. These measures included price controls, export taxes, royalty increases and several amendments to federal tax legislation aimed at preventing pre-emption of the resource tax base by provincial levies.[1] In addition, a new Crown corporation, Petro-Canada, was formed to undertake oil and gas exploration and development. Recently, new lease and royalty regulations for frontier area exploration requiring increased Canadian participation and imposing higher federal royalties on any major finds have been announced.

In the light of these developments, this paper considers the financial position in which the industry currently finds itself and in particular, the adequacy of incentive arrangements in the light of certain proposed policy objectives. In short, what kinds of opportunities are being provided to encourage the reinvestment of industry cash flows? How are these related to the return on investment the petroleum industry needs today? Will cash flows, even if reinvested, be adequate?

The answers to these questions will have a significant impact on determining the most likely future course of Canadian oil and gas supplies. If cash flows to the industry are inadequate for the self-financing of needed future expansion then even government-enforced reinvestment cannot assure adequate investment for future needs. On the other hand, substantial cash flows, unaccompanied by suitable reinvestment incentives, would likely be redirected to alternative investments, again resulting in a deteriorating petroleum supply position. Conversely, profit opportunities above the cost of capital could attract substantial external investment funds to supplement any inadequacy in internally generated cash. Evidence of responsiveness to profit opportunities is abundant in the international petroleum industry of which the Canadian industry is a segment.

Given the nature of the issues, the empirical evidence which we have collected must necessarily relate to industry averages or sampled company statistics. Such data will invariably be unrepresentative of some specific company or situation but is sufficient to identify general trends. Orders of magnitude and direction of movement in the quantities measured are useful indicators even if particular estimates are imprecise. With this understanding, we present our findings which are based on currently available information.

II. RECENT TRENDS

TABLE 1
Return on Investment in Petroleum and Other Industries

	1972	1973	1974	1975	% Growth
			(Million $)		
Petroleum and Coal Industries					
After Tax Income...............	418	613	787	743	
Deferred Taxes................	50	88	164	191	
Long-term Interest	56	57	64	86	
Total Return	524	758	1,014	1,020	25%
Invested Capital	5,101	5,689	6,503	7,500	
R.O.I.	10.3%	13.3%	15.6%	13.6%	
Mineral Fuels					
After Tax Income...............	393	581	689	957	
Deferred Taxes................	29	40	164	161	
Long-term Interest	48	55	59	64	
Total Return	470	676	912	1,182	36%
Invested Capital	5,763	6,358	7,043	7,935	
R.O.I.	8.2%	10.6%	12.9%	14.9%	
All Industries					
After Tax Income...............	5,265	7,540	9,226	8,694	
Deferred Taxes................	446	790	1,195	1,111	
Long-Term Interest............	1,285	1,485	1,760	2,084	
Total Return	5,711	8,330	10,421	9,805	20%
Invested Capital	80,338	87,439	96,435	106,673	
R.O.I.	8.7%	11.2%	12.6%	11.2%	

Source: Statistics Canada. *Industrial Corporations, Financial Statistics.* Fourth Quarter 1975.

A great deal of public concern has focused on the profitability of the oil industry and the degree to which the increase in prices has accrued to the benefit of the oil companies. Table 1 indicates reported book rates of return which have been achieved in the petroleum industries. Overall industry average figures are presented for comparative purposes.

Discussion of the adequacy of these rates of return is reserved for the section below on the cost of capital. It should be noted that, even treating deferred taxes as part of return on investment (rather than as an increased liability), the rate of return on invested capital for the two industry categories which include oil and gas production are only marginally above all-industry averages. Other activities, such as coal mining, petroleum refining and marketing are included in the statistics reported in Table 1. Growth in invested capital appears in all three cases to be closely related to total returns, indicating no influx of external capital into the Canadian petroleum and coal industry despite the major upward shift in the international petroleum price which occurred in 1973. It seems safe to conclude that in this period, opportunities in the Canadian petroleum industry did not attract significant new investment from outside sources.

Cash flows were available to the domestic industry and the amounts spent on finding and developing new sources of energy are indicated by the analysis of sources and uses of funds shown in Table 2:

TABLE 2
Sources and Disposition of Funds —
Petroleum Industries

	1972	1973	1974	1975
		(Million $)		
Sources				
Net Income and Deferred Taxes	890	1,322	1,804	2,052
Depreciation	344	370	394	427
Depletion	244	305	345	354
Total Cash Flow	1,478	1,997	2,543	2,833
Uses				
Dividends	225	295	360	524
Exploration, Development and Facilities	1,094	1,213	1,425	1,557
Other Investments	159	489	758	752
	1,478	1,997	2,543	2,833

Source: Statistics Canada. *Industrial Corporations, Financial Statistics*, Fourth Quarter 1975. Reported figures are the sums of "Petroleum and Coal" and "Mineral Fuels" industries.

We notice from the above that the percentage of available cash flow allocated for the development of new supplies dropped from 74% in 1972 to only 55% in 1975. With dividends increasing on a proportionate basis from 15% to 18%, the remainder of the funds available appear to have been invested elsewhere. Industry behaviour must be interpreted to imply either that the available opportunities for oil and gas investment in Canada have diminished or that the incentives provided to the industry have been insufficiently attractive to encourage the reinvestment of cash flows.

TABLE 3
Replacement Costs for Crude Oil Equivalents

	1966	1967	1968	1969	1970	1971	1972	1973	1974	1975	Total
Additions to Oil and Gas Reserves (MMSB Equiv.)	2,128	1,242	1,240	1,542	762	690	156	461	896	317	9,435
Exploration, Development and Facility Costs (MM$)	688	803	813	891	900	1,042	1,095	1,212	1,424	1,557	10,425
Replacement Cost ($/B)	0.32	0.65	0.66	0.58	1.18	1.51	7.02	2.63	1.59	4.91	1.10
5 yr. Centered Moving Avg. ($/B)	—	—	.68	.92	2.19	2.59	2.79	3.54	n.a.	n.a.	

Source: Canadian Petroleum Association data on reserves and expenditures.

III. EXPLORATION RESULTS AND PROFITABILITY

Part of the explanation of the above industry actions can be found by considering the effectiveness of exploration expenditures in recent years. Using a conversion factor of 10 thousand cubic feet of gas to 1 barrel of oil equivalent, Table 3 opposite indicates the cost of replacing a barrel of oil.[2] Because of the lag between expenditures and results, individual year data are not too reliable, and a moving average is used to eliminate excessive year-to-year variability.

Table 3 clearly indicates a trend toward substantially higher costs of replacement with the average over the most recent five years being more than five times greater than the corresponding value in 1970. This average, over the last five years, of $3.54 per barrel is over three and a half times greater than the overall ten year average.

The implications are clear. Even with no further deterioration in finding rates companies must earn a substantially increased share of the gross revenue per barrel if new ventures are to maintain rates of return on investment at current industry levels.

Using the latest five year average replacement costs of $3.54 per barrel, an investment analysis was carried out to determine the prospective returns available from exploration investment.[3] It was assumed that the domestic price of oil would, in conjunction with stated government policy, move to a real price at the world level of $12.00 per barrel (in 1976 dollars) by 1978. The results of such an investment under currently applicable federal taxation provisions (assuming that the investor has sufficient taxable income against which to write-off expenditures as quickly as possible) and under the approximately 26% royalty level (currently imposed by Alberta on "new" oil) are shown in Table 4.

Table 4 shows that the corporate share of the $12 revenue drops from a nominal $2.50 if timing considerations are ignored to a loss of $0.44 per barrel if a 15% discount factor is used. This is due to the lengthy payback period which is estimated at 11.18 years. The real rate of return from the investment was evaluated at 8.98% which, under assumptions of a 5% long-run inflation in prices would be equivalent to a nominal rate of return of around 14%. As prospective rates of return these rates appear, from industry behaviour, to be insufficiently attractive to induce a major step-up in exploration.

TABLE 4

Profitability Analysis — Oil Exploration in Western Canada

	Undiscounted ($ per bbl.)	%	Discounted at 15% ($ per bbl.)	%
Gross Revenue..................	$12.00	100.0	$4.09	100.0
Exploration, Development and				
Facilities......................	3.54	29.5	2.56	62.6
Operating Costs.................	1.01	8.4	0.34	8.3
Net Revenue..............	7.45		1.19	
Royalties	3.14	26.2	2.08	50.9
Federal Taxes	1.44	12.0	(0.36)	(8.8)
Provincial Taxes	0.37	3.1	(0.09)	(2.2)
Net Income...............	2.50	20.8	(0.44)	(10.8)

R.O.I. = 8.98%   Payback Period = 11.18 years

It should be noted that the major factor inhibiting profitability are royalties which rise from a nominal 26.2% share of total benefits when timing is ignored to a 50.9% share after discounting. Reduction of the royalty percentage to a nominal 10% resulted in a doubling of the real R.O.I. to 16.48% indicating that investment opportunities could be made substantially more attractive by royalty adjustment.

The recently announced federal government land and royalty regulations for northern exploration contain provisions for a base royalty of 10%. However, the additional "profit tax" on highly productive fields imposes an additional royalty of 40% of the excess profit above a certain level of return (roughly 25%). Since the distribution of oil or gas pools in nature is such that a small number of all pools will contain the vast bulk of total reserves, it can be concluded that the effective royalty rate will substantially exceed 10%. For example, if 20% of all exploration and development expenditures produce 70% of all reserves, then the effective royalty rate on the productive pools would be around 33%. With the remaining reserves paying a 10% royalty, the effective overall average royalty rate would be around 26%, the level of current provincial royalties. Unless substantially *lower* per barrel costs are incurred in northern exploration (an unlikely possibility), the industry can expect no more than the above returns on the average.

IV. REQUIRED RETURNS ON INVESTMENT

The prospective rates of return estimated above look impressive, at least at first glance when viewed through the eyes of a generation which grew up in a world where 6% was "the" interest rate, or the ceiling rate for chartered banks, and in which a 10% rule-of-thumb was frequently used as an estimate of the cost of common share equity to corporations. However, it is *only* when judged by such yardsticks that rates of return on petroleum exploration look impressive. They look much less impressive in a world in which bond yields exceed 10%, interest rates on prime first mortgages are in the 11%-12% range, and equity investors in low-risk public utility common stock are permitted to earn rates of return in the 13%-15% range by public utility commissions. Simple comparisons with interest rates should, admittedly, be made only with caution, in the light of a complex tax system in which the net after-tax return from a given return on equities will, for many taxpayers, exceed the net from an equivalent before-tax interest income, while for others, interest income (up to $1,000) is exempt from tax while neither dividends nor capital gains are so exempt. The fact is that in the last decade or so, traditional notions of what constitutes an appropriate rate of return have become untenable, as mounting inflation rates and perceived political risks have pushed costs of capital funds, as measured by the prospective yields which investors require in order to induce them to commit funds to particular undertakings, to levels that have no counterpart in the memories of living Canadians.

Under such circumstances, the only way to determine whether a given prospective rate of return in petroleum exploration is adequate to attract capital is to undertake a careful examination of the relative riskiness of petroleum exploration in comparison with other investment opportunities currently available, and to determine what rate of return premium, if any, over prospective rates of return available on these alternatives, is required to make investment in petroleum exploration as attractive as the alternatives.

It is a commonplace within the industry that petroleum exploration is a very risky business indeed. This assessment is based on the low probability of success on any given wildcat well, and is as beside the point as the contrary assertion that, by virtue of the law of large numbers, success is assured in the aggregate and that the industry is, in effect, risk free. While the numbers involved are never large enough to produce a stable discovery rate for a single company, nor even for all of the companies operating in a given area, this purely technological interpretation of risk ignores the problems of changing marketability, prices, royalties and tax rates which have recently been the primary generators of effective risk in the industry. In any event it is preferable to produce a quantitative measure of risk which is in some degree comparable with a similar measure applied to other companies in other industries.

Unfortunately, there is no generally accepted measure of risk which can be used for this purpose. There is general agreement that investors' risk is associated with the possibility of variations in the income stream to be received, and/or with the loss of part or all of the capital sum invested. The latter can, of course, be linked to the former as it reflects an anticipated reduction in, or cessation of, the income stream generated by the investment. Risk is essentially forward-looking and attempts to quantify risk by measurements applied to historically-observed variables can be no more than partially successful. There is also disagreement, at the theoretical level, with respect to precisely what aspects of risk enter into the determination of the risk premiums that investors require.

It is currently fashionable, in academic circles, to identify risk premiums as associated exclusively with systematic risk, which can be defined as that portion of risk which cannot be eliminated in a well-diversified portfolio. Systematic risk is measured by the so-called Beta coefficient of the Sharpe-Lintner Capital Asset Pricing Model.[4] The Beta coefficient for a particular security is simply a measure of the relative responsiveness of that security's price to changes in the prices of the market generally. The measure of risk derived from this model is the Beta coefficient β_i; if $\beta_i = 1$, then the security in question is judged to be equal, in risk, to the market as a whole. If $\beta_i > 1$, the security is above average in risk, while if $\beta_i < 1$ it is less risky than average. Proponents of this risk measure do not deny that there are components of risk which are not captured by β_i. They assert, however, that, since investors can get rid of these other components of risk by diversifying their portfolios, they do not require any compensation for bearing them.

While the underlying theory behind the use of β_i as a risk measure is attractive, empirical evidence in support of its use are far from compelling. Computed values of β_i for individual securities are quite unstable from one period to the next[5] and tests of the ability of β_i to explain variations in yields do not permit rejection of the alternative hypothesis that these are related to total risk and not just to its systematic component.[6]

As applied to oil company shares in the current context, the credibility of β_i is also weakened by the fact that the increases in political risks since 1970 have frequently led to price movements in directions opposite to the market as a whole, and have thus reduced computed values of β_i below the values which would have been computed if political risks had not increased. It can, of course, be argued that political risks are unsystematic; whether investors will be persuaded that they are irrelevant is less clear. A more convincing argument might be that political risks have always existed, at least potentially, and that the losses which have been incurred to date have reduced the potential for further loss, and that the reduced β_i values reflect a genuine reduction in risk. We do not find this explanation particularly appealing either. While β_i is, in our view, a very imperfect measure of risk, it is frequently used as a measure of risk and, as the systematic risk it purports to measure is a significant component of total risk, it is a measure which is worth examining.

We have computed β_i statistics for a sample of 157 Canadian companies, representing all the non-financial companies included in the *Financial Post* computer data bank meeting certain criteria with respect to data continuity, minimum trading volume, etc.[7] Monthly closing prices for the shares of companies in the sample were collected from Toronto Stock Exchange records, and β_i was calculated using monthly price changes over the period July 1970 - July 1975, using changes in the TSE industrial index as the independent variable. In the sample, there were 22 oil companies, of which 4 were integrated major oil companies and 18 independents. Computed β_i values for these companies are shown in Table 5. β_i values for the major companies are in excess of 1.0, suggesting that these companies are riskier than the weighted average of all companies in the TSE index; those of the independents are higher still. Given the likelihood that β_i underestimates risk, for the reasons noted above, the general proposition that petroleum exploration is well above average in terms of risk is supported.

For reasons noted above, we are less than happy with β_i as a measure of risk. For use as evidence in public-utility hearings where we have given rate of return testimony, we have developed a more comprehensive ordinal risk measure which, while less precise, appears to us to capture more of what is comprehended in the relatively broader but vaguer notions of risk held in the investment community and by investors in general. Companies are ranked in terms of risk as measured by five variables, the ranks are summed and the resulting risk measure is the sum of the ranks obtained on the five measures. Finally, companies are once again ranked in order of the sum of the ranks so obtained. The lowest-ranked companies are the least risky.

TABLE 5

**Computed Values of β_i — Canadian Oil Companies'
Common Shares**

	β_i
A. Integrated Major Companies	
Texaco Canada Ltd.	1.021
Gulf Oil Canada Ltd.	1.085
Shell Canada Ltd.	1.130
Imperial Oil Ltd.	1.171
Average	1.102
B. Independents	
Scurry-Rainbow Oil Ltd.	0.650
Union Oil Co. of Canada Ltd.	0.992
Alminex Ltd.	0.998
PanCanadian Petroleum Ltd.	1.165
Murphy Oil Co. Ltd.	1.242
Hudson's Bay Oil and Gas Co. Ltd.	1.339
Husky Oil Ltd.	1.418
Canadian Superior Oil Co. Ltd.	1.429
Pacific Petroleums Ltd.	1.661
Canadian Industrial Gas and Oil Ltd.	1.661
Western Decalta Petroleum Ltd.	1.741
Canadian Export Gas and Oil.	1.803
Home Oil Co. Ltd.	1.850
Canadian Occidental Petroleum Ltd.	1.859
United Canso Oil and Gas Ltd.	1.921
Numac Oil and Gas Ltd.	1.973
Dome Petroleum Ltd.	2.004
Ranger Oil (Canada) Ltd.	2.024
Average	1.541

In addition to β_i, the measures used include:

1. the maximum percentage shortfall in annual earnings per share below a 10-year trend line;

2. the mean absolute percentage deviation of annual earnings per share about a three-year moving average;

227

3. the maximum drop in share price over a 12-month period;

4. the standard deviation of monthly share price changes.

Ordinal rankings of the oil companies in the sample, using this more comprehensive measure of risk, are reported in Table 6. Once again, they confirm the industry's self-image; oil exploration is a relatively risky business. The mean ranking of the integrated majors is 50th; that of the independents, which are more heavily concentrated in exploration and development, is 118th.

TABLE 6
Ordinal Risk Measures for Canadian Oil Companies' Common Shares

	Rank (out of 157)
A. Integrated Major Companies	
Shell Canada Ltd.	42
Gulf Oil Canada Ltd.	49
Texaco Canada Ltd.	52
Imperial Oil Ltd.	57
Average	50
B. Independents	
Alminex Ltd.	60
Pan Canadian Petroleum Ltd.	70
Hudson's Bay Oil and Gas Ltd.	91
Pacific Petroleums Ltd.	103
Canadian Industrial Gas and Oil Ltd.	105
Murphy Oil Co. Ltd.	107
Scurry-Rainbow Oil Ltd.	110
Husky Oil Ltd.	114
Dome Petroleum Ltd.	115
Union Oil Co. of Canada Ltd.	121
Western Decalta Petroleum Ltd.	125
Home Oil Co. Ltd.	127
Canadian Superior Oil Ltd.	135
Canadian Occidental Petroleum Ltd.	136
Canadian Export Gas and Oil Ltd.	143
Numac Oil and Gas Ltd.	105
Ranger Oil (Canada) Ltd.	152
United Canso Oil and Gas Ltd.	157
Average	118

While some of the independents qualify as low risk using β_i, presumably because of the unsystematic character of their individual risk, none so qualify using the ordinal measure. Nor do the majors appear comparable in risk to public utilities which are found, mostly, at the low end of the risk spectrum. Table 7 shows the distribution of utilities and oil companies within quintiles of the sample. It clearly indicates the major oil companies to be significantly riskier than utilities, while the independents are riskier still.

TABLE 7
Risk Quintile Rankings
Petroleum Companies and Public Utilities

Quintile	Utilities*	Major Integrated Oils	Independent Oils
I	10	—	—
II	1	4	1
III	—	—	2
IV	—	—	8
V	—	—	7

* Telephone, Natural Gas, Electric (includes Gas Pipelines)

Before examining what these risk levels mean in terms of required rates of return, it is perhaps worth considering the extent to which they reflect the true risk characteristics of the industry. As noted earlier, since they are based on past data, they can reflect only those portions of risk which have, as it were, come home to roost during the period to which the observations relate, while much of the relevant current risk is future-oriented. The major imponderable is political risk, in the broader sense which includes not only domestic political risks but the possible domestic repercussions of international events. As indicated earlier, domestic political events, including the raising of royalty rates by the producing provinces, tax "reform", and the conflicting claims of federal and provincial authorities to ever-increasing shares of wellhead revenues, have had an effect on the historical record, particularly since 1973. As noted however, they operated perversely to reduce computed risk by at least one of the measures used. While the federal government appears to have let up on the industry to some degree, the response of Nova Scotia to the latest crude price increase, and responses in Ontario to the Isbister Royal Commission report suggest that the road ahead may not be altogether smooth. However, the risk rankings are relative, and while a more inclusive risk measure might place even more oil companies in the highest risk class, the basic picture would likely be changed but little.

What do these risk rankings mean in terms of rates of return required to attract and retain equity capital? Unfortunately, the evidence is fragmentary. The only bodies which produce such estimates for public consumption on a fairly careful basis are public utility commissions, which must deal with the problem in carrying out their regulatory responsibilities. The numbers so produced, however, relate to companies which are significantly lower in risk than oil companies. Nevertheless, they provide a starting point. Table 8 lists rates of return allowed, on common shareholders' equity, for a number of utilities operating in Canada. β_i statistics and risk ranks for the utilities are also shown in Table 8. The rates of return in Table 8 are, of course, nominal rates.

TABLE 8
Allowed Rates of Return on Common Equity
for Certain Canadian Utility Companies

Company	Return Allowed-%	β_i	Risk Ranking
Bell Canada	12.0	0.235	1
B.C. Telephone	13.3*	0.409	2
Calgary Power	15.0	0.875	6
Consumers' Gas	14.0	0.531	3
Northern & Central Gas	14.4**	0.976	10
TransCanada PipeLines	16.7	0.898	31
Union Gas	15.0**	0.669	5
Average	14.3	0.656	8.3

* Allowance stated as a range 12.8-13.8%
** Restated to reflect allowances for return on deferred tax reserve.

Use of β_i to estimate required risk premiums on common stocks is apt, in our view, to underestimate required risk premiums to the extent that the latter incorporate an allowance for unsystematic risk. Given the importance of the unsystematic political factor, this is apt to be of particular significance in the present case. However, estimates so based may be useful as indicators of minimum requirements, as long as it is recognized that actual requirements may be somewhat greater. The theoretical model from which β_i was developed suggests that the risk premium, over the "risk-free" interest rate will be proportional to β_i. The mean rate of return allowance awarded the utilities in Table 8 is 14.3%, their mean β_i value is 0.656. Using the current treasury bill rate of 9.0% as an estimate of the risk-free rate (long-term bonds are not risk-free and have $\beta_i > 0$),[8] the risk premium for stock having $\beta_i = 1.0$ can be estimated at 8.08%. Applying this to the typical major company, with $\beta_i = 1.10$ gives a risk premium of 8.9%, for a required equity rate of return of 17.9%. Applying it to a typical independent, with $\beta_i = 1.54$, gives a risk premium of 12.4%, and a required equity rate of return of 21.4%.

These rates of return, approximately 18% for major integrated companies and 21.5% for independents, would, if earned, make investment in the petroleum industry about as attractive as investment in the utilities listed in Table 8 on a risk-adjusted basis. To the extent that unsystematic risk enters into investors' consideration, these estimates must be adjusted upward, since unsystematic risks are important in the oil industry but relatively insignificant for most utilities. We have not made such an adjustment, but regard the resulting estimates as minimal estimates which do not compensate for all aspects of risk. The required rates of return for major integrated companies are lower than for independents, in our view, because of the mix of activities in which they are engaged. Refining and marketing are less risky than exploration and production, and investors will be satisfied with lower rates of return in these activities, but there is no evidence to suggest that required rates of return on particular exploration and development investments by major companies are any less than on similar investments by independents. Accordingly, we adopt 21.5% as a conservatively low estimate of the nominal rate of return which would provide rewards for risk-bearing which are comparable to those earned by utilities.

The above rate of return estimates related, of course, to common share equity funds only. To some degree, exploration and development can be financed, at least by established companies, using debt funds which are less costly than equity. Debt financing is available for development investment only, and then on a basis which affords an ample margin of safety to the lender. Capital structure ratios vary widely (Table 9). However, we would estimate that the "typical" exploration-production operation could use 16.67% debt. This ratio is relatively low, reflecting the risk characteristics of such operation. Most small oil companies' debt is privately placed, but we would estimate our "typical" exploration production operation, with the capital structure cited, could borrow at 11.5% under mid-1976 conditions.

TABLE 9
Debt Ratios of Canadian Oil Producers, 1974

	(1) Total Assets	(2) Current Liabilities	(3) Permanent Funds	(4) Of Which Debt:	(5) Debt Ratio %
Alminex Ltd.	39.6	1.5	38.1	—	0
PanCanadian Petroleum Ltd.	382.5	68.5	314.0	89.9	28.6
Hudson's Bay Oil and Gas Co. . . .	487.3	109.5	377.8	52.0	13.8
Pacific Petroleums Ltd.	596.7	61.2	535.5	133.7	25.0
Murphy Oil Co. Ltd.	128.1	49.9	78.2	21.6	27.6
Scurry-Rainbow Oil Ltd.	71.2	5.8	65.4	17.3	26.5
Husky Oil Ltd.	393.5	92.3	301.2	102.1	33.9
Dome Petroleum Ltd.	414.0	98.5	315.5	110.9	35.2
Union Oil Co. of Canada Ltd.	201.5	24.5	177.0	—	0
Western Decalta Petroleum Ltd.. .	60.6	6.7	53.9	15.3	28.4
Home Oil Co. Ltd.	381.8	55.7	326.1	68.1	20.9
Canadian Superior Oil Ltd.	188.0	25.9	162.1	—	0
Canadian Occidental Petroleum Ltd.	138.6	7.5	131.1	18.8	14.3
Canadian Export Gas and Oil Ltd.	19.9	2.0	17.9	—	0
Numac Oil and Gas Ltd.	35.3	1.3	34.0	9.3	27.4
Ranger Oil (Canada) Ltd.	32.8	5.0	27.8	—	0
United Canso Oil and Gas Ltd. . . .	18.3	1.2	17.1	—	0
Average					16.6

Source: *The Financial Post Survey of Oils, 1976,* Canadian Industrial Gas and Oil, included in Table 3, excluded as company merged, data not reported.

Allowing for the tax deductibility of interest, the effective after-tax rate of return requirement to producers becomes:

	Rate	Per Cent of Capital	Weighted Rate
Debt................	5.75	16.67	.95%
Equity	21.50	83.33	17.92%
			18.87%

This is the number which must be compared to the rates of return cited in Section III above in determining whether an adequate incentive to invest exists. Our figures suggest that it does not. It is, of course, possible that finding costs will decline, below the levels experienced in recent years, although the evidence on which to predict such a decline is slim indeed. If such a decline were to occur, the gap between requirements and prospects would of course be narrowed.

Our projections, however, seem to be consistent with the federal government's finding:

> "that the effective rate of return on the production of resources in the producing provinces will be in the range of 12% to 13% after taxes if future price levels for domestic oil and natural gas continue to move towards (sic) international levels and reflect future rates of inflation."[9]

In our view, the problem does not lie there but in the complacent observation which follows:

> "The federal government believes that this constitutes a reasonable and competitive return for the petroleum industry with regard to known reserves."[10]

The risk premium proposed is, with respect to investment in public utilities, negative. Our analysis suggests that the disparities in risk, compared to public utilities are major, if not extreme, and that a significantly greater risk premium must be provided if funds are to be attracted to, or even retained in, oil and gas production.

V. THE REINVESTMENT QUESTION

We have not made any distinction between the rate of return needed to attract capital and that needed to retain capital currently employed in the industry. Financial theory recognizes no such distinction, except for the need to cover underwriting costs on newly-raised funds. Present tax and royalty structures provided certain credits against tax and royalty liability which can only be claimed if funds are reinvested.[11] Our analyses allow for the claiming of such credits. If funds are not reinvested, available rates of return are significantly reduced.

It is our view that the existence of such allowances and the implicit reasoning which underlies them, are a major ingredient contributing to the present level of political risk in the industry. The notion that rates of return need be adequate (even by the government's standards) only if reinvestment takes place appears to involve the assumption that corporate earnings are not beneficially owned by corporate shareholders, and that nominal title to them can be retained only if reinvestment takes place. Otherwise the state is entitled to confiscate a significant fraction of them. The shareholder derives no benefit from earnings until they are received as dividends or invested in assets which will lead to future increases in dividends. In a wasting asset industry with a shrinking resource base, such as oil, the shareholder must anticipate the day when it will no longer be possible to invest in oil production. At this point, if the present fiscal climate continues, he will be taxed at the higher rate. Reinvestment reduces current dividends, and cannot lead to worthwhile dividend growth if present regulations persist. Under such circumstances, reinvestment is a bloodless form of Russian roulette, and is, or should be, further deterred by the realization that no property rights in corporate earnings are recognized except as a temporary expedient to induce reinvestment. Once reinvestment is impractical, there is every reason to expect that even the remaining pittance will be unceremoniously seized.

To a significant degree, the oil companies have brought this on themselves by stressing, in presentations to government, the need to generate profits as a source of funds for reinvestment purposes. While such propositions may be well-meant, they are incorrect in a country with a well-functioning capital market, and practically invite the conclusion that if reinvestment is not needed, profits are unnecessary.

It is clear, analytically, that the required before-tax rate of return under a dual-tax rate regime, in which a higher tax rate is applied to profits which are not reinvested than on profits which are reinvested, shifts to a level determined by the effective tax rate on *distributable* earnings rather than by the temporarily lower nominal rate. The effectiveness of this tax policy in inducing reinvestment will depend critically on the level of other opportunities available to investors on a before-tax basis.[12]

This factor might be irrelevant if, for reasons of reluctance to disinvest in the corporate going concern, "good corporate citizenship" or whatever, corporate managements were willing to reinvest earnings at prospective rates of return which did not fully compensate for the higher ultimate tax rate, providing the level of earnings they were willing to so reinvest was sufficient to generate the desired or required rate of growth in output. Present shareholders would ultimately lose most or all of their investment, but the oil and gas would be available. If available cash flows are *not* adequate, then funds will have to be attracted from the market at prospective yields which reflect the higher taxes.

Given current industry conditions, the prospects of oil and gas self-sufficiency through industry reinvestment can be considered by projecting industry performance. In considering this projection, we restrict attention to oil and gas production only, ignoring other parts of the integrated companies (such as refining, marketing or other investments).

Cash flows which will be available from production of *current* reserves (without reinvestment) are shown in Table 10:

TABLE 10
Projected Cash Flows from Current Reserves
(Without Reinvestment)

	1977	1978	(Million $) 1979	1980	1981	Average 1977-2005	
Gross Revenues.....	$ 8,888	$10,482	$10,273	$10.074	$ 9,882	$ 8.182	100%
Operating Costs	852	822	804	788	771	748	9.1
Crown Royalties	3.300	4.173	4,043	3,915	3,789	2,812	34.4
Federal Taxes.......	1,067	1,564	2,082	2,251	2,281	1,834	22.4
Provincial Taxes	160	268	440	504	525	455	5.6
Cash Flow........	$ 3,509	$ 3,655	$ 2,904	$ 2,616	$ 2,516	$ 2,332	28.5%

These projections assume that oil and gas prices will increase to $9.75 per barrel and $1.50 per MCF (at Toronto) by 1977 and to $12.00 and $1.75, respectively by 1978. Thereafter, prices are assumed to increase with inflation at 5%. Current production rates were assumed to decline by 7.8% for oil and 4.3% for gas with no further exploration or development expenditures. No allowance has been made for additional investments which may be required to produce existing reserves, though some investment, e.g., for additional development wells, for workovers of existing wells, etc., will undoubtedly be required. There will thus be some over-statement of the rates of return. Assuming that the average finding and development cost of current reserves of oil and gas was $1.10 per barrel equivalent, (the past ten year average)and that in 1975 dollars this is equivalent to $2.64, then the lifecycle real rate of return would be 6.72%, or, assuming an average 5% inflation, a nominal rate of 11.72%. Thus, despite the projected increase of 50 per cent over 1975 prices, rate of return to the oil industry from past investments will remain moderate.

The projections on gross revenues should be compared with actual industry revenues of $6,143.4 million in 1975 and estimates of $6,774.0 million for 1976. Of the $1,594 million of further increase in gross revenues between 1977 and 1978, the increased industry share (without reinvestment) would amount to only $146 million with increased royalties and taxes consuming the rest. As the initial earned depletion and development write-offs are substantially exhausted by 1979, income taxes will jump by a third resulting in a reduction of cash flows by $751 million.

Given that fast write-offs and earned depletion regulations are intended to encourage reinvestment of funds by reducing current income tax liabilities, it is important to consider the total industry cash flows including new investment in oil and gas. In fact, if the level of production is to be maintained at the 1975 level of 609 million barrels of oil and 2,360 thousand cubic feet of gas then an annual reinvestment expenditure of $2,991 million (in 1975 dollars) would be required assuming the $3.54 per barrel equivalent replacement cost. Additionally, to meet a 5 per cent growth in domestic demand, a further addition to reserves of approximately 56 per cent of production would be required to maintain a reserve to production index of around 11.1 years. This creates the need for a total reinvestment expenditure of $4,666 million per year. An industry projection under the assumption of *constant* finding and development costs of $3.54, with 5 per cent growth in production and 5 per cent inflation rate is shown in Table 11:

TABLE 11
Projected Cash Flows with Reinvestment

	1977	1978	1979	1980	1981	Average 1977-2005	
			(Billion $)				
Gross Revenues	9	11	12	13	15	52.8	100%
Operating Costs	1	1	1	2	2	3.8	7.2
Crown Royalties	3	4	4	4	4	13.9	26.3
Federal Taxes	0	1	1	1	1	3.9	7.4
Provincial Taxes	0	0	0	0	0	0.9	1.7
Operating Income..	5	5	6	6	8	30.3	
Exploration, Development and Facilities...........	5	5	6	6	7	25.3	47.9
Net Cash Flow	0	0	0	0	1	5.0	9.5%

Several observations may be made concerning the above scenario. The most evident is that, even with the assumed constant finding cost, it is highly questionable whether the industry can be self-financing over the next five years given the total lack of any margin of safety. Additionally, no provision has been made for the payment of dividends or any other application of cash other than in oil and gas investment. We conclude that the industry will have to rely on the capital market to support even moderate market growth and that unless rates of return, after tax, without reinvestment gimmicks, allow it to do so, Canada will become increasingly dependent on foreign sources of supply.

VI. CONCLUSIONS

The apparent net withdrawal of funds generated in petroleum production in Canada for investment elsewhere raises a serious practical question about the adequacy of incentives to invest in the industry. These have been seriously reduced by the holding of prices below world market levels, and by various fiscal measures intended to convert "economic rents" into government revenues. The available evidence suggests that a lifecycle nominal rate of return of 11.72% or a real rate of 6.72% will have been earned on existing reserves by the time they are depleted, under existing legislation and scheduled price increases. Returns on current investment, with the reinvestment incentives in the present tax and royalty system, are approximately 14% nominal, and 9.0% in real terms. The adequacy of these rates of return must be judged in the light of available yields on other investment opportunities. Comparison with precisely equivalent alternatives is difficult, because of the significantly higher risks encountered in petroleum exploration. However, making adjustments for the apparent difference in risk levels and using allowed rates of return on equity investment in public utilities as a yardstick, required rates of return on equity investment in petroleum exploration appear to be in the neighbourhood of 21.5% nominal, or 16.5%

in real terms. Allowing for the use of debt financing, overall required rates of return drop to the 19% range (14% real). These rates are substantially in excess of rates of return currently being realized or presently available on typical investment opportunities. Seen in this light, the withdrawal of funds is scarcely surprising. It is unlikely, even without further withdrawals, that dependence on imports can be held at present relative levels without attracting new investment through the capital market. Some improvement in incentives will be required if the present rate of self-sufficiency is to be maintained. Prices should be allowed to escalate to world levels as soon as possible. However, the analysis indicates that, under the present fiscal regime, this alone will be inadequate to restore incentives, as royalties will absorb too large a share of the available income. Some reduction in royalties will be required. The analysis relates to Alberta, but similar conclusions apply to frontier areas where effective royalty rates, including "profit taxes", appear to be at comparable levels.

Notes

[1] These measures, and their successive impacts on the incentive structure facing the industry are outlined in our earlier paper "Changing Incentive Structures in Petroleum Exploration", Proceedings, 27th Tax Conference, Canadian Tax Foundation (November 10-12, 1975), pp. 174-187.

[2] The conversion factor of 10 deliberately understates the comparative Btu content of gas; it is to be construed as an economic, rather than as a physical conversion factor, and recognizes the higher cost (per Btu-mile) of transporting gas. Equivalent prices per Btu at the city gate mean lower prices, per Btu, for gas at the wellhead.

[3] The evaluation was carried out using POGO, Profitability of Oil and Gas Opportunities, Petroleum Software International Ltd. (GE. Mark III Time Sharing System).

[4] For the underlying theory, see W.F. Sharpe, *Portfolio Theory and Capital Markets* (New York: McGraw Hill, 1970).

[5]M. Blume, "On The Assessment of Risk", *Journal of Finance* Vol. XXVI (March, 1971).

[6]M.H. Miller and M. Scholes, "Rates of Return in Relation to Risk: A Re-examination of Some Recent Findings" in M.C. Jensen, ed., *Studies in the Theory of Capital Markets* (New York, Praeger, 1972).

[7]The specific criteria were that: (i) earnings per share were available for 1964 to 1974; (ii) monthly prices were available for the period July 1970 to July 1975; (iii) that the trading volume of the Stock on the Toronto Stock Exchange in 1974 was at least 100,000 shares.

[8]See J. McCallum, "The Expected Holding Period Return, The Term Structure of Interest Rates and Investment in the Government of Canada Bond Market", (Unpublished Ph.D. Dissertation, University of Toronto, 1973).

[9]Canada, Department of Energy, Mines and Resources, *An Energy Strategy for Canada: Policies for Self Reliance* (Ottawa, 1976), p. 38.

[10]*Idem.*

[11]For a discussion of these and their consequences see T.S. Tuschak, *A Federal Perspective on the Tax Treatment of the Petroleum Industry*, in *op. cit. supra* n.1, pp. 157-173.

[12]The proof is omitted here for reasons of space but will be provided by the authors on request.

Editor's Introduction

Theoretical economic advantages from the operation of markets under free trade are well known. However, in the case of energy resources such advantages are constrained by other objectives and concerns: national security; balancing trade between manufactured and raw materials; sensitivity over foreign ownership and the like. Professor McKie's essay concerns energy relations between the United States and Canada. He outlines the dramatic changes in energy policy frameworks between the two countries which have taken place over a relatively short period of time, 1969 to 1976. In 1969 it seemed that a continental energy policy could be developed to offer mutual security and economic benefits. The United States would provide ready access for any surplus Canadian petroleum; security guarantees would be negotiated to protect import-dependent Eastern Canada. Canadian frontier resources might be developed on a joint basis. In short, markets without barriers would allocate energy resources between the two countries; non-market factors such as security of supply would be handled by intergovernmental agreements. How different is the picture today. Continental harmony in energy does not exist. Trade restrictions abound. Cooperation in the development of new energy resources is minimal. Canadian economic nationalism would preclude any substantial direct involvement by the United States in developing Canadian energy resources. A comprehensive mutual energy policy is unattainable. Notwithstanding this sombre situation, Professor McKie points to some remaining areas of beneficial cooperation, including: reciprocity in transportation; petroleum exchanges; emergency measures in the event of oil embargoes; and United States capital investment in energy enterprises where mutual advantages can be negotiated. Under current circumstances the opportunities are limited, but should not be discarded.

United States and Canadian Energy Policy

JAMES W. McKIE

Dean
College of Social and Behavioral Sciences
and
Professor of Economics
University of Texas at Austin

THE AUTHOR

James W. McKie is Professor of Economics at the University of Texas at Austin where he received his A.B. in 1943 and his M.A. in 1947. He received his A.M. in 1949 and his Ph.D. in 1952, both from Harvard University. He was born in California in 1922.

The recognition of Dean McKie's scholarship has been marked by Fellowships, Offices and Special Appointments by the Ford Foundation, by U.S. government departments and task forces, and by corporations, journals, institutions and associations. Among the positions he has held and which give him unique insights into the energy problem were Chief Economist to the U.S. Cabinet Task Force on Oil Import Control, 1969-70 and member, Advisory Committee on Emergency Planning and Sub-committee on Emergency Energy Capacity, National Academy of Sciences/National Research Council, 1972-73.

Dean McKie has written extensively on energy regulation, exploration, conservation and policy. His "The Oil Crisis in Perspective — the United States," was published in *Daedalus*, Fall, 1975, and reprinted in Raymond Vernon, (ed.), *The Oil Crisis*, (New York, W.W. Norton, Inc., 1976). His work, "The Political Economy of World Petroleum," appeared in *The American Economic Review*, May 1974. Dean McKie's "Balancing the Demand and Supply of Oil," in John J. Schanz, (ed.), *Balancing Supply and Demand for Energy in the United States*, Denver, Rocky Mountain Petroleum Institute and the University of Denver, 1972, was substantially reprinted as "Energy Policy and the Long Run" in Samuel P. Ellison, (ed.), *Toward a National Policy on Energy Resources and Mineral Plant Foods*, Austin, Texas, Bureau of Economic Geology, The University of Texas, 1973.

United States and Canadian Energy Policy

JAMES W. McKIE

Dean
College of Social and Behavioral Sciences
and

Professor of Economics
University of Texas at Austin

I. A VIEW FROM SOUTH OF THE BORDER[1]

Not long ago, a study of Canadian-American energy relations shrewdly summed up the current outlook by saying, "The future does not hold any remote possibility of a continental energy policy".[2] Recent events may warrant a still more pessimistic view: the future may not even hold any possibility of a continental energy market. From the point of view of an American observer, these predictions are distressing. Nor are they easy to understand. Eight or ten years ago all the lines of economic and political interest seemed likely to converge to a quite different policy: North American cooperation or even unification on energy, and specifically on petroleum. It is therefore of some importance to determine how we got into this predicament, and whether we are likely to remain in it.

The following discussion focuses on oil primarily and gas secondarily; it has little to say about other forms of energy, which up to date (with occasional exceptions) have not been of primary concern in energy policy relations between the United States and Canada.[3] This paper reviews the background and outlook as seen from the United States. The author has done his best to learn and understand Canadian views of these matters, to the extent that they may differ from those in the United States, but some divergences of interpretation and of opinion will doubtless remain. And so will divergences of interest; we must assume that each country will follow its own. Even the most optimistic advocate of closer ties between Canada and the U.S. would not have the temerity to construct and maximize a joint welfare function for the two countries.

The situation and outlook at the end of the 1960's

That the interests, both economic and political, of Canada and the U.S. in energy actually converged to a very significant extent, while diverging in some other ways, was the dominant opinion south of the border, and possibly north of it, until the end of the sixties. Perhaps we can get a picture of the reasons for this opinion by looking briefly at a cross-section of the North American energy problem as it stood at that time.

Energy relations between the U.S. and Canada have included several elements, of unequal importance: electric power, uranium, coal, natural gas, and oil. Net exports of electric power from Canada to the United States reached a high of less than 5 per cent of total Canadian output in the early 1960's; by the end of the decade exports and imports were pretty much in balance. Flows across the border have been determined largely by location of surplus and off-peak capacity in relation to local markets.[4]

Both countries produce uranium, but over the long run the U.S. is expected to be a net importer of uranium for electric power generation. The 1960's were years of slump in total North American demand, since military use of uranium had fallen drastically while nuclear power reactors were still in an early stage of development. Potentially, however, Canada's reserves of uranium presented much the same case as its other energy and mineral resources: large future demands from the U.S. industrial economy, and growing resistance to export from those wishing to develop Canadian industry instead. No reverse flow of technology from the U.S. to assist that development, including nuclear power development, has seemed likely in view of the rapid progress of Canada's own nuclear-technology capabilities during this period.

Coal has tended to move in the opposite direction, from the U.S. toward Canada. In 1969, imports supplied over half of Canadian requirements. However, there were large supplies in Western Canada which could not reach Eastern Canadian markets under the price structure prevalent at that time.

During the 1960's, Canadian exports of natural gas as a percentage of its total output rose from under 25 per cent to over 40, but even at the end of the decade Canada supplied less than 4 per cent of total U.S. consumption. At that time it appeared that the known reserves of Canadian gas could supply only a declining fraction of the demand south of the border in the future, and that exports would fall sharply both in absolute amount and as a percentage of Canadian production unless large new deposits should be discovered and developed offshore and in the Canadian Arctic.[5]

The major energy resource affecting trade between the two countries has been oil. The United States became a net importer of oil in 1948, and by 1968 was importing nearly 3 million barrels of crude and products per day — over one-fifth of its total consumption. Exports of oil from Canada to the United States rose from 151,000 barrels per day in 1957 to 470,000 in 1968, or from less than one-third to nearly one-half of Canadian production.[6] By then, Canada was the second largest supplier of imported oil to the United States. At the same time Canada was itself a large importer of oil; throughout this decade the Canadian market east of the Ottawa River used imported oil, chiefly from Venezuela. In fact, her imports were greater than her exports until 1969.

TABLE 1
The U.S. — Canada Oil Balance[1]
(Thousand Barrels Per Day)
A. 1968

	U.S.	Canada	Total
Consumption and Changes in Stocks	13,068	1,208	14,276
Domestic Production	10,453	1,013	11,466
Exports	195	470	
Imports:			
From Outside North America:			
From Western Hemisphere	1,705	480	2,185
From Eastern Hemisphere	635	135	770
Total, Non-North American	2,340	615	2,955
From North America[2]	470	50	
Total Imports	2,810	665	

B. 1974

	U.S.	Canada	Total
Consumption and Changes in Stocks	16,390	1,845	18,235
Domestic Production	10,485	2,000	12,485
Exports	220	1,045	
Imports:			
From Outside North America:			
From Western Hemisphere	2,445	430	2,875
From Eastern Hemisphere	2,655	430	3,085
Total, Non-North American	5,100	860	5,960
From North America[2]	1,025	30	
Total Imports	6,125	890	

Sources: [1]American Petroleum Institute, *Petroleum Facts and Figures,* 1971: Canadian Petroleum Association, *Reserves of Crude Oil, Natural Gas Liquids and Natural Gas in the United States and Canada,* 1972, British Petroleum Company Ltd., *BP Statistical Review of the World Oil Industry,* 1968 and 1974. Refinery gain is deducted from products figures. The various sources are not fully consistent, and the figures shown may not reconcile exactly when different sources are compared. The table is intended to suggest orders of magnitude.
[2]"North America" means north of the Rio Grande. Mexico is included with "Western Hemisphere Outside North America".

The established Canadian oil provinces in Alberta, British Columbia and Saskatchewan (the Western Sedimentary Basin) were nearing their peak of development by the end of the 1960's. It was estimated that their potential capacity for production, with some small additional investment in surface facilities and gathering lines, would be about 2.3 million barrels per day. Total Canadian production in 1968 was less than half that amount. There was not much remaining opportunity for new discovery and development in that basin. The future of oil in Canada lay in the frontier provinces — offshore in the Atlantic and in the Arctic — and in the Athabascan Tar Sands. The latter held hundreds of billions of barrels in possible reserves, but the technology for economic recovery had not been developed. Capital costs of development in both the new provinces and the Tar Sands were bound to be very high.

The oil trade policies of the two countries must be set in the context of the time. The 1960's (like most of the 1950's) was an era of surplus capacity, in both countries. The shut-in capacity in Alberta was greater, relative to Canadian potential, than shut-in capacity in Texas and Louisiana was relative to total U.S. potential, but it was substantial for both. And in both cases a large fraction of the total market was being supplied by imports — a fraction which could have absorbed most or all of the shut-in domestic production if prices had had a different relationship from the one that actually prevailed. Few were then contemplating an oil shortage. Producers in both countries were seeking to expand market outlets for domestic production.

Both countries were, in fact, operating what amounted to a cartel-type restriction on production, which maintained domestic prices above the levels prevalent on world markets. Both had to make pragmatic adjustments to the pressure of cheap imports by allowing imports in under controlled conditions while protecting the market position of the domestic industry to the extent possible.

But their viewpoints were not symmetrical. Canada was interested in developing markets — in Eastern Canada if possible, in the United States if not — at prices reflecting a premium above the world oil prices that prevailed at the end

249

of the 1960's. At the same time the people of Eastern Canada preferred those low world prices to such an extent that a political compromise was necessary: imports were to be allowed in as far west as the Ottawa River, with the rest of Canada reserved for domestic producers.[7]

The United States had long given up any illusions of regaining its position as a major exporter of oil. It was preoccupied with limiting imports and supporting prices, but it had no convenient device like the Ottawa Valley to use as a boundary. Moreover, it was beginning to perceive a national security problem in the flow of oil imports into the U.S. Whatever policies it adopted toward the economic and security aspects of oil imports, Canada would have a significant place in the overall scheme.

Quantitative projections

Projections of Canadian petroleum supply made in 1969 appeared highly favorable. One such estimate (never published)[8] was that the discoveries in the Canadian Arctic would probably amount to over 50 billion barrels of recoverable reserves, and explorations in Hudson's Bay and offshore Nova Scotia and Newfoundland would yield another 27 billion. The Western Basin fields were approaching maximum output potential and the beginning of decline, but could probably maintain 2.5 million bbl/day for a decade, and after that the frontier areas should come on stream rapidly. Natural gas liquids in Alberta should add another .5 million bbl/day. By 1980, it was estimated, Canadian production of oil with free access to the U.S. market at the protected U.S. price could be as high as 5 million bbl/day under optimistic assumptions about production from new frontier areas and tar sands, but at least 3.5 million, including natural gas liquids, under more conservative projections. Since total Canadian consumption was projected at 2.0 million bbl/day in 1980 and half of that might be supplied from non-North American sources, some 1.5 to 4.0 million might be available for export to the U.S.

North America as a whole (north of the Rio Grande) in 1980 was expected to produce about 17.5 million bbl/day if real prices for the two countries held at 1970 levels, and to consume about 21.5 million bbl/day; the balance of 4.0 million bbl/day could be imported mostly from relatively secure sources in the Western Hemisphere. Thus it appeared on the basis of these optimistic forecasts that a mutual security arrangement buttressed by mutual economic benefit was at least within reach for the two countries.

The security issue

The U.S. policy of limiting oil imports, begun in the late 1950's, was always rationalized on the basis of national security. The Presidential proclamation of March 10, 1959, imposing mandatory controls on imports of oil and petroleum products, invoked security as its principal ground, though the Presidential statement accompanying it noted that, "the new program is designed to insure a stable, healthy industry in the United States capable of exploring for and developing new hemisphere reserves to replace those being depleted".[9] Apparently the economic health of the domestic U.S. industry was itself an element in security. These twin elements of security and economic protection-ism have been intermingled since, though the weight of the security element tended to grow as the time went on.

How did Canada fit into the security objective? The reference to "hemispheric reserves" in President Eisenhower's statement was unclear. Most imports coming into the United States at the time were in fact "hemispheric", produced in the Western Hemisphere by American-owned companies. Not much originated in any country which was then considered hostile to the United States. Imports from all Arab countries as late as 1969 were less than one-fifth of total imports to the U.S. But the Mandatory Oil Imports Program did not at first distinguish among points of origin in fixing the overall import quota, which was eventually set at 12.2 per cent of domestic production for the area east of the Rocky Mountains. (Imports into the western third of the country were controlled by a somewhat different formula.) Nor did the Program make any real effort to define "security" or the threats to security.

Yet is was apparent that imports from Canada must present a different kind of security problem from imports originating elsewhere. The first recognition of that fact was a kind of "exemption" of Canadian oil from import ticket allocations distributed to U.S. refiners. The total from Canada, however, had to be subtracted from the overall allocated quota which was not increased when imports from Canada increased. This arrangement conferred an advantage on Canadian supply. It was rationalized in the form of an exemption (within the overall quota) for "overland" imports, implying a greater threat to security from waterborne imports — a spurious basis for a legitimate purpose.[10] The result was a steady expansion of Canada's share of the total import quota, which in turn provoked complaints from other producing nations less favorably treated and from domestic producers unfavorably positioned with reference to Canadian competition. It appeared to some observers in the United States that Canada was shipping oil to the U.S. to take advantage of high U.S. prices and replacing it in Eastern Canada with imports at much lower world prices. As a result of these pressures, the two governments negotiated an agreement in 1967 setting limits (increasing over time) on Canadian crude oil shipments into the U.S. east of the Rockies. But the agreement, lacking any enforcement mechanism, was not effective.

At the end of the 1960's, therefore, the United States looked on Canadian oil as more "secure" in some undefined way than other foreign supply, but still a competitive threat to the domestic industry. Imports from Canada had to be controlled primarily for economic reasons — an extraordinarily shortsighted view.

If there was a "security" problem in Canadian oil from the U.S. standpoint, it lay in the possibility that the oil would be diverted to domestic Canadian use after U.S. consumers had become dependent on it. Assessment of that risk required thinking about the probable hazards — of shortages rather than surpluses. The threat was not military but political and economic. An embargo of oil by non-North American suppliers could affect Canada as well as the United

States, and half of Canadian consumption was dependent upon such imports. True, there was enough surplus capacity in the Canadian oil industry as late as 1969 to cover those requirements if the means of transportation to Eastern Canada could be improvised, but if that excess were drawn into the American market it could no longer provide the same guarantee. Hence mutual guarantees, for sharing of supplies in time of emergency, would be necessary for the mutual security of the two countries. Of course in 1969 few people took the threat of embargo seriously, notwithstanding the growing vulnerability of the U.S.

The possibility that foreign producers would one day be able to control supply and exact monopoly prices was likewise given little consideration; but if that did occur, the question of prices for Canadian oil at home and in the United States was bound to arise. Mutual price guarantees might have been part of an energy pact.

The opportunity for a North American energy bargain

In retrospect, the optimistic assumptions and quantitative projections of 1969 seem to have been merely wishful thinking. Had they materialized, they could have provided the basis for a U.S.-Canadian energy policy. But the year 1969-70 was perhaps the last year that such a policy bargain could have been attempted, since the old order in petroleum began to change very rapidly after that.

It appeared that the two countries could both secure benefits from the following, under the overall estimates of energy supply availability and costs that were then current:

1. Unlimited access to the U.S. market for Canadian oil, at a common price level for both countries.

2. Security guarantees for the Eastern Canadian oil market, in the form of a joint plan for reallocation in case of interruption of imports, including perhaps maintenance of a security reserve in Canadian fields.

253

3. Similar security plans for the United States, to include limitations on non-North American imports and a security reserve of storage and/or reserve production capacity in U.S. fields.

4. Joint development of the Canadian Arctic oil and gas resources, under Canadian control but with massive contributions of U.S. capital.

5. Commitment of large U.S. capital resources to aid in construction of oil and gas pipelines up the Mackenzie Valley,[11] in a form that would guarantee Canadian control but with a joint agreement to transport both Canadian and Alaskan Arctic production to both Canadian and U.S. markets.

6. A similar plan for joint development of the Athabascan tar sands, which also called for very large capital investments.

7. Agreements for the export of natural gas in excess of Canada's own projected needs, including supplies forthcoming from the Arctic, to the U.S. at prices reflecting its true market value. (Such an agreement would probably have affected U.S. price ceilings on natural gas also.)

The operation of the market — for oil and gas and for investment capital — would have aided in the achievement of these results, but security policy and other political considerations would have required complex inter-governmental agreements as well. In the event, none of these things happened.

The Task Force recommendation
In February, 1970, the U.S. Cabinet Task Force on Oil Import Control recommended replacement of import quotas with a tariff system that would admit Canadian oil to the United States after July, 1972, free of tariff[12] and essentially on an unrestricted basis, if an energy pact could be con-

cluded by then providing for the security of Eastern Canada and possibly harmonizing U.S. — Canadian policies on pipeline transportation, access to natural gas, and other related energy matters.

This recommendation was not followed by the President, nor was any other recommendation of the Task Force. No negotiations on an energy bargain were begun. Instead, the United States Government in March 1970 unilaterally imposed import quotas on Canadian oil. That event signalled a decisive turn away from energy cooperation between the two countries, even though the quotas were soon removed.

II. FROM SURPLUS TO SHORTAGE: THE REVERSAL OF POLICY

"Continental harmonization", for all of its economic attractions to both the U.S. and Canada at the time it was proposed, was probably already politically unacceptable in Canada. The prospect of exporting well over half of Canada's oil and gas production to the United States over an indefinite future was not one which the Canadian public could have been expected to greet with enthusiasm. Since then the environment for such a joint policy has become forbidding indeed.

The recent coalescence of such a large number of unfavorable influences on the U.S. - Canadian energy relationship has been truly remarkable. But there are long-standing antagonisms in Canada against American economic power.

The background: fears of economic domination

The problem has arisen from several elements:

1. Intercoupling of foreign trade with the U.S. to a degree that many Canadians have regarded as excessive, particularly in view of the fact that this trade was a great deal more important to Canada than it was to the U.S. Approximately two-thirds of Canadian merchandise exports in 1973 went to the United States; a slightly higher proportion of its merchandise imports came from the United States.[13] On the

other hand, Canada was the largest single foreign supplier of the U.S. (25 per cent of total imports in 1973) and the largest foreign market (21.5 per cent of exports). Over 75 per cent of imports from Canada, including practically all raw materials, came into the U.S. duty-free. Canadian merchandise exports were about 20 per cent of her GNP, versus about 6 per cent in the U.S.[14] The issue of trade proportions and reciprocity had been significant in Canadian politics at least since before World War I, the government of Sir Wilfred Laurier having fallen in 1911 because of its proposals to enlarge reciprocity between the two countries. The infamous U.S. Smoot-Hawley Tariff of 1930, which closed much of the American market to Canadian exports for a time and greatly intensified the depression in Canada, has not yet been forgotten there. Nor has the more recent import tax surcharge of 10 per cent imposed suddenly by the Nixon administration in August, 1971. Though only about one-fourth of U.S. imports from Canada were affected, Canadians interpreted the surcharge (and U.S. refusal to exempt Canada from it) as self-seeking protectionism.

2. Export of raw materials. In 1961, export of crude materials including agricultural products accounted for 37 per cent of the value of all Canadian exports; by 1973 this figure had fallen to 33 per cent. Only 22 per cent of exports to the U.S. in 1973 were in these categories.[15] Yet the image of Canada as an exporter primarily of products of forest, mine, water and land, tended to persist as a political issue. To paraphrase a familiar Canadian slogan, "no nation wants to be a hewer of wood and drawer of water for its neighbors", and to those who held this view a North American petroleum compact meant more of the same.

3. Ownership of Canadian resources by foreigners, again principally by corporations and individuals based in the United States. In 1970, for example, 76 per cent of Canada's oil and gas assets (by value) were controlled by non-residents, and 61 per cent were owned outright by foreigners. Over 60 per cent of capital employed in manufacturing was subject to foreign control.[16] Residents of the United States accounted for about 80 per cent of total foreign ownership.[17]

TABLE 2
The Foreign Trade of Canada, 1973
(Millions of Dollars, Canadian)[1]

	Imports		Exports	
	Total	From U.S.	Total	To U.S.
Live animals, food, feed, tobacco and beverages	1,981	992	3,123	979
Crude materials[2]	2,016	780	5,019	2,734
Fabricated materials	4,282	2,824	8,194	5,698
Manufactured end products	14,777	11,695	8,308	7,161
Special transactions	247	192	45	40
Total	23,303	16,483 (70.1%)	24,719	16,612 (67.2%)
Per cent in first two Categories	17.2	10.8	32.9	22.4

Source: [1]*Canada Year Book*, 1974, Tables 18.27 and 18.28.
    [2]Including crude oil but not refined petroleum products.

TABLE 3
The Foreign Trade of
The United States, 1973
(Millions of Dollars, U.S.)[1]

	Imports		Exports	
	Total	Percent	Total	Percent
Live animals, food, feed, beverages and tobacco	9,494	13.7	13,622	19.4
Crude materials	5,014	7.2	8,380	11.9
Fuels and related minerals	8,174[2]	11.8[3]	1,671	2.4
Chemicals	2,463	3.5	5,749	8.2
Machinery and transport equipment	21,076	30.3	27,869	39.7
Other manufactured goods	21,462	30.9	11,112	15.8
Other transactions	1,794	2.6	1,842	2.6
Total	69,476	100.0	70,246	100.0
With Canada:	17,443	(25.1%)	15,073	(21.5%)
Per cent in first three categories		32.7		33.7

Source: [1]*Statistical Abstract of the United States*, 1975, Tables 1366 annd 1368. Import and export figures are not on an equivalent basis to those in the Canadian table (Table 2).
    [2]In 1974 this item rose abruptly to $25,350 million.
    [3]In 1974 this percentage was 25.1.

What these elements added up to in many Canadian minds was colonialism. Development of resources and investment was controlled from outside for the primary benefit of foreigners. The revenues of materials extraction were collected from foreign buyers, but the rents and profits were captured in turn by foreigners, via foreign-controlled companies. All that was left in Canada from the sale of its raw materials were the relatively small payments to local factors of production and small local taxes; even the capital equipment came largely from the United States. And since oil and gas extraction are not labor-intensive industries, development of those did little to create employment in Canada. (It was U.S. policy, for example, to refine in the United States the crude oil produced in Canada; even the Task Force recommendations called for prevention of export of refining capacity to crude-producing countries through a differential tariff on refined products.) The industries of metropolitan places in Canada would not benefit at all. And, after 1970 when the Canadian dollar was "floated", increased foreign-exchange earnings from growing exports of oil and gas caused the Canadian dollar to appreciate, making exports of goods and processing components manufactured in Eastern Canada more expensive. Some journalists interpreted these effects as "exporting Canada's resources and importing unemployment".[18]

The facts show that U.S. exports of crude materials and other products of extractive industries as late as 1973 were as great relative to total exports as Canada's were relative to her total exports, (Tables 2 and 3). It was true that the United States imported more raw materials than Canada imported, but that was a measure of Canada's advantages in using its own. U.S. absorption of finished and fabricated goods from Canada was far greater than its absorption of raw materials and fuel from that source, and nearly as great as Canada's imports of finished and fabricated goods from the United States.

But whether such attitudes were strictly "rational" in the economic sense or whether the more extreme viewpoints were held by a majority of Canadians is beside the point. They appeared as one facet of Canadian nationalism.

There were others, all part of the long Canadian struggle for national identity which in economic matters tended to take the form of continental separatism.[19] Further reference to the political and cultural aspects of nationalism would be out of place here. The important thing for this discussion is that nationalism and separatism did influence energy policy, and that the influence tended to accelerate markedly after 1969, producing a new orientation of Canadian policy by the middle 1970's.

Curiously enough, these viewpoints were almost unperceived in the United States — which indeed may have added to their credibility in Canada. Americans considered Canadian resources as freely available for American use. Hostility between peoples of the two countries was unthinkable. It never entered the head of the average American that some Canadians would find this attitude patronizing. The famous Canadian traits of reticence and polite reserve in dealing with foreigners did not promote enlightenment. The U.S. treated energy policy toward Canada almost abstractedly — a very odd approach in view of the fact that Canada was its second-largest supplier and a much more important one at the time than the Middle Eastern countries with which U.S. policymakers were preoccupied.

Revision of the forecasts

The optimistic forecasts of what Canadian oil and gas production was to be during the '70's and '80's soon went down the drain. By 1973 it no longer appeared that large new supplies would soon be forthcoming from Canadian frontier provinces. Not much oil was found in the Arctic, and none offshore in the Pacific. Gas discovery in the Arctic was moderately encouraging, but it was not likely to reach the market for a long time.[20] Atlantic offshore exploration experienced delays and disappointments; expectations were revised downward substantially. Production of oil in any quantity from the Athabascan Tar Sands had to be postponed indefinitely as the pilot developments encountered unforeseen technical difficulties and escalating costs. And "excess" capacity in the Western Sedimentary Basin turned out to be somewhat less available than had been thought, while depletion steadily reduced the potential output there.[21] Canadian production increased from 1.077 million barrels per day in 1969 to 2.115 million bbl/day in 1973, by which time it was apparently near short-run capacity. It was clearly not going to be possible to get anywhere close to the contintental security targets of oil availability for 1980 and afterward that the American government had hoped would be achieved by then.

Other elements of the continental energy balance forecast also turned unfavorable. U.S. onshore production of oil peaked in 1972 when the Southwestern fields reached 100 per cent of potential capacity, and has declined since. Offshore development was disappointing, and was also restrained by newly-imposed policies and rules of environmental protection. Natural gas supply, under the disincentives of ceiling-price regulation, began to fall while demand stimulated by those same artificially low prices grew very rapidly. The Alaskan oil pipeline which was to bring oil from the Alaskan Arctic to the Gulf of Alaska to be transhipped by sea to the main American market was repeatedly postponed. This delay in turn set back any possible alternate or supplementary route through the Canadian Arctic which might have brought more Canadian oil to market in the future. Nuclear power development lagged well behind projections.

In both countries, demand for oil and gas accelerated well beyond forecasts. In the United States, new environmental protection regulation forced a massive conversion from coal to oil and gas. By 1973 demand growth had mopped up the surplus capacity both north and south of the border.

By the middle of 1973, therefore, the North American countries faced a new situation. Production of crude oil and natural gas liquids in the United States had fallen to 10.9 million barrels per day, while consumption had risen to the equivalent of 16.8 million. Canadian production was 2.1 million, of which 1.3 million was exported to the U.S.; Canadian demand was 1.8 million bbl/day of which 1.0 million was imported.[22] The net overseas import balance for the two countries combined was almost 6 million bbl/day, only about

3.5 million of which could be obtained from other Western Hemisphere sources. Moreover, Canada had little or no remaining available capacity, certainly not enough even under forced-draft production to cover the needs of Eastern Canada in case imports from the Middle East (over half a million bbl/day) were cut off. And demand forecasts for gas in Canada indicated that any new supplies likely to be developed by 1980 could be absorbed in the domestic economy. A North American security combination seemed far less accessible now.

Let us review the events in the world oil economy leading up to the embargo of October 1973.

Changes in the world oil economy, 1970-76

Demand for energy accelerated rapidly all over the world after 1969. The virtual disappearance of spare capacity during the next four years removed the main cause of low world prices. They began to move above the low levels which they had reached in the 1960's — as low as $1.00 per barrel f.o.b. Persian Gulf. The rise was kicked off by an extended shutdown of the Trans-Arabian Pipeline in 1970, which caused pressure on the available transportation capacity to Europe from the Middle East. Meanwhile, a revolution in Libya had toppled the pro-Western government, and its nationalistic successor adopted a policy of conserving its oil reserves and limiting production. Kuwait and then Saudi Arabia, the largest producer in the Eastern Hemisphere, decided to follow similar policies and to restrain expansion of production there.

In these new circumstances, the Organization of Petroleum Exporting Countries (OPEC) which for ten years had ineffectually tried to stabilize or raise oil prices, quickly acquired real control over the international oil market. Prices were revised upward in negotiations in Libya, 1970-71, and in Teheran, early in 1971. We need not dwell on the details. By August, 1973 prices for crude at some North African sources had risen to $5.00 per barrel — above the domestic U.S. and Canadian prices. Imported oil in Eastern Canada was becoming more expensive than the domestically-produced commodity.

261

Then came the embargo, and the increase in posted prices to $11.65 for Arabian light crude, and rapid movement of actual transactions prices for crude from OPEC countries to and above that benchmark. The embargo marked a double epiphany for the United States and Canada: it revealed the true dimensions of the security problem, and it presented a new structure of prices at home and abroad. The latter bore special significance for Canada. The changed situation revealed in late 1973 has continued up to the present.

The development of Canadian-U.S. energy policy, 1970-76
Canada is not a member of OPEC. It would be comforting to the American point of view to be able to report that the two countries stood together to resist OPEC exactions, to insulate the North American market against them, and to forge a common security policy after the end of the Arab embargo in March 1974. But that could hardly have been expected. The U.S. and Canada did cooperate remarkably well during the embargo and Canada did what was possible to alleviate the oil crisis on the continent with emergency production and improvisation of special procedures. Both countries have since joined with others in the International Energy Agency emergency sharing scheme. Prices, however, were another matter, and so was the longer-run question of Canadian supply of the American market.

The most visible signal of a change in the policy of the Canadian government actually came before the embargo, when it imposed export controls, first on natural gas in 1970 and then on oil in March 1973. The Prime Minister made a noteworthy speech in December 1973 advocating abolition of the Ottawa River barrier — to permit the movement of Canadian-produced oil *eastward* via pipelines to be constructed to Montreal and points east. Meanwhile, the Federal Government of Canada had frozen the domestic price of oil but had imposed an export tax to collect the difference between that and the rising price of oil in the U.S. Domestic prices were allowed to rise from $3.80 to $6.50 per barrel after the world price increases of December, but the government adopted an express policy of adding an export tax at a level that would normally equalize the price of Canadian oil with the price of other U.S. imports in Chicago.[23] By 1974 this tax had reached $6.40 per barrel. Ultimately, the export tax supported a subsidy to the eastern provinces which were importing oil that was now higher in price than Canadian-produced oil. The government's announced policy was to have a single oil price for consumers everywhere in Canada.

Thus the Canadian policy took advantage of OPEC prices externally without binding Canada to OPEC agreements. The producer rents of oil began to flow massively into the hands of Canadian Federal and provincial governments. But the overriding policy for Canada was to reserve oil for domestic home use. Some of the rents were to be transferred to consumers in Eastern Canada. The government also set up a national oil company, Petro-Canada, more or less on the model of the national companies of other major oil-producing countries. It went into business on January 1, 1976, and at first was to be confined to a "competitive" role in exploration and production.[24] In August it acquired Arco's Canadian producing properties for $350 million.

It must be said that the external price policy is entirely in the national interests of Canada, which cannot itself set world prices for oil. Its producers are simply meeting that price in the principal external market. The export tax may divert part of the revenues to the government, but exporting companies would sell at the price paid in the U.S. for other imports, with or without the tax. Nevertheless, the imposition of the export tax was resented in the United States.

Domestically, Canadian oil prices remained stabilized at $6.50 per barrel for over a year, and then were allowed to rise to $8.00 — still $3.00 to $4.00 per barrel below the price of imported oil. In early 1976 the Federal government issued a policy statement calling for a gradual increase of domestic Canadian oil prices to world prices, while continuing to restrict and eventually phase out exports and greatly reduce imports of oil.[25] The domestic price was to rise to $9.75 by the end of the year.[26] Soon after the embargo, the Government advised the U.S. not to expect any more oil imports from Canada after 1983, and began phasing down the permitted level — to about 725,000 barrels per day in 1975, 510,000 bbl/day in the first half of 1976, and an expected 385,000 bbl/day later in 1976 after the pipeline extension to Montreal is in operation. In 1975 the government also moved the termination date for most exports up two years, to 1981.[27]

Export policy on natural gas developed similarly. Restrictions on exports to the amounts "surplus to Canadian requirements" actually were imposed earlier than those on oil. No new export licenses for gas have been granted since 1970. The government also moved to increase export prices, setting a border price of $1.00 per MCF effective January 1, 1975, and mandating further large increases early in 1976.

While Canada was moving toward a policy of self-sufficiency, or rather "self-reliance", the United States was doing something similar, at least on paper. "Project Independence" aimed at sharp reductions in oil imports by 1985. The published plan made no special reference by name to Canadian or other Hemispheric sources. But it did refer cryptically to "secure" oil.[28] At a projected oil price of $7.00 per barrel, total U.S. imports in 1985 were estimated at 12.4 million barrels per day of which 6.2 would come from "secure" sources; at a price of $11.00, total imports would be 3.3 million bbl/day of which 2.1 million would come from secure sources.[29] Was all of this to be Canadian? We do not know; but neither projection fitted in with Canadian intentions, which were that in the long run, Canadian oil was to be totally insecure, i.e. unavailable, to the U.S. Perhaps the FEA did not take that intention seriously. But U.S. energy policy has remained diffuse and ineffectual, its attitude toward Canadian energy undefined, and its expectations of Canadian policy confused, right down to the present.

III. ALTERNATIVES

Canada seems so firmly committed to a policy of energy "self-reliance" and curtailment of export of oil and gas that it may be futile for a non-resident even to contemplate alternative forms of relationship for the U.S. and Canada. But, as we have seen, policy reacts to a mixture of events and political attitudes, and can change significantly in a very short period of time. It may not be amiss for an American observer to comment on the alternatives available to the two countries including the Canadian options as seen from the outside, while disclaiming any intention - or opportunity - to meddle in Canadian affairs.

A policy of self-sufficiency

It should be remembered that energy policy is not solely a matter of economics. As a *security* policy, self-sufficiency in energy may be seen as a desirable goal by any country that has the means to achieve it. It is not, of course, the only way by which an industrialized country can protect itself against a repetition of 1973-4. At the moment, Canada can achieve security in petroleum more easily than the United States can. It would not have to resort to massive storage, reservation of spare capacity, subsidies for exploration and development, taxes on lower-priority uses, and price guarantees to nearly the same extent as the United States in order to minimize the threat of a cut-off of oil imports by 1985 or so. Its primary security objective is to complete the pipeline to Montreal.

Neither country is pursuing autarky or energy isolation in the literal sense. The U.S. proposes to continue to import oil from "secure" sources, whatever they may be. Canada expects to be a net importer of oil in the near future. It will continue to export gas declared surplus to Canadian requirements. It is not clear to an outside observer whether the Canadian policy is conceived in Canada primarily as a matter of security or of economics. The two elements are doubtless intermingled, as they are in the United States, but domestic "needs" have different implications depending on which meaning is uppermost.

265

The economic impact of export restrictions

If there were no security issue — no threat of curtailment of imported sources of oil — and no export restrictions, no U.S. import quotas, no price controls in either country, and no other impediments to trade across the border, oil imports would tend to follow the pre-embargo pattern. The oil price in both the United States and Canada would rise to the higher world price, in both Eastern Canada and the eastern seaboard of the United States. The wellhead prices of domestically-produced oil meeting that competition would be determined by transportation costs netted back to the point of origin. The geographic relations are such that the "natural" flow of Western Basin oil after Western Canada was supplied would be southward, into the U.S. Middle West, as before, rather than to Montreal. Thus Canada would be both an exporter and an importer, even though her domestic production almost equalled domestic consumption on balance. (The U.S. import balance would be affected as to source, but not as to amount.) If the continental oil price floated on the world price, the net Canadian foreign-trade balance on oil would be greater than from an alternative policy of restricting oil exports, eliminating imports, and keeping the domestic price below what it would otherwise have been.

Considered as an economic policy, without reference to security of political issues, would quantitative restrictions on exports to meet domestic needs be an optimum policy for any country similarly situated? We can see a few difficulties with it.

One is the meaning of the "needs" of the domestic economy for oil and gas in the long run. With an infinite time horizon, every possible quantum of fuel in the earth's crust would be needed for domestic use at some time in the future, assuming that the nation survives and that no cheaper substitute appears. The Government of Canada has not taken that position in making its projections;[30] but once hoarding begins it tends to produce its own justifications. More important is the question of levels of use: domestic conservation and the role of possible substitutes in the future energy balance. These depend on relative prices — of inputs, processes, and products. If total domestic production exceeds future domestic demand at world prices, a quantitative limit on exports would tend to depress domestic prices to levels that will cause the reserved amount of energy to be used, i.e. "needed", domestically. Under those circumstances, prices of domestic oil could rise to world price levels, or remain there, as *An Energy Strategy for Canada* advocates, only if production were restricted. If, on the other hand, capacity production in Canada were insufficient to satisfy domestic demand at world prices, export restrictions could serve only to deflect output to domestic markets that were somewhat less profitable or more costly to reach than export markets in the United States. Either outcome might, of course, be defended as augmenting Canada's national security, but the economic benefits are less clear. (Similar statements would be applicable to similar policies in the United States.)

The classical model of the economic benefits of free trade must of course be modified when applied to real situations. Prices for oil on world markets are not exactly competitive, as long as OPEC controls them. Most of Canada's trade is with one country, very much larger than itself and less sensitive to the price and employments effects of trade; dollar for dollar the task of adjustment to changes is thrown disproportionately on Canada. For all that, Canada *does* have a comparative advantage in some extractive industries and in a free-trade world would export those products while importing other goods that might embody cheaper labor or capital or more advanced technology.

The problem mentioned earlier — that oil and gas are high-rent products whose rents have also been exported to foreign owners — could be alleviated by a policy of taxation in Canada designed to capture those rents and hold them as Canadian credits on the balance of payments. That would not require quantitative restrictions on exports. What the existing policy does is to transfer some of the rents to consumers and petroleum-using industries within Canada.

To the extent that export restrictions keep domestic oil and gas prices below world prices, the Canadian consumer benefits from them but loses by foregoing some cheap imports of other goods that would otherwise have been available. The terms of trade probably deteriorate, but domestic employment demand probably increases. The industries that use much low-cost energy are able to expand exports, but the ultimate beneficiary of the subsidy then is the foreign (mostly U.S.) consumer of what is exported. Furthermore, these exporting industries also may be foreign-owned. Canadian consumers and industries will consume more oil at low prices, and will fail to use substitute fuels and processes that would be attractive at higher prices for petroleum.

If export restrictions keep domestic prices down, the Canadian industry loses incentives to develop new supplies whose costs are above the domestic price, but which might have been developed at the higher world price. Employment may gain in the (subsidized) export industries, but suffer losses in the unsubsidized industries whose markets are curtailed. These are familiar effects of trade restrictions. Economic theory holds that they produce on balance a loss in welfare for an economic system in equilibrium, and make it run less efficiently. The apparent gain in employment is frequently lost elsewhere in the system, and with a net loss in real income as well.[31]

Recognizing the disincentives of low domestic prices, the 1976 Ministry report quotes with approval a statement by the Economic Council of Canada:

"The policy of keeping oil prices to Canadian domestic consumers below the price of alternative supplies cannot be maintained for very long; and if it were pursued as a medium-term objective, it could serve to delay needed energy-conserving technological change, hasten the depletion of existing reserves, delay the provision of supplements and alternatives, lower the potential volume of savings, and perhaps foster abortive development of energy-intensive industries dependent upon the hidden subsidy for cheap oil and gas."[32]

The government proposes to forestall these effects by moving to world price parity for domestic oil and gas, but offers no analysis of the possible adverse effects of export restrictions on economic efficiency under that policy.

We do not know what would happen to Canadian policy if world prices should again fall to very much lower levels than the domestic oil price, and remain there indefinitely. One may speculate that the Canadian government would have to improvise policies to sustain minimum prices and protect domestic markets against imports — a policy also very likely to be adopted to a degree in the United States. A minimum price of $7.00 is already guaranteed by the IEA agreements of 1975.

Does Canadian development depend on export restrictions?
There is no evidence that the relatively free trade policy for oil and gas followed by Canada for many years before 1973 has hampered growth of its industries or its GNP, though we have no reliable estimate of where its economy would be now if it had adopted stringent forms of protectionism vis-à-vis the United States, in 1940, for instance.[33] As an example of what full integration of the petroleum economy can do to a local economy, we might look at the experience of Texas during the same period. It too was still primarily an extractive economy as late as the 1930's; it has experienced massive inflows of capital from other regions; its industry and resources were largely owned by non-Texans; its per capita income in 1940 was significantly less than that of the regions that controlled most of its resources. Anti- "colonialist" populism was a staple of Texas politics as late as 1945. Yet the full integration of the Texas petroleum economy with the rest of the United States does not appear to have left it in a relatively underdeveloped condition. Growth of manufactures and manufacturing employment has been more rapid in Texas than elsewhere in the country. Its extractive industries have continued to thrive alongside manufacturing. Its cities are booming, its tertiary activities are continuing to grow in complexity, its rural economy is healthy, and its per capita income has moved closer (though still not up to) the U.S. average. And though its oil and gas resources have now reached the stage of depletion, it has successfully made the transition to balanced growth.[34]

All this took place during a period of petroleum surplus, not the period of energy scarcity that is expected for the next couple of decades. The experience of Texas and Alberta, respectively, does not demonstrate that *other* states and provinces benefited equally from an unhampered market in energy resources. But it may suggest that development of manufacturing employment and exports is likely to result from more specialization and division of labor and reciprocal trade rather than from self-sufficiency. Again, the economic argument does not address itself to the question of security.

What is now possible?

That a comprehensive common energy policy for the United States and Canada is unattainable at present must be conceded. It is probable that both countries will follow a high-price policy for petroleum even if world prices should fall, to stimulate domestic supplies and encourage development of substitutes — though price controls in both countries at present tend to work in the contrary direction. Canadian policy intends to shift the security problem largely to the United States. Domestic Canadian coal from the Western provinces in the future may replace American coal in Canadian markets under the price structure that is now emerging. Aside from exchanges of surplus electric power, marginal additional natural gas sales, and trade in uranium, what remains of continental energy relations? Naturally if huge new supplies of oil and gas should be discovered in either country, the outlook might be substantially changed, but that is improbable. Canada's future production of oil is not likely to exceed her own consumption, and exports to the U.S. under *any* export policy are not likely to constitute a large fraction of U.S. consumption.

The opportunities have not vanished, though they certainly do not add up to anything like a continental market.[35]

1. The geography of the two countries offers a number of advantageous opportunities for reciprocal transportation routes and for exchange of oil and refined products along the northern tier of states.

270

2. Canada might be persuaded to release additional supplies of oil and gas for export under a bilateral agreement with the U.S. binding the latter to accept more processed and semi-processed goods instead of raw materials - refined products rather than crude oil, for example.

3. The position of the refineries in the Maritimes presents some interesting possibilities for access to U.S. products markets. These refineries must operate on imported oil. At present their total capacity considerably exceeds what the local Canadian market requires. The remaining "natural" market for those products is in the north-eastern United States. They would displace other products that the U.S. could refine domestically from imported crude.

4. U.S. capital investment in the enormously expensive enterprises of the Arctic gas pipeline and the Tar Sands development might still be desirable, even necessary, from the Canadian point of view. Contracts with governmental guarantees calling for sale to the U.S. of any "surplus" resulting from those developments would be one way of providing for mutuality of benefit.

5. Parallel to any new U.S. petroleum investment, Canadian policy might provide for conversion over time of existing equity investments to debt, returning control to Canada. If current sales of oil and gas to the U.S. are permitted, or if the Canadian balance of payments with the U.S. shows a surplus, repatriation (liquidation) of U.S. investments in Canadian oil could be stipulated by inter-governmental agreement.

6. The U.S. could agree to renegotiate the Columbia River Treaty for electric power, on a fairer basis.

7. The U.S. might choose to adopt the CANDU reactor in the development of its own program of nuclear power generation.

8. Additional coordination between the two governments of emergency petroleum measures in case of embargo, relating to transportation, border exchanges, and allocation of

emergency production, will probably be seen as mutually desirable. These measures would be quite secondary to the major effort of coping with the shortages resulting from an embargo, which would presumably be governed by the IEA emergency sharing agreement among the OECD countries.

These are small and mean opportunities, compared to the large vision of a unified continental energy policy that once was seen by some in the United States. Some of these possible arrangements would violate the canons of efficient economic organization. They would not simulate the results of free trade. Even so, a lot of mutual good will is necessary even to get that far.

If a defensive and suspicious turn in American foreign economic policy should begin strongly to affect U.S. relations with Canada, the results could be calamitous. Up to date, the United States has grieved and murmured over the unfavorable developments in Canada on energy policies, but has not attempted to retaliate; any injuries to Canadian interests by U.S. actions during the past few years, as earlier, have been done almost absentmindedly.

The shape of the more distant future cannot be discerned with any confidence. Among the possible scenarios of the future let us assume one that validates pessimistic projections of discovery of conventional hydrocarbon resources in the world, including both Canada and the United States. Suppose that it also features (1) high and rising world prices of oil and gas, and rapid depletion of conventional reserves; (2) massive increases in coal production and the successful development technology of coal hydrogenation, in both countries; (3) extensive exploitation of the Athabascan Tar Sands; (4) successful development and control of the breeder reactor in many countries some time after 2000. This model, not an implausible one, includes a near-term "backstop" for energy supply in the form of coal, and a more distant one in the form of nuclear power. ("Backstop" simply means that abundant supplies of energy will be available at higher real costs than the present prices of oil and gas.) Domestic energy prices would tend to move upward with world prices.

272

If these things should come to pass, then both Canada and the United States will use up their domestic reserves of conventional oil and gas first, substituting synthetic oil and coal as time goes on. Without massive new discoveries of Arctic gas or development of abundant Tar Sands production, the combined oil and gas resources of the two countries could not possibly sustain existing levels of energy consumption for long, let alone high growth rates in consumption; and the rest of the world may be lagging the North American situation by a mere 15 years or so.

A Canadian policy of keeping oil for domestic use would probably not postpone the period of transition to alternatives very much if world supplies of conventional hydrocarbons really are in a phase of rapid depletion. Nor would it necessarily leave Canada in the best position to make a successful transition to a world in which the country no longer had a comparative advantage in energy. If the North American continent were to shift first to coal and then to nuclear power as its main energy source, which seems likely, constraints imposed by depletable energy-resource endowments would virtually cease to operate. Trade between the two countries would no longer include a major energy-resource component. Meanwhile, cheap energy, so long a staple element in both the domestic economies and the foreign trade of both Canada and the United States, is probably gone for good.

Notes

[1] The author is indebted to Gaylen Duncan, Richard Mancke, William Stevenson, and Campbell Watkins, as well as to several anonymous critics, for helpful comments on an earlier draft of this paper. Any remaining defects and errors are solely his own responsibility.

[2] Leonard Waverman, "The Reluctant Bride: Canadian and American Energy Relations", in E.W. Erickson and Leonard Waverman, eds., *The Energy Question: An International Failure of Policy*, Volume 2: *North America*. Toronto and Buffalo: University of Toronto Press, p. 218.

[3]For simplicity, we shall leave Mexico out of the discussion and speak of "North American" problems as if they included Canada and the United States alone. If Mexico again becomes an important exporter of oil, of course, her location in North America could begin to affect the energy policies of both countries to the north in a significant way, but that is worth a separate study.

[4]The primary point of contention in electric power has been the sale by Canada under the Columbia River Treaty of 1964 of power essentially at a fixed price for 60 years, which terms have since been characterized as a windfall for the United States. This transaction should not obscure the mutual benefits available to both countries from continued development of an electric power "grid". Larrett Higgins, "Electricity and Canadian Policy", in Erickson and Waverman, *Op. cit.*, pp. 172, 182 ff.

[5]American Gas Association, *Gas Facts*, 1971, cited in Richard E. Hamilton, "Natural Gas and Canadian Policy", in Erickson and Waverman, *Op. cit.*, p. 151.

[6]See Table 1.

[7]As a government policy, this arrangement was recommended by the so-called Borden Report *(Second Report of the Royal Commission of Enquiry on Energy*, 1960).

[8]The components were supplied by officials of the Canadian government and persons in the Canadian oil industry to the staff of the Cabinet Task Force on Oil Import Control.

[9]See the texts of these documents in *The Oil Import Question*, A Report on the Relationship of Oil Imports to the National Security by the Cabinet Task Force on Oil Import Control (Washington: U.S. Government Printing Office, February 1970), Appendix C.

[10]The "overland exemption" meant that imports from Canada *across the Great Lakes* had to be allocated by ticket distribution to refiners, presumably to minimize the threat from hostile submarines on Lake Huron. At the other border it also created the absurd "Brownsville loop" where seaborne cargoes were landed, transported under bond in trucks across the border into Mexico and back again, and reloaded on the tankers as "overland imports" for transportation to final destination in the U.S.

[11]One authoritative estimate was that a 48-inch gas pipeline from the Arctic to Calgary would be economical, even though it would be the largest gas line ever built on the North American continent. Its cost was estimated at $5 billion. The same author estimated the costs of an oil pipeline from Prudhoe Bay to Edmonton at $3.4 billion in 1976 prices. To these figures would have to be added several hundred million dollars in annual investment cost for exploration and development of petroleum resources in the Canadian Arctic. Judith Maxwell, *Energy from the Arctic: Facts and Issues* (Montreal and Washington: C.D. Howe Research Institute and National Planning Association, 1973), Chapters 2 and 3. In 1970, gross domestic capital formation in Canada was about $18 billion.

[12]*Report*, pp. 94, 106. The then-existing small tariff of 10.5 cents per barrel would be continued on Canadian oil, but the tariff for Eastern Hemisphere oil would rise to $1.455. (At the time, the "world price" was less than $1.25 f.o.b.). Provision was made for possible delay in the preferential provisions for Canada.

[13]*Canada Year Book*, 1974 (Ottawa: Information Canada, 1974), Table 21.31, pp. 820-21. Current receipts in Canada's balance of payments in 1972 amounted to about 25 per cent of its Gross National Product.

[14]See *Statistical Abstract of the United States*, 1975; *Canada Year Book*, 1974. See also Tables 2 and 3.

[15]See Table 2. The "automobile pact" in the meantime was responsible for a considerable expansion of trade in fabricated goods and components between the two countries. In 1973, automobiles and auto parts accounted for nearly one-third of their mutual trade — over $5 billion in exports each way.

[16]*Canada Year Book*, 1974, p. 807.

[17]*Ibid.*, Table 21.33, p. 823.

[18]The above may be too bold a characterization of what the economic nationalists in Canada actually thought, but it represents what some media of public opinion were saying.

[19]A good background study is James Eayrs, "Sharing a Continent: The Hard Issues" in John Sloan Dickey, ed., *The United States and Canada*, (The American Assembly, 1964) pp. 55-94.

[20]The Canadian Arctic Gas Study Limited (CAGSL) was formed in 1972 to investigate the problem of transporting gas from Prudhoe Bay and the Beaufort Sea. In 1975, the Canadian government began hearings on permit applications for the section of the gas line from the Mackenzie Delta to southern Canada.

[21]According to the Canadian Petroleum Association *Statistical Yearbook*, proved producible crude oil reserves in Canada peaked in 1969.

[22]Figures are from *BP Statistical Review of the World Oil Industry:* 1973 (London: British Petroleum Ltd., 1974).

[23]J.G. Debanne, "Oil and Canadian Policy" in Erickson and Waverman, *Op. cit.*, Vol. 2, pp. 125-148. This article also gives interesting details of the internal struggle over tax and price policy among the Federal government, the Provincial governments and private economic interests.

[24]See "Aspects of Canadian Energy and Investment Policy", Address by the Hon. Alastair Gillespie, Minister of Energy, Mines and Resources, before the Traffic Club of Pittsburgh, Pennsylvania, January 22, 1976.

[25]Ministry of Energy, Mines and Resources, *An Energy Strategy for Canada: Policies for Self-Reliance* (Ottawa, 1976).

[26]*Wall Street Journal*, May 19, 1976, p. 3.

[27]These figures were recommended by the National Energy Board of Canada in its reports on Canadian energy supplies and requirements. They were obtained from press accounts of the reports. The government may allow some small amounts to continue to flow to dependent Northern Tier refineries in the U.S. even after the general cutoff date.

[28]Federal Energy Administration, *Project Independence* (Washington: U.S. Government Printing Office, 1974). "While zero imports is achievable, it is simply not warranted economically or politically. Some imports are from secure sources. Others are from insecure sources but they can be insured against through emergency demand curtailment measures or standby storage." (p. 44) The "secure" sources are nowhere specified in the report.

[29]*Ibid.*, Table 1-15, p. 35.

[30]The projections of "exportable surpluses" of *gas* by the National Energy Board have been quite straightforward, but still arbitrary: it has estimated Canadian sales

over a 30-year period, then arrived at a "Canadian reserve requirement" by multiplying consumption in the fourth year by 25. Demand was estimated without a model of relative fuel prices. Reserves in excess of this requirement would support an exportable surplus. It has recently increased the stringency of its estimates of Canadian requirements by adding the requirement of "deliverability" from Canadian sources. The government did not use a similar formula for its estimates of *oil* requirements in Canada, but seems to have relied mainly on extrapolation. I am indebted to Dr. Paul G. Bradley of the University of British Columbia for information on the gas reserve formula. See National Energy Board, *Report to Governor in Council*, August 1970; Department of Energy, Mines and Resources, *An Energy Policy for Canada*, 1973; and Richard E. Hamilton, *Op. cit.*

[31]This paragraph is indebted to the persuasive analysis by Waverman, *Op. cit.*, pp. 231-33.

[32]*Economic Targets and Social Indicators*, Eleventh Annual Review of the Economic Council of Canada, 1974, p. 60, quoted in *An Energy Strategy for Canada, Op. cit.*, pp. 126-7.

[33]For an interesting projection of the Canadian economy in 1970 *ex visu* 1958, see Richard E. Caves and Richard H. Holton, *The Canadian Economy: Prospect and Retrospect* (Cambridge: Harvard University Press, 1959.) Though the forecasts of Caves and Holton were remarkably accurate in many respects, they overestimated the percentage of Canadian exports that would take the form of raw materials and agricultural products in 1970 by a considerable amount and correspondingly underestimated the percentage of manufactured goods in the total value of Canadian exports. Projections of the distribution of the Canadian labor force overestimated somewhat the percentage to be employed in agriculture, mining, and other extractive industries and underestimated service employment, but were very close on manufacturing, trade and transport.

[34]It may be justly objected that the relation between Texas and the rest of the United States is total integration, not merely free trade in petroleum. Trade in other goods between the United States and Canada has not been entirely free of restrictions on imports. On the other hand, factor movements between the U.S. and Canada up to about 1970 were extraordinarily free, though not as free as within a single country. Other principal economic differences — in currency, monetary and employment policy, taxation, and subsidies — do not set the U.S. off from Canada nearly as much as from most other countries. An intermediate model like the EEC could furnish an illuminating comparison.

[35]See *An Energy Strategy for Canada, Op. cit.*, Part II, Chapter 3, for further discussion of some of these possibilities.

INDEX

histories of, 146-148
divestiture of, 174, 200, 201, 206
nationalization of, 187
government regulation of, 174
and OPEC, 186-187, 194, 199
Competition
among companies, 133-143, 174
anti-trust policy, 136, 143
and government enterprises, 150
and public utilities, 155-156
see also Monopoly
Conference on Industrial Energy
Conservation, Canada, (1976), 74
Conference on International
Economic Cooperation, 207
Conservation
and economic growth, 72-80
function of price in, 74
industries and, 74
government policy re, 79, 266
practices, 205
Consolidated Natural Gas, 101
Consumer Price Index, Canada, U.S.,
(1955-1974), 144
Consumers' Gas, 230
Continental Oil Company, 141
Coombs, James A., 60-61, 67
Cross-price elasticity, 51

Davis, John, 59
deChazeau, Melvin G., 137-138
Demand for energy
effect of price on, 2, 44, 60-68, 76,
90-93, 199, 267
Canadian domestic, (1958 and
1973), 49
historical evidence, 58-60
factors affecting, 48-60, 67-68
in relation to GNP, 59-60
projecting, 69-72
effect of, on price, 90-93, 109-110,
180
prorationing, 152, 205
world, 174-177, 261-262
forecast, 175, 182-183
Deminex, 146
Denny, M., 61, 67
Department of Energy, Mines and
Resources, 71-72, 240
Dinning Commission, 100
Dome Petroleum Ltd., 227-228, 232
Duchesneau, Thomas D., 142

Economic Council of Canada, 268
ELF group, 146
Embargo, Arab Oil, 161, 164,
181-182, 196, 215
Energy Strategy for Canada, 267
Ente Nazionale Idrocarburi (ENI),
147
ERCB
see Alberta Energy Resources
Conservation Board
Exploration, oil
investment in, 2, 8, 221-224
companies in, 7, 36, 190, 199
process, 8-10
effect of prices on, 8-10, 92
discoveries, 18-35
government in, 36-40, 151, 215
offshore, 250, 260
Petro-Canada, 215
Exports: Canada-U.S., 55, 247-250,
255-259, 265-273
Exxon Corporation, 137, 184, 185
in 'seven sisters', 134, 184

Federal Oil and Gas Corporation
(FOGCO), 151
Fenn Big Valley field, (1950), 96
Financial Post, 226
First National City Bank, 163
Flanagan, R.J., 157
Fortune magazine, 163
France, 146, 186
see also Compagnie Française de
Petroles (CFP)
Fuss, M., 62, 65, 67-68

Geological Survey of Canada, 21, 41
GNP, Canada, 59, 70-74, 256, 269
Golden Spike field, (1949), 96
Gorbet, F.W., 61, 65, 67-68
Government
in exploration, 7, 36-40
as regulator, 98, 103-105, 117,
118, 131-133, 143, 145,
157-160, 165, 166, 215
as operator of enterprise, 126, 132,
143, 146-152, 165, 166
as deterrent to competition, 138,
151
British, 147-148
see also Petro-Canada

Gross national product, *see* GNP
Gulf Oil
    Canada Ltd., 103, 227-228
    U.S., 134
    in coal, 141
    in 'seven sisters', 134, 184

Home heating oil, 178
Home Oil Co. Ltd., 227-228, 232
Hubbert, M.K., 24-29
Hudson's Bay Oil and Gas Co. Ltd.,
    227-228, 232
Husky Oil Ltd., 227-228, 232
Hyndman, R., 65, 67-68

Imperial Oil Ltd., 227-228
Import(s)
    Canadian, 55, 179, 247, 250, 257
    price, 78, 106, 156
    subsidies, 109-113
    quotas, 153, 202
    policy, U.S., 175, 178-183, 204,
        250-253
    'overland' exemption, 179, 274
    CTF recommendations, 180-183
    U.S., 251-253, 264
    export balance, Canada-U.S., 248
    'Brownsville loop', 274
    see also U.S. Cabinet Task Force on
        Oil Import Control
Income elasticity, 53
Indonesia, 193, 197
    see also Southeast Asia
International Energy Agency, 262,
    272
Interprovincial pipeline, 204, 262,
    264
Investment
    in petroleum exploration, 2, 36-40,
        190
    taxes, 78
    returns, 105, 216-239
    foreign, in Canada, 218, 256, 271
    risk, 224-233
Iran, 193, 197
    Shah of, 187
Iraq, 193, 195-197
Isbister Royal Commission, 230
Israel, 186

Japan, 186
Jenkins, G.P., 105
Joarcam field, (1949), 96
Johnson, William A., 140

Kahn, Alfred E., 137-138, 155
Kendrick, John W., 163
Khazzoom, J. Daniel, 61, 67
Kuwait, 193, 197, 209, 261

Leduc field, (1947), 96, 100
Libya, 193, 197, 209, 261

MacAvoy, Paul W., 155
Mackenzie Valley pipeline, 69, 254
McRae, Robert, 62, 68

Mancke, Richard B., 156
Manitoba, 95
Market(s)
    government controls in, 40, 138,
        174
    prices in free, 93
    regional, 94-96, 271
    world, 175-177
    in a cartel, 191-194
    Canada-U.S., 245-273
Medicine Hat reservoir (1904), 19
Mexican National Oil Company
    (PEMEX), 151
Mexico, 195-196, 209
Mobil Oil group, 137
    in 'seven sisters', 134, 184
Money supply, Canada, U.S.,
    (1955-1974), 144
Monopoly
    of producing nations, 181, 188
    oil companies and, 133-143, 165,
        201
    government enterprise as, 151
    in public utilities, 155-156
    see also Cartel; OPEC
Monte Carlo method,
    definition of, 41
Moody's, 164
Moore, Thomas Gale, 155
Murphy Oil Company Ltd., 227-228,
    232

279

282

Fraser Institute Books in Print

PUBLIC PROPERTY?
The Habitat Debate Continued

Essays on the price, ownership and government of land. Edited by **Lawrence B. Smith,** Associate Chairman, Department of Political Economy, University of Toronto and **Michael Walker,** Research and Editorial Director, The Fraser Institute, Vancouver.

Twelve Canadian economists examine the operation and importance of land markets and the impact of government regulation, control and ownership on the supply and price of land. Essential reading for all those concerned with the future of landownership in Canada.

Contributors include: **David Nowlan** of the University of Toronto (on the land market and how it works); **Larry R. G. Martin** of the University of Waterloo (on the impact of government policies on the supply and price of land for urban development); **Stanley W. Hamilton** and **David E. Baxter,** both of the University of British Columbia (on government ownership and the price of land); **Jack Carr** and **Lawrence Smith,** both of the University of Toronto (on public land banking and the price of land); **James R. Markusen** and **David T. Scheffman,** both of the University of Western Ontario (on ownership concentration in the urban land market); **Stuart McFadyen** of the University of Alberta and **Robert Hobart** of the Ministry of State for Urban Affairs (on the foreign ownership of Canadian land) and **Michael A. Goldberg** of the University of British Columbia (on housing and land prices in Canada and the U.S.).

278 Pages   •   7 Charts   •   20 Tables
$5.95 paperback ISBN 0-88975-014-9 $12.95 hardcover ISBN 0-88975-017-3

FRIEDMAN ON GALBRAITH
. . . and on curing the British Disease

Why is it that the economic mind behind the Prime Minister has few, if any, followers in the economics profession? Why is it that John Kenneth Galbraith's theories have become widely accepted when there is a total lack of support for them? Is Galbraith a *scientist* or a *missionary*? Milton Friedman, Nobel Laureate in Economics 1976, addresses these and other questions about Galbraith as economist and prophet in this Fraser Institute book. Whatever the reader's view of Galbraith, this book by Friedman is must reading. It is said that Canada and other countries are on the same path as Britain— to some, the *British Disease* is the logical ending of Galbraith's story. In the second essay in this book, Professor Friedman outlines a cure for the British Disease: the principles that Friedman develops in this essay are of immediate Canadian interest as they point out the necessity to adopt gradualist corrective policies *now* before the more jarring policies currently required in the U.K. are necessary here.

66 Pages   • $3.95 paperback   •   ISBN 0-88975-015-7

WHICH WAY AHEAD?
Canada after Wage and Price Control

Fifteen well-informed Canadian economists assess the controls programme, suggest the reasons why it should be ended, and propose policies that should be adopted after controls end—**policies to give Canada a healthy and internationally competitive economy —policies for restraint in the public sector—policies to meet the critical double-headed challenge of low inflation and full employment.** Contributors include Jack Carr, Tom Courchene, John Helliwell, David Laidler, Richard Lipsey, Michael Parkin, Simon Reisman, Grant Reuber and Michael Walker.

376 Pages • 5 Charts • 9 Tables • $4.95 paperback • ISBN 0-88975-010-6

THE ILLUSION OF WAGE AND PRICE CONTROL
Essays On Inflation, Its Causes And Its Cures

A look at the causes of inflation and an examination of responses to it in Canada, the United States and the United Kingdom. Contributors include Jack Carr, Michael Darby, Jackson Grayson, David Laidler, Michael Parkin, Robert Schuettinger and Michael Walker.

258 Pages   •   16 Charts   •   7 Tables
$5.95 paperback ISBN 0-88975-001-7   • $2.95 pocketbook ISBN 0-88975-005-X

HOW MUCH TAX DO YOU REALLY PAY?
Introducing The Canadian Consumer Tax Index

Have you ever stopped to think what you pay your federal, provincial, and municipal governments in taxes? Have you ever wondered how much hidden tax you pay on all of the things you buy? This Fraser Institute Guide asks and answers two basic questions: Q: Who pays for government? (A: You do!) and Q: How much do you pay? By reading this book, you will see for the first time how astronomically the Canadian CONSUMER TAX INDEX has risen over the past fifteen years. And if you want to, you can actually calculate how much tax you really pay and your real tax rate.

120 Pages • 6 Charts • 22 Tables • $2.95 paperback • ISBN 0-88975-004-1

To: The Secretary,
     The Fraser Institute,
     626 Bute Street,
     Vancouver, British Columbia. V6E 3M1
     Canada.

PUBLICATION ORDER FORM

Please send me:

_____ copies of _____
_____ copies of _____
_____ copies of _____

Enclosed is payment in full of $_____ or credit card no.: Chargex # _____ Mastercharge # _____

Signature: _____

Name: _____

(please print)

Organization: _____

Address: _____

_____

--->✂

MEMBERSHIP REQUEST FORM

Dear Sir:

Please send me information on how I can become a member of the Fraser Institute.

Name: _____

Title: _____

Organization: _____

Address: _____

_____